Encounters at the Edge
of the Muslim World

Encounters at the Edge of the Muslim World

A Political Memoir of Kyrgyzstan

Eugene Huskey

ROWMAN & LITTLEFIELD
Lanham • Boulder • New York • London

Published by Rowman & Littlefield
An imprint of The Rowman & Littlefield Publishing Group, Inc.
4501 Forbes Boulevard, Suite 200, Lanham, Maryland 20706
https://rowman.com

Unit A, Whitacre Mews, 26-34 Stannary Street, London SE11 4AB,
United Kingdom

British Library Cataloguing in Publication Information Available

Library of Congress Cataloging-in-Publication Data
Names: Huskey, Eugene, 1952– author.
Title: Encounters at the edge of the Muslim world : a political memoir of Kyrgyzstan /
    Eugene Huskey.
Description: Lanham, Maryland : Rowman & Littlefield, 2018. | Includes bibliographical
    references and index.
Identifiers: LCCN 2018016751 (print) | LCCN 2018022842 (ebook) | ISBN
    9781538117095 (electronic) | ISBN 9781538117071 | ISBN 9781538117071 (cloth :
    alk. paper) | ISBN 9781538117088 (pbk. : alk. paper)
Subjects: LCSH: Kyrgyzstan—Politics and government—1991– | Kyrgyzstan—Histo-
    ry—1991–
Classification: LCC DK918.6 (ebook) | LCC DK918.6 .H88 2018 (print) | DDC 958.43/
    086—dc23
LC record available at https://lccn.loc.gov/2018016751

To the memory of Bolot Djigitekov

Contents

List of Figures

Preface and Acknowledgments

On a fall day in 2004, I entered the chambers of a federal district judge in Orlando with a group of visiting jurists in tow from Uzbekistan. The judge, like "Gaston" from Disney's *Beauty and the Beast*, had used antlers in all of his decorating. Heads of wild animals stared down at us ominously from the dark, wood-paneled walls of his chambers. Once the Uzbek visitors had oriented themselves to the unusual surroundings and exchanged pleasantries with the judge, the ranking member of the delegation—a justice on Uzbekistan's Supreme Court—invited the judge to visit her Central Asian country. After a stony silence, the judge replied, "I'll never travel to a country that ends in 'Stan'."

Uttered three years after the 9/11 attacks, these words expressed a widely held belief in the West that the Muslim-majority countries around Afghanistan held little interest—and much danger—for Americans and other Westerners. But the popular image of Central Asia as uniformly hostile and uninviting does not do justice to the political and cultural diversity of the region, where more than 70 million people live in five demonstrably different countries. It is especially unfair to the smallest and most democratic of the former Soviet Central Asian states, Kyrgyzstan.

The pages below tell the story of Kyrgyzstan from its origins in the Soviet era through its first quarter-century as independent country. They also tell my own story as a scholar who was fortunate enough to begin studying the country-to-be under Gorbachev and then to experience its birth and emergence as a new state. Unlike a traditional work of contemporary history, this book blends personal narrative with essential background on Kyrgyzstan's geography, history, culture, and political development. At the core of the narrative are encounters with a remarkable cast of characters, from presidents to ordinary citizens, who reveal the very human challenges of navigating the transition from communism to a new order, where identities, property, and the rules of the political game were constantly in dispute.

Predictably for a work that was a quarter-century in the making, there are many people to thank. First are the untold number of Kyrgyzstani citizens who were keen to show me their country and to answer questions about their government and their lives with refreshing honesty. I am especially grateful to the over one hundred politicians, journalists, social activists, and government officials who sat for in-depth interviews; many of them became friends and some collaborators. At the risk of omitting Kyrgyzstanis who made a signal contribution to this work—and of offending some who will not feel comfortable being mentioned alongside their political adversaries—let me express my deep appreciation to Roza Otunbaeva, Zamira Sydykova, Kubatbek Baibolov, Gulnara Iskakova, Askat Dukenbaev, Shairbek Juraev, Dinara Oshurakhunova, Asel Doolotkeldieva, Naryn Ayip, Anara Kerimbaeva, and Nurbek Omuraliev.

I owe a special debt to Joe Mozur, who accompanied me on my first trip to Kyrgyzstan and who read and offered corrections and perceptive comments on the entire manuscript. Students in my course at Stetson University on Central Asian Politics and Society read the book in draft form and alerted me to passages that would pose challenges for the general reader, as did James Russo, a student assistant. Another student, Lindsay McGrath, submitted a lengthy critique that pushed me to rethink the balance between personal narrative and background material. Scott Horton always found time in his hectic schedule to put me in touch with the right people in Kyrgyzstan and the United States and to share critical documents on developments in Central Asia. A longtime colleague, Bill Fierman, provided invaluable comments on the manuscript and kept my inbox full with the latest news and analyses about Kyrgyzstan. Because travel to Central Asia is not an inexpensive proposition, I am particularly thankful for funding from the National Council for Eurasian and East European Research (NCEEER), the International Research and Exchanges Board (IREX), the Open Society Institute, and Stetson's Program in Russian, East European, and Eurasian Studies (SPREES).

During this book's long gestation, my wife, Janet Martinez, and daughters, Sarah and Charlotte, were constant sources of support as well as good sports about my frequent trips abroad. Janet and Charlotte also served as welcome research companions on a visit to Kyrgyzstan at a low point in the country's history. I am also indebted to my editor at Rowman & Littlefield, Susan McEachern, for embracing a manuscript that defied traditional genres, and to her editorial assistant, Katelyn Turner, for lightening my load.

My final word of thanks goes to Bolot Djigitekov, without whom Kyrgyzstan might have seemed a Stan like any other to me. He may not have seen his native land achieve statehood, but he was always convinced of its special place in the world. This book is dedicated to his memory.

Note on Usage

Kyrgyz is used to describe persons who are ethnic Kyrgyz. Kyrgyzstani is used for citizens of Kyrgyzstan, whatever their ethnic origin. When referring to place names, I use the term appropriate to the era about which I am writing. Thus, in the Soviet era the capital city is Frunze and the republic is called Kirgizia or the Kirgiz Republic. Thereafter, Frunze becomes Bishkek and Kirgizia becomes Kyrgyzstan or the Kyrgyz Republic.

Chapter One

Conversations with Bolot

My introduction to Central Asia came in the fall of 1979 in a dormitory at Moscow State University. There I befriended a hall mate, Bolot Djigitekov, a thoughtful and soft-spoken young scholar who was writing a dissertation on the Korean religious leader, Sun Myung Moon. Bolot was the rare student in Moscow from the remote Soviet republic known then as Kirgizia; rarer still was his access to English-language newspapers housed in the special depositories of the Lenin Library, which were off-limits to all but the privileged few whose work required exposure to the "capitalist press." A regular reader of

Figure 1.1.   Map of Kyrgyzstan

1

The Times of London, he conversed with an authority and worldliness that was unusual for a Soviet citizen of his day, never mind a young man from the country's little-known periphery.

In our initial encounters, Bolot and I spoke of the two competing political and economic systems that shaped us. The discussions soon turned, however, to his native Kirgizia, whose landscape and customs he described in colorful detail. In languid conversations that seemed to last for hours, he painted a picture of a land of towering mountains where his traditionally nomadic people would tend sheep in the lowlands during the winter and then drive them into verdant high mountain valleys—known as *jailoo* in Kyrgyz—in the summer. Exhibiting the respect for elders that is a hallmark of traditional cultures, he spoke often of his grandfather, a shepherd who had a cultish reverence for meat befitting a people who lacked ready access to grains and vegetables. When Bolot pronounced the word for meat—*miaso* in Russian—it seemed to linger on his own tongue.

Midway through my nine-month stay in Moscow on the Soviet-American academic exchange, Bolot's cousin arrived from Kirgizia for a visit. Having heard that he worked as a shepherd, I was not prepared for the thoroughly modern young man I met. He was decked out in fashionable clothes with a degree from a technical college and a swagger that contrasted sharply with Bolot's Zen-like demeanor. As the cousin was quick to tell me, work in the pasture freed him from the stifling supervision found in most urban employment. It also provided opportunities to make money on the side, or *nalevo*, a reference to the illegal activity that allowed workers to supplement their meager state salaries. Evidence of earnings gained *nalevo* was everywhere, even in the heart of Moscow. Unable to find a taxi willing to bring a rented refrigerator back to our dorm, a fellow student flagged down an ambulance and negotiated a fare. Returning one day to the university from the center of Moscow, I stopped an empty city bus that had just completed its route and, for three rubles, enjoyed a ride home as the sole passenger. Among those on the make in Moscow was Bolot's cousin, who treated me to an extravagant dinner. I soon realized that the lavish meal was to be a prelude to a deal in which I was to supply him with items that could only be obtained in shops open to foreigners or the handful of Soviet citizens who had access to hard currency.

As I got to know Bolot better, I came to understand the depth of his attachments to both his Soviet and Kyrgyz identities. Like most Kyrgyz of his generation, he was a proud Soviet citizen who recognized the advances in education, industry, and infrastructure that Soviet power had brought to his native land. And yet his Kyrgyz identity seemed to exert a stronger pull than his Soviet loyalties.[1] The USSR had wanted to create a new Soviet man who would set aside affinities with any particular ethnic group, but it unwittingly perpetuated the "nationalities question" by creating separate republics named after ethnic communities and by branding each citizen with an ethnic label. Bolot was born in the Kirgiz Soviet Socialist Republic and carried a passport and other official documents that identified him as an ethnic Kyrgyz. He was the rare graduate student from his republic who was not granted admission to Moscow State University as part of an affirmative action quota of "national specialists" from Central Asia.

Despite efforts by the Soviet government to reduce ethnic differences to cute curiosities like those portrayed by Disney's "It's a Small World," tensions between cultural groups occasionally broke through the carefully cultivated facade of inter-ethnic harmony. One evening in our dorm at Moscow State University, a fight between two male students, one Russian and the other Kazakh, turned into a brawl between two ethnic groups. University authorities stepped in quickly to defuse the tension.

In those days, religion was a subject that few Soviet citizens spoke about openly, and Bolot was no exception. Raised on the periphery of the Muslim world, in a communist society intent on relegating religion to the dustbin of history, Bolot gave no indication that the religion of his forefathers, Islam, had shaped his identity. Yet closing mosques and removing Islam from the public square did not completely strip Kyrgyz identity of its Muslim rituals and sensibilities. In a land where religion was not a choice but a birthright, one did not have to observe the five pillars of faith to retain a sense of belonging to the Muslim world.

Shortly before my departure from Moscow in late April of 1980, Bolot's wife, Anara, came to my room to reveal something that Bolot had hidden from me for months during our candid conversations: he had leukemia. A difficult disease in any country, at any time, it was an especially harsh sentence in the Soviet Union in the Brezhnev era. Bolot and I parted knowing that these conversations might be our last. Not long after returning to London to complete my dissertation, I received a letter from Bolot asking if I could send a small piece of medical equipment needed for his treatment. Aware that the item would likely be confiscated by Soviet postal authorities, I arranged to have a kind British Airways pilot transfer the equipment to a contact in Moscow. Whether because of his declining health or the unreliable mail of that time, it was the last contact I had with Bolot. Two years later, I received a letter from his wife informing me that he had succumbed to his illness.

In the Soviet era, Kirgizia was one of the many areas of the USSR that was off-limits to foreigners.[2] In his own way, Bolot had lifted this travel ban for me and set me on a journey that would eventually lead to his homeland.

Chapter Two

From Moscow to Bishkek (or Kirgizia, Kirgizstan, Kyrgyzstan)

At the end of the 1980s, I received a call from Jerry Hough, a Duke University professor and America's leading Sovietologist. Hough was assembling a team of young scholars to study the fifteen republics of the Soviet Union, whose relations with Moscow were changing rapidly due to the reforms of Mikhail Gorbachev. Because of the highly centralized nature of earlier Soviet politics, and the difficulties that foreign scholars encountered in traveling outside of Moscow and a handful of other Soviet cities, few American social scientists had expertise in the more remote republics of the USSR. When Hough approached me about joining the project, he lacked specialists for four Muslim-majority republics on the Soviet Union's southern rim—Azerbaijan, Kirgizia, Tajikistan, and Turkmenia. Even though my research to that point had focused on the politics of Soviet law, I told him without hesitation to sign me up for Kirgizia. I qualified for the assignment, Hough later quipped, because I was the only American who could locate Kirgizia on a map.

Over the next three years, from 1989 to 1992, the fifteen members of this research team examined the different approaches to public policy being pursued by their republics, on issues ranging from economic reform to language laws. These three years turned out to be a momentous period in Soviet, and world, history. Our research, which began with a focus on the major political subdivisions of the USSR, turned into an analysis of the emergence of fifteen independent post-communist countries. From experts on the Soviet republics, the members of our group became country specialists on the world's newest states, some of which, like Kirgizia, had never experienced statehood before.

For those of us working on the lesser-known republics, access to sources presented an enormous challenge. In the pre-internet age, when even the

5

largest American libraries contained few holdings on territories like Kirgizia, one had to rely heavily on USSR-level materials, such as the census, for information on individual republics. Fortunately, the Soviet Union generously subsidized subscriptions to periodicals, and so, with funding from Duke, I was able to receive at my door, often within a week of their publication, the major daily newspaper of Kirgizia, *Sovetskaia Kirgizia*, and a monthly literary-political journal, *Literaturnyi Kirgizstan*.

These seemingly meager sources were a godsend for a Sovietologist. Even the changing mastheads of the periodicals told a political story. At a time when language and symbols marked the front lines in the battle for republican self-assertion, what to call the republic in a newspaper's or journal's title became a subject of political conflict. Where the Communist Party newspaper, *Sovetskaia Kirgizia*, initially retained the longstanding Russian name for the republic in its title (Kirgizia), the literary-political journal, published by the local writers' union, abandoned that usage in favor of Kirgizstan. A word of Persian origin, "Stan" is a widely used designation for country in the Turkic-speaking world, of which the Kyrgyz are a part.

When I opened an issue of *Sovetskaia Kirgizia* in February 1991—packaged as usual with the distinctive Soviet address band around the tri-folded paper—I was taken aback. It was no longer *Sovietskaia Kirgizia* but *Slovo Kyrgyzstana* (The Word of Kyrgyzstan); the next month, *Literaturnyi Kirgizstan* arrived with a new cover and a new name: *Literaturnyi Kyrgyzstan*. These changes, which brought the republic's name into full conformity with the orthographic rules of the Kyrgyz language, were more than scholarly curiosities; they signaled a shift in power toward those who sought to revive Kyrgyz language and culture, even at the expense of Russian. The republic's rapid journey at the end of the Soviet era from Kirgizia to Kirgizstan to Kyrgyzstan anticipated the flood of toponymic changes that would be unleashed by the rise of an independent Kyrgyzstan at the end of 1991.

The scholars working on Jerry Hough's project gathered twice a year at Duke to present their research findings and to participate in seminars led by top Western and Soviet experts and officials. One such Soviet visitor was Chingiz Aitmatov, Kyrgyzstan's most famous native son, indeed its only famous native son. The child of a Tatar mother and a Kyrgyz father, Aitmatov grew up in the small town of Sheker, along the border of the Kirgiz and Kazakh Republics. His family embraced the efforts of the Bolsheviks to modernize Central Asia along communist lines and, after receiving an education in agricultural institutes in Kyrgyzstan and neighboring Kazakhstan, Aitmatov turned to writing fiction, first in his native Kyrgyz, and then in Russian. In the mid-1950s, while on a two-year course at the Maxim Gorky Literature Institute in Moscow, his work attracted the attention of leading Soviet and Western writers, including the well-known French Communist, Louis Aragon. The publication of his short stories in 1958 in the premier

Soviet literary-political journal, *Novyi mir*, cemented his reputation as one of the leading non-Russian writers working in the Soviet Union.[1]

As Aitmatov's fame grew, through new literary works as well as films based on his writing, he emerged as a pillar of the Soviet cultural establishment. With that designation came political obligations, from serving as a deputy in the rubber-stamp Soviet national parliament to assuming leadership roles in the writers' unions of the USSR and the republic of Kirgizia. When Gorbachev came to power in 1985, he cultivated Aitmatov—"his favorite author"—as an ally in his efforts to reform Soviet culture and to include more non-Russian voices in the halls of power in Moscow. From an important figure in cultural affairs, Aitmatov became an actor on the big stage of Soviet politics in the late 1980s.

It is testimony to the public authority of the Kyrgyz writer in this period that Gorbachev chose Aitmatov—from among the 2,500 members of the Congress of People's Deputies—to place the Soviet leader's name in nomination for the role of chairman of the USSR Supreme Soviet in May 1989. Aitmatov's speech nominating Gorbachev did not conform to the sycophantic ritual that had characterized speeches supporting party leaders in earlier decades. It was instead a brutally honest assessment of the ways in which "the spiritual ascent of our society" revealed "totalitarian dogmatism" and the "cult of military intimidation"—a comment that did not endear Aitmatov to the Soviet armed forces. Again in stark contrast to earlier traditions, Aitmatov even recognized that the increasingly harsh criticism of Gorbachev as leader under perestroika was "quite understandable and fully in the spirit of genuine democracy."[2]

Aitmatov's speeches in the Congress of People's Deputies revealed his intolerance for the yawning gap between official ideology and Soviet reality. That he was an enemy of humbug was apparent in his insistence that while the Soviet Union "conjectured, ordained, and expatiated as to what socialism should or should not be, other peoples have already got it, built it, and are enjoying its fruits." By those other peoples he had in mind what he called "the flourishing, law-governed societies of Sweden, Austria, Finland, Norway, Holland, Spain, and, across the ocean, Canada."[3]

Aitmatov's public recognition of the artificial distinction between the socialist and capitalist camps had come as early as 1986, when he helped to bring together prominent cultural figures from East and West at the Issyk-Kul' Forum in Kyrgyzstan. This forum advanced the idea, revolutionary at the time in the communist world, of the superiority of universal values over class interests.[4] Even in the pre-Gorbachev era he had made his criticisms of Soviet socialism known to some members of the cultural establishment. In one of these conversations, the editor of a major publication "frowned, sadly shook his gray head, and said—'In 1937 you would have been put up against the wall and shot for saying that.'"[5] Aitmatov responded that he didn't doubt it, since "he had his own family experience on that account," a reference to the murder in 1938 of his father, Torekul Aitmatov, a prominent Kyrgyz leader, at the hands of Stalinist authorities.

Chingiz Aitmatov's remarks at the Congress of People's Deputies were also noteworthy for their defense of the cultural rights of ethnic minorities. Although some read his statements as a call for far-reaching de-russification, Aitmatov advocated a middle path, which lay between the Russian chauvinists who favored Russian cultural hegemony and the radical nationalists who wished to eliminate Russian cultural and linguistic influence in their republics. As a Kyrgyz writer who was bilingual in Kyrgyz and Russian, Aitmatov recognized the value of Russian as a window on world culture. He was at the same time, however, an uncompromising critic of those in Moscow who belittled the reputation of ethnic minorities or constrained their cultural development. For example, he departed from his mentor, Gorbachev, in vigorously criticizing the central press and television for their crude campaigns against the Kazakhs and Uzbeks following the riots in Alma-Ata, Kazakhstan, in 1986 and the ensuing cotton scandal in Uzbekistan. He warned against the danger of cultural stereotyping and imposing collective guilt on an entire people when the real villains were the political elites. We must not, he said, "pander to philistines."

Aitmatov also took up the cause of deported peoples, especially the Crimean Tatars and the Germans, who were "banished, scattered, and humiliated during the war years, [and who] . . . still suffer from political discrimination."[6] His proposed solution in the German case was to grant them an autonomous region, an idea that, if implemented, might have stemmed the exodus of the approximately 100,000 ethnic Germans who left independent Kyrgyzstan in the 1990s. In short, when Aitmatov arrived in the United States in April 1991 to participate in the Duke workshop, he was one of the Soviet Union's most distinguished public figures.

Aitmatov's initial stop in this country was Central Florida, where he would give a lecture to a packed hall at Stetson University, my home institution. Not used to sitting in coach or flying through Florida's notorious thunderstorms, Aitmatov arrived in Orlando in ill humor after a long trip from Europe. Accompanied by Joe Mozur, an American Aitmatov specialist and a Russian linguist, he perked up quickly when he observed a dazzling lightning display above downtown Orlando. The unusually intense storm, now retreating from the city, produced expressions of childlike awe on Aitmatov's face. By the time we arrived at the university, he seemed reassured that his brief American trip would be productive.

The next morning, the three of us set off for Cape Canaveral, the real draw for Aitmatov in Central Florida. The contrast between the Kennedy Space Center and the Soviet space complex at Baikonur, Kazakhstan, could not have been greater. Instead of the bleak and polluted cosmodrome on the

Figure 2.1.   Chingiz Aitmatov at Stetson University sporting a gift from the institution, a Stetson hat (with the author). October 1991

Kazakh steppe, which figured prominently in Aitmatov's most famous novel, *The Day Lasts More Than a Hundred Years*, Aitmatov found on Cape Canaveral a space center coexisting with a natural park, which had eagles and alligators and orange trees. With Baikonur as his frame of reference, he seemed unable to accept that rocketry and nature could exist in relative harmony, or that ordinary citizens would be allowed to take bus tours around a sensitive installation like a space center.

In those days, the tours permitted visitors to view the launch pads up close, and on one of the stops we walked to an observation deck from where we could see the launch sites and the ocean, some 200–300 yards in the distance. While looking out across the dunes to the Atlantic, an orca whale rose from the ocean, as if beckoned by the magnetism of Aitmatov. A native of Florida who had spent part of his childhood surfing the Atlantic waters near the Cape, I had never seen a whale before, never mind such a display of nature's bravado. The sight of the whale rising from the ocean clearly made an impression on Aitmatov, who would include whales as ubiquitous figures—referenced over eighty times—in one of his last novels, *The Mark of Cassandra*, published in 1996.

The time that Joe Mozur and I spent with Aitmatov in Florida and later North Carolina was not to be our last encounter with Kyrgyzstan's favorite son. As the Soviet Union collapsed a few months later, we finalized plans for a visit in early June 1992 to the newly independent country of Kyrgyzstan. Because our route took us through Frankfurt, and then on to Moscow and Bishkek, the Kyrgyz capital, we arranged to meet with Aitmatov in Luxembourg, where he had been serving as the Soviet—and later Russian—ambassador to that small European principality. After a short train ride from Frankfurt Airport, we passed through large iron gates and expansive grounds to arrive at the Château de Beggen, the nineteenth-century estate that served as the home of Ambassador Aitmatov.

Over a leisurely dinner at the estate with Aitmatov and his wife, Maria, we discussed his reasons for accepting an appointment as Soviet ambassador to Luxembourg in late 1990. In Aitmatov's telling, he wanted a refuge from the daily political drama that engulfed him in Moscow, a refuge that would allow him to return to full-time writing, and so Gorbachev proposed the Luxembourg option. Aitmatov's outspokenness had clearly alienated powerful forces in the Soviet capital, including reportedly some elements in the military, but in his diplomatic version of events, the decision to retire from the center stage of Soviet politics was voluntary and motivated by a desire to practice his craft as a writer. Aitmatov would continue to serve as Russian ambassador in Luxembourg until 1994, when he began a long-running appointment in Brussels as the Kyrgyzstani ambassador to the Benelux countries, the EU, and NATO.

Much of our dinner conversation at the Château de Beggen was devoted to arrangements for our visit to Kyrgyzstan. Whether because of our status as two of the first American scholars to visit his homeland, the reception we'd shown him in the United States, or traditional Kyrgyz hospitality, Aitmatov did not just wish us well on our travels. He informed us that he was putting his car and driver at our disposal in Bishkek, arranging our placement at the Academy of Sciences, and notifying numerous contacts, including his sister, of our impending arrival. As we discovered in Kyrgyzstan, merely mentioning to strangers that we knew "Chingiz Torekulovich"—the polite rendering of Aitmatov's name—prompted a smile of recognition and respect and served as an unrivaled letter of introduction.

Standing between us and our arrival in Kyrgyzstan was a connection through Moscow. In the Soviet era, and even well into the post-communist period for many Russian cities as well as capitals of the former republics, air connections with the outside world were only possible through Moscow. When we arrived at the Moscow airport that served Central Asian countries, Domodedovo, we found a scrum of passengers waiting to have their suitcases wrapped in layers of rugged cellophane tape to prevent theft by baggage handlers. Thinking that I would avoid these problems by taking the bag with me on the flight, I boarded to find that I had been assigned a middle seat for the more than four-hour flight to Bishkek. Opening the overheard bins, it was immediately apparent that my sizable suitcase would not fit into the narrow opening. With passengers scrambling to find their places, I stuffed the suitcase into the space in front of my seat, which eliminated all leg room, forcing me to sit cross-legged on top of the seat. With an oversized passenger sitting next to me on the aisle, it took only a few minutes for me to realize that I had to do something. Recalling instinctively the lessons learned during an academic year in Moscow, I did what any good Russian would have done in this circumstance: I made a scene. A few seconds later, a flustered flight attendant arrived and found me an empty seat. Embarrassed and relieved, I resolved to always pack light when traveling in the former Soviet Union.

As we were taxiing to the runway, the flight attendant began to make the usual announcements heard on any Soviet flight, except this time they were in Russian and Kyrgyz. Only at this point did I realize that although we'd booked flights on the flagship Soviet airline, Aeroflot, we were now flying "Kyrgyzstan Aba Joldoru," the recently created Kyrgyzstani airline that was spun off from Aeroflot when the USSR collapsed. Looking around the plane, I noticed that there were crates of mineral water obstructing the rear exit door. Missing pieces of carpet revealed plywood on the floor. It was an Iliushin IL-62 aircraft, a workhorse of the Soviet passenger fleet, whose rear fuselage was often held up by a support wheel to prevent it from tipping backwards as passengers and cargo were loaded and unloaded. As we took off from Moscow for Bishkek, I couldn't help but think that with the breakup of the Soviet national airline, the small, remote republic of Kyrgyzstan may not have received the best equipment in the fleet.

Chapter Three

The Present Is History

Having studied a territory for years without ever laying eyes on it, I approached our arrival in Bishkek with more than a little anticipation, and trepidation. After flying for hours above the flat expanses of Russia and Kazakhstan, the famed mountains of northern Kyrgyzstan, the Ala-Too Range, finally came into view. They rose sharply out of the fields of the Chu Valley, where we landed in the late afternoon sunlight at Manas Airport, fifteen miles west of the capital. Surrounded by farmland, the airport was a small, sad facility that exuded Soviet-era neglect. Once out of the terminal, however, we encountered another world, with mountains dominating the skyline and the unhurried gait of a farmer driving his cattle across the main road into Bishkek. It was a far cry from Moscow, and a reminder of the diversity and grandeur that was once the Soviet Union.

Bishkek was in every respect a Soviet city. Because the traditionally nomadic Kyrgyz left few architectural traces—the only ancient monument in the northern half of the country is Burana Tower, constructed by predecessors to the Kyrgyz, the Karakhanids, in the eleventh century—the Kyrgyzstani capital was a product of Russian colonial and Soviet design. There were a few hints of Islamic architecture in the city: in the entranceway to the Osh Bazaar, Bishkek's main market; in the buildings surrounding the main square; and on the decorative terraces of some of the newer apartment buildings. However, low, unadorned functional structures built after WWII of stone, brick, or concrete dominated the core of the Kyrgyzstani capital. Butting up against the modern, compact central city were residential neighborhoods with the feel of a Russian village. Just across *Jibek Jolu* (Silk Road Street), a few blocks from the main square, some Bishkek residents lived in one- and two-story wooden houses arranged haphazardly among fruit trees and small gardens.

Arriving in Bishkek in late spring, the eclectic architecture was barely visible amid the greenery that cloaked the city. At the heart of the capital was a wide, tree-lined boulevard dotted with rose gardens, park benches, and swings for children. Named in the Soviet period after the first Bolshevik secret police chief, Dzherzhinsky, the boulevard assumed the Kyrgyz name for freedom, Erkindik, shortly after Kyrgyzstan gained its independence.

Running along each side of Erkindik, and several other main north-south arteries in the capital, were narrow concrete channels that directed the mountain runoff through the city and into the Chu River beyond. Small dams above the city regulated the flow of water into town, while thin pieces of wood placed in vertical grooves in the concrete served as makeshift sluice gates along the streets for city workers who periodically flooded the boulevard to irrigate trees and gardens. For those sitting or strolling along Erkindik in the summer months, when temperatures could exceed 100 degrees, the flow of mountain water was a natural air conditioner.

Bishkek was not just a Soviet city but a Russian city, at least at our arrival in June 1992. While the ethnic Kyrgyz remained concentrated in the rural areas, Russians and Ukrainians moved in large numbers into Frunze—to use the Soviet-era name for Bishkek—to assume jobs in industry, transport, and education after WWII.[1] Because of this influx of Russians and other European peoples, the Kyrgyz made up less than 10 percent of the capital's 200,000 citizens at the end of the 1950s. As the city grew over the succeeding decades, to over 600,000 citizens by the end of the Soviet era, the higher birth rate of the ethnic Kyrgyz and the increased migration from villages to the cities began to reduce the Russian share of the population. Yet the last Soviet census, conducted in 1989, showed that the ethnic Kyrgyz still made up less than a quarter of their own republican capital.[2] Among the capitals of the fourteen non-Russian republics, only Almaty, in neighboring Kazakhstan, rivaled Bishkek as a center of Russian life.

Worried about their fate—and their children's fate—in a Kyrgyzstan unmoored from the Soviet Union, a steady stream of ethnic Russians and other European peoples, including Germans, had begun to leave Kyrgyzstan as the USSR unraveled.[3] Yet in the early months of post-communist Kyrgyzstan there was no sign that the influence of the Russian language was waning in Bishkek. Although the republic had introduced a new language law in 1989 calling for the revival of Kyrgyz, little progress had been made in implementing its provisions by 1992. In fact, the Kyrgyz language was virtually absent from the streets of the capital during our stay. Signs were still in Russian, and ethnic Kyrgyz rarely spoke their mother tongue in Bishkek, even among themselves. One reason for that was the decades-long dominance of Russian in the schools of the capital. When we arrived, only three of the city's sixty-nine primary schools offered Kyrgyz as the primary language of instruction.[4] Kyrgyz parents understandably chose Russian-language education for their children as a way of improving their life chances in a Soviet Union where Russian was the language of opportunity. As a result, a generation and more of ethnic Kyrgyz raised in the capital had little facility in their native tongue. They also had little interest in elevating the role of the Kyrgyz language because it would have given an advantage to their ethnic kin in the country-side, who spoke better Kyrgyz.

In a visit to the outskirts of the capital, I encountered some of these country Kyrgyz, recent arrivals from rural communities who were squatting on land because there was no housing to be had in the city. Known as "the builders" (*zastroishchiki*), these squatters provided willing recruits to one of the first grassroots political movements in independent Kyrgyzstan, called *Ashar*, whose demands for inclusion in the political and economic life of the city raised concerns in the government and the local Russian community. With Russians possessing some of the best jobs and housing, one Kyrgyz complained to a local paper that he felt like "a guest in his own home."[5] The resentment of the newly arrived Kyrgyz extended not just to the members of other ethnic groups but to the Russified Kyrgyz raised in the capital. The new arrivals referred disparagingly to these denizens of Bishkek as "Kirgiz" rath-er than "Kyrgyz"—evoking the Russian spelling and pronunciation (Keer-geez) of the name.

Because scholars visiting Kyrgyzstan needed an institutional placement in order to receive a visa, Chingiz Aitmatov had arranged for us to be attached to the Academy of Sciences of Kyrgyzstan during our stay. Housed in a sprawling mid-twentieth-century building on the western edge of central Bishkek, the academy was composed of numerous institutes aligned with traditional academic disciplines. Our placement was in the Institute of Lin-guistics and Literature, which had an informal section devoted to Aitmatov Studies (*Aitmatovedenie*). Our contact there was Melis Akmataliev, a young Kyrgyz specialist on Aitmatov whose work tended to blur the distinction between scholarship and hagiography. His first name, Melis, suggested that he was born to parents who were devoted Communists—Melis is the acro-nym in Russian for Marx-Engels-Lenin-and-Stalin. The name, common in the Soviet era, was far from the most revolutionary-sounding appellation in the USSR. Parents wishing to express their devotion to the communist order had numerous naming options to choose from, including Elina, a diminutive form of Electrification and Industrialization, and Vilorik, composed of the first letters in Russian of Vladimir Il'ich Lenin Freed the Workers and Peas-ants.

Arriving as guests of Chingiz Aitmatov, we found ourselves in the awk-ward position of enjoying the hospitality he arranged for us while recoiling from some of the hero-worship of the writer that we found on display. Early in our stay, Melis inducted us into the Aitmatov Club, an organization he headed that was devoted to advancing the reputation of Chingiz Torekulovich. To formalize our induction into the club, Melis signed and presented us with red folding membership cards, which resembled in shape, color, and size the membership cards carried by Communist Party members in the Soviet era. In discussing the mission of the Aitmatov Club, Melis and other devotees of the distinguished Kyrgyz writer spoke of him with a respectfulness that often edged into adoration.

The pride that Melis and other Kyrgyz felt in their successful kinsman was certainly understandable and heartfelt. How many authors from any country, never mind a small, fledgling state, had sold over 80 million copies of their books and had their works translated into 176 different languages?[6] Chingiz Aitmatov was also more than a prolific author: his literary and political activity had helped to transform his society. Yet the extraordinary deference accorded to Aitmatov by Melis and many other Kyrgyz reminded me that societies celebrating Great Men, especially those among the living, were always in danger of succumbing to the authoritarian temptation. As Bertolt Brecht put it, unhappy the land that is in need of heroes.

Shortly after arriving in Bishkek, we received an invitation to have an early afternoon dinner at the home of Aitmatov's sister, Roza, a physicist who lived on the outskirts of Bishkek. It was our first chance to get out of the city, and as we drove south toward the mountains, through alleys of birch trees, we passed well-kept houses typical of the small Russian or German settlements ringing Bishkek. The houses were one-story structures with high roofs, each occupying what was called a private plot of land in the Soviet era. Although modest in scale and design—the post-communist McMansions favored by a growing nouveau riche class had yet to appear—these houses were highly sought after by the country's elite because of their distance from the noise and pollution of the city. In this village-like setting, Roza lived in a tasteful brick house with intricate wooden designs beneath the roof line and large rose bushes in full bloom along the drive. One outside wall resembled a work of abstract art, with alternate bricks painted white and an earthy red.

A quiet, deliberate woman a few years younger than her famous brother, Roza greeted us respectfully and invited us inside. Spread across the living room floor was a thick white cloth dotted with small plates that held fresh fruits and vegetables and an array of Kyrgyz appetizers. We took our seats on the floor with legs folded in traditional Kyrgyz fashion and marveled at the feast in front of us. Some of the offerings were familiar—sliced tomatoes and Russian vodka—but others were culinary novelties for us, from the traditional Kyrgyz flatbread, *naan*, which is a heavier, thicker version of its well-known Indian cousin, to *manty*, large steamed dumplings filled with ground lamb and onions. Even as a southerner used to eating with his hands, I was not quite prepared for the challenges of maintaining a semblance of propriety while biting into *manty*, out of which oozed a greasy liquid. Following the appetizer course, Roza's husband, Esenbek, brought out the main dish, a large plate of meat cut into unfamiliar slices. Biting into a piece with a large bone attached, I recognized the taste of garlic, but the flavor of the meat itself, though pleasant enough, was unfamiliar. Inquiring about the dish, we learned that it was horsemeat, once a Kyrgyz staple that is now reserved for special occasions because of its expense.

After dinner, Roza and Esenbek drove us toward the nearby settlement of Chon-Tash, stopping in a barren field whose only distinguishing marker was a small, low metal fence on a rise in the earth that covered a building in ruins. Surveying the scene, Roza explained solemnly that this was the site of a mass grave that held the remains of 137 members of the Kyrgyz political and cultural elite who had been killed in early November 1938 by Stalin's secret police.[7] Among those executed was her father, Torekul. In 1937, he had been a high-ranking Communist Party official in the republic who was recalled from his studies at the Institute of Red Professors in Moscow and arrested. Branded a "bourgeois nationalist," an accusation leveled at an entire genera- tion of indigenous leaders in non-Russian republics, his repression ushered in a period of intense russification of Kirgizia.

For the next twelve years, ethnic Russians with no previous experience in Kirgizia led the republic as Communist Party first secretaries. The ethnic Kyrgyz who took the place of Torekul Aitmatov and other party and govern- ment officials working under the first secretaries generally lacked the educa- tion and sophistication of their predecessors. The result was a crude syco- phantism toward the Russians, evident in the comments about them made by a Kyrgyz leader in the Brezhnev period. First Secretary Turdukan Usubaliev expressed his "gratitude to the Great Russian people . . . whose ardent love and devotion to the socialist motherland and to Lenin's glorious party have always been and will always be a source of inspiration and a splendid exam- ple and model for the Kirgiz people."[8]

Our trip to Chon-Tash came just a year after the discovery of the mass grave. The mystery surrounding their father's fate had weighed on Chingiz and Roza their whole lives, and the emotions unleashed by the unexpected revelation were still apparent in Roza's face as she approached the site. Chingiz and Roza had grown up as "enemies of the people," the label given to the relatives of those repressed in the Stalin era; the correspondence their mother received from the authorities after Torekul's disappearance stated that their father had been sent to a distant labor colony, without the right to send or receive letters. A few years later, while Roza was still a teenager, the policies of Nikita Khrushchev brought the rehabilitation of her father, and millions of other repressed citizens, but no word on his fate.

The grave might never have been unearthed had a woman not come forward with a secret entrusted to her by her father on his deathbed, a secret that she kept for almost thirty years, until she felt the political moment was right. Her father had worked in the 1930s as a cook for the NKVD, the secret

Figure 3.1.   The site of a mass grave of Stalinist-era victims near the town of Chon-Tash. The victims included Chingiz Aitmatov's father, Torekul. From right to left, Chingiz Aitmatov's driver; the author; Joe Mozur; and Roza Aitmatova. June 1992

police, which maintained a retreat for its personnel on the site of an old brick factory in Chon-Tash. After executing the 137 persons in a basement of the NKVD headquarters in central Bishkek, the authorities concluded that the brick factory was the only place that the bodies could be buried without arousing suspicion. In a disused brick firing kiln measuring ten by ten by ten feet, the NKVD stacked all of those killed, shoveling in dirt between the layers of corpses. For years after the mass burial, local residents claimed to see on clear nights a luminescent glow rising from the site, later attributed to the decaying of the remains.

After unearthing the bodies, only five persons among the 137 could be definitively identified. One of them was Torekul Aitmatov. Handed a typed indictment issued by the visiting military tribunal from Moscow that condemned them to death, Aitmatov and three other individuals had placed the document in their pockets, where they remained. The other identified victim went to his death wearing clothing with his name sewn inside. To honor the memory of all who died in the massacre, Chingiz Aitmatov, his sister Roza, and other relatives of the dead, as well as thousands of ordinary citizens of Bishkek, attended a solemn reinterment of the bodies in August 1991. They were laid to rest in 137 individual plots near the mass grave in Chon-Tash. In 2000, the Kyrgyzstani government created a moving memorial on the site, anchored by a large *tunduk*, the wooden crossties at the top of a yurt that serve as a symbol of the country. Perhaps the most poignant memorial to Torekul Aitmatov, though, was the book published by Roza Aitmatova in 2013, *The Blank Pages of History*, which recounts not just the death and strange afterlife of Torekul, but the role of an absent father in the life of a girl growing up in Soviet Kirgizia. [9]

Chapter Four

Hope Abounds

The gruesome discovery in Chon-Tash served to unite people of all backgrounds in the country, but the collapse of the old regime brought an inevitable struggle over the redistribution of political and economic power in independent Kyrgyzstan. Eager to speak to someone in government about the challenges facing the new Kyrgyzstani state, I walked along Erkindik one morning to the Foreign Ministry, which was housed in a small and unassuming white wooden building within a stone's throw of the recently opened American Embassy. Arriving unannounced, I explained to the kindly old doorman—security was not an issue in those days—that I wished to speak to the foreign minister. To my surprise, they ushered me into her office within minutes. A diminutive dynamo with a ready smile and staccato speech, Roza Otunbaeva greeted me as if I were an old friend. Only later did I learn that, following the example of Gorbachev, she addressed virtually everyone with the familiar form of "you" (*ty*), which Russians usually reserve for close friends and family or those much younger than themselves.

At forty-one, Roza Otunbaeva was only two years older than I, but she had already had a highly successful career in the Soviet and Kyrgyz capitals. After receiving a PhD in the mind-numbing field of dialectical materialism, an intellectual backwater even by Soviet standards, she taught "DiaMat" for several years at Kyrgyz State University before rising through the ranks of the local party apparatus to the position of foreign minister and deputy prime minister of the Kirgiz Republic. In one of the many oddities of the Soviet system, each of the fifteen republics had its own foreign ministry, intended in part to buttress the myth that the USSR was a voluntary union of republics that could secede from the country. After several years as "Foreign Minister" of Kirgizia, Roza moved to Moscow to work in responsible positions in the foreign ministry of the USSR. When the Soviet Union fell apart in December

1991, she faced a difficult career choice: assume the post of Russian ambassador to Malaysia or return to her native Kyrgyzstan to become the country's first foreign minister. She chose the latter, and when I arrived in her office to find the country's foreign ministry staffed by only four or five professionals, I began to understand what it meant to build a diplomatic service—and a new state—from scratch.

After listening attentively while I explained my interest in her new country, Roza quickly ran through a list of interviews that she would arrange for me. It was to be the first of many kindnesses that she would extend me over more than twenty years. When we ended our conversation just after noon that day, she invited me to join her for lunch in the Cabinet dining room in the White House, the modern, seven-story building that in those days housed both the presidency and parliament. Although I was more than a head taller than Roza, I struggled to keep up with her as she dashed across the wide plaza that separated the Foreign Ministry from the White House. When we walked into the dining room on a corner of an upper floor, the several male ministers seated at the table, deep in conversation, glanced at me with suspicion, surprised to find a foreigner in their midst. To establish my bona fides, Roza explained to her colleagues how important it was that American scholars like me tell the story of Kyrgyzstan in the West. Ever the energetic saleswoman to the world for Kyrgyzstan, Foreign Minister Otunbaeva realized, like the country's first president, Askar Akaev, that her remote and resource-poor land would only rise from obscurity if it garnered the attention and aid of larger, more powerful countries.

It did not take long for news of the presence of two American scholars in Kyrgyzstan to spread through the capital. Shortly after my meeting with Roza Otunbaeva, the new deputy minister of tourism called to insist on taking Joe Mozur and me to a resort on the shores of Issyk-Kul', where some of the world's tallest mountains surround a mile-high lake with sand beaches and clear, turquoise waters. The tourist official's goal was to attract well-heeled Western visitors to a site that had long been a retreat for cosmonauts, Communist Party leaders, and other members of the Soviet elite. The Kyrgyz may not have had the energy or mineral resources possessed by other Central Asian countries, like Kazakhstan and Turkmenistan, but they figured in these heady first months after independence that they could make good on their president's branding of their country as the Switzerland of Asia.

Pulling up to our hotel in the early morning with a driver in his government-issued Volga, the deputy minister initially seemed uncomfortable with the prospect of making the three-and-a-half hour trip to Issyk-Kul' with two strange Americans. He breathed a sigh of relief when he saw that we both spoke Russian. As we traveled east from the capital along the Chu Valley, with the Ala-Too Mountains to our right, he began laying out his ideas for the development of Issyk-Kul' as a tourist destination. When I asked whether security would be a problem during the long drive from the capital to the lakeside resorts, he replied that escorts toting machine guns could accompany Western tourist buses if desired. Sensing that that was not the response we hoped for, he quickly added that visitors could make the journey in a fraction of the time in Soviet army helicopters, which Kyrgyzstan had inherited from the old order. The deeper we got into the conversation, and the longer we stayed in Kyrgyzstan, the more we realized the dearth of understanding in the country about how politics and markets worked in the West.[1]

If the Kyrgyzstani deputy minister had his blind spots about the expectations of Western tourists, I was ignorant about the real source of danger to visitors to Issyk-Kul'. It came not from highwaymen along the route but careless or drunken drivers on the treacherous roads that connected Issyk-Kul' with the Chu Valley. An hour-and-a-half east of the capital, the route to the lake entered a series of canyons where the grade was steep and the road dropped precipitously in places to the raging Chu River below. Stopping at an overlook midway up a windswept canyon, Joe and I cautiously approached the edge of the roadway. All around us were treeless mountain slopes peppered with rock slides that spilled into the brown waters churning hundreds of feet beneath us. Landslides, avalanches, and earthquakes: these were the natural perils that the Kyrgyz had confronted for centuries.

Driving out of the canyons and into the Issyk-Kul' valley, we encountered a very different landscape, where bare mountains gave way to an alpine-like setting, with abundant trees and vegetation. One of the world's largest and deepest inland lakes, Issyk-Kul' creates its own microclimate, which moderates temperatures in summer and winter. In the Soviet era, waters near the southern shore had functioned as a testing site for torpedoes. Small vacation houses and hotels well past their prime dotted the lake's northern shore, which had long been a favorite of tourists from Russia and other Soviet republics, as well as Kyrgyz city dwellers escaping the country's hot summers. Normally bustling with vacationers, the beaches we saw that year were virtually empty because of the economic crisis brought on by the collapse of the Soviet Union.

It was along the northern shore, just shy of Cholpon-Ata, the main tourist town, that we pulled into an old resort shaded by a stand of pine trees. There an associate of the deputy minister joined us for a sumptuous lunch, heavy with meat and vodka, and discussions became more serious about how we might cooperate to bring tourists to Kyrgyzstan from the West. Despite repeated assurances that we were scholars and not businessmen, the Kyrgyz seemed reluctant to believe that not all Americans were deal-makers. At one point in the conversation, I found it difficult to determine whether the ideas about tourist development were part of a private business venture or an initiative of the state. Whatever the intentions of our Kyrgyz companions that

Figure 4.1.   A beach on the north shore of Lake Issyk-Kul'. Summer 2008

day, the use of government office to amass personal fortunes soon became a serious problem in this newly independent state.

Following the meal, Joe and I headed to an abandoned beach with our hosts, and lacking a swimsuit, I shed my clothes after much prompting and headed into the water. Hoping to plunge quickly into the chilly lake, I began running headlong, but the water receded so gradually from the shore that I had to take several long leaps before going under. Pulling myself out of the clear, cold lake after only a few seconds, I stood up to find that my breath had left me entirely, and it was several minutes before I could breathe normally. A frightening experience that I'd never had before, or since, it was a warning about swimming in icy water at high altitude after drinking vodka.

As we were readying to leave for the return trip to Bishkek, Joe and I began speaking with the driver while the deputy minister and his associate were settling the bill in the restaurant. The driver asked out of curiosity what a dollar bill looked like, and I pulled one out of my wallet and told him to keep it. When our hosts returned to find the driver studying the greenback, they asked for dollar bills as souvenirs as well, and we gladly obliged, though with a sense of embarrassment that the American currency could be such a novelty in the country, especially for highly ranked officials. Unlike in Moscow and St. Petersburg, where black marketeers had traded rubles for tourist dollars on the streets for well over a decade, Kyrgyzstan had not been exposed to Western visitors in the Soviet era, which ensured that our encounters with Kyrgyzstani citizens during our stay were exercises in mutual discovery.

After following events in Kyrgyzstan from afar largely through the lens of a single Bishkek daily, I spent what free time we had on this first trip to Bishkek reading and collecting other newspapers and magazines, which sold for pennies apiece in Bishkek's ubiquitous kiosks. One publication in particular, *Res Publica*, caught my eye because of its lively writing style and its willingness to criticize the government of the day. Finding the address of the editorial offices on the back page of the paper, Joe and I headed out one afternoon to pay a call on the journalists behind *Res Publica*. Ducking into an unkempt and dimly lit entranceway typical of Khrushchev-era walk-ups throughout the Soviet Union, we found a door marked "Res Publica," knocked, and walked in. Working in a two-room apartment with bare floors and spare furnishings was a small group of young reporters who looked like they'd stepped out of a Kerouac novel. They had just put that week's paper to bed, and to mark the unexpected arrival of two curious Americans and the completion of another issue of their paper, this young collective produced from nowhere the "loaves and fishes" that always seemed to materialize in this part of the world when there was something—anything—to celebrate. Over vodka, bread, and cucumbers, we talked into the evening about the challenges of running an opposition-oriented newspaper in a post-communist country as well as the first stirrings of organized political activity in Kyrgyzstan.

The paper's editor-in-chief, Zamira Sydykova, was a thirty-two-year-old graduate of the journalism faculty of Moscow State University. After working for several years as a reporter for the newspaper of the Young Communist League of Kirgizia, she established *Res Publica* in early 1992, just after the collapse of the USSR. *Res Publica* was in the forefront of a rapidly changing media landscape in Kyrgyzstan. Legacy newspapers attached to government institutions, like *Slovo Kyrgyzstana*, continued to write in the wooden, formulaic style that had characterized Soviet journalism. *Res Publica* and a handful of other independent publications broke free from these financial and stylistic shackles and published trenchant pieces on issues that the government ignored or sought to suppress, such as the demands of recent migrants for land on the outskirts of the capital. It was on the pages of *Res Publica*, and in interviews arranged by Zamira with opposition figures, that I began to appreciate the vulnerabilities of the emerging political order in Kyrgyzstan.

Figure 4.2.   Newspaper kiosk in Bishkek. May 2009

Kyrgyzstan did not yet have officially recognized political parties, but there were already activist groups that had been organizing since 1989. The most important of these was the Democratic Movement of Kyrgyzstan (DDK), an umbrella organization that united diverse groups seeking the reform of the political and economic systems. The leader of the DDK, Djypar Djeksheev, was a member of the country's cultural elite, like many of those pushing for change in Kyrgyzstan. In an interview in his modest office, he outlined to me the movement's platform, which could have been written by any moderate party in the West: a secular state; equal rights for all ethnic groups; the privatization of property, including the distribution of state land to the peasants; and a reduction in the size of the bureaucracy. On the sensitive issue of language policy, the DDK favored gradually de-emphasizing Russian and moving toward a single state language, Kyrgyz, which in their view should be written in the Latin rather than the Cyrillic alphabet.[2] Originally written in Arabic script, the Kyrgyz language was rendered in the Latin alphabet from 1926 to 1939, when the Soviet government decided to bring it into line with Russian, which uses Cyrillic.

Shortly after the meeting with Djeksheev, I interviewed the head of a spin-off group of the DDK, Asaba, which was led by Asan Ormushev, the author of a dissertation on the history of the Kyrgyz working class. Asaba was the first openly nationalist political group in Kyrgyzstan and an unabashed advocate of a Kyrgyzstan for the Kyrgyz. According to Ormushev, because the economic standing of the Kyrgyz had lagged behind that of other ethnic groups in the Soviet era, in the transition from communism the state needed to introduce policies that privileged the titular group, meaning the people after whom the country is named. In his words, "at first you have the right of nations, and later the rights of man." Only by raising the level of the Kyrgyz, he argued, could they compete effectively with other groups. On the controversial issue of land reform, Asaba insisted that the ethnic Kyrgyz should be the sole owners of real property; non-Kyrgyz would only be able to lease land. It would be forty to fifty years, he conceded, before the country might be ready to embrace equal private property rights for all ethnic groups. On the language question, Asaba also advanced a maximalist position, arguing that all official documents should be issued in Kyrgyz alone by January 1, 1993, and Russian should lose its position as the main language of inter-ethnic discourse.[3]

Asaba had first gained notoriety in 1991 when it organized an almost 300-mile people's march to commemorate the seventy-fifth anniversary of the Kyrgyz uprising against the Russians in 1916, an event known in Kyrgyz as the Urkun.[4] At a time when Russian settlers were moving into some of the best farmland in northern Kirgizia, the Tsar issued an order to conscript ethnic Kyrgyz to fight in the First World War. Rebelling against this edict, some Kyrgyz attacked Russian settlers, which led to massive repression by Russian army units garrisoned in the region. The result was the flight of hundreds of thousands of Kyrgyz, up to a third of their total population, across the Tien Shan Mountains into western China. Many Kyrgyz died on the journey, in winter, across mountains at the roof of the world.[5] Some descendants of Kyrgyz caught in the Urkun still live in China's Xinjiang province today, though most survivors and their children returned to the USSR after the 1940s. Understandably, the Urkun remains a politically charged symbol in the country, and those hoping to mobilize discontented ethnic Kyrgyz, or challenge Russian influence, have invoked the memories associated with what some have called a genocide to advance their political goals.

Although political opinions diverged among those interviewed, most of the voices I heard during our two-week stay in Kyrgyzstan expressed excitement bordering on disbelief about the rapid movement of Kyrgyzstan from a dependent territory of the USSR to an independent state. The political, economic, and cultural ground that had seemed unshakeable in the Soviet era had shifted irreversibly in Kyrgyzstan over a few short months. Amid the unwinding of the Soviet way of life and the emergence of an as yet dimly understood post-communist order, a spirit of optimism prevailed, especially in official circles. Yet the critical tasks facing the new state were still to be addressed: the privatization of property, the development of competitive political institutions, the adoption of a new constitution, the establishment of a national currency, and the shaping of a new national identity that could satisfy the aspirations of the core nation, the Kyrgyz, while protecting the interests of the country's minority groups, which in this period made up almost half of Kyrgyzstan's population. Even at this early moment of Kyrgyzstan's history as an independent country, we met some persons who viewed themselves as potential losers in the transition from communism: members of ethnic minorities, including an Armenian, a Dungan, and a German, and some figures in the cultural and scientific communities who worried about the ability of the new state to finance their pursuits.

It was easy to forget the scope of the challenges facing the country at a time when the world was being disrupted, and anything seemed possible. Landing in Moscow in the late evening on our return trip, we taxied toward the terminal and, as the plane came to a halt, we looked out over the right wing to see a Toyota sedan approaching the plane. As we walked down the stairs to the tarmac, the young Russian driver opened the car doors and invited us inside. With American pop music playing from the rear speakers, we sped off toward Sheremetovo Airport for the final leg of our trip home. Our modestly priced airport transfer, arranged during our earlier connection through Moscow, seemed too good to be true, and at the time I should have known that when anything goes, the moment is fleeting.

Chapter Five

Traveling the Chu Valley

Last Stop, the President's Office

The euphoria at the birth of a new nation soon gave way to a more sober assessment of the challenges facing Kyrgyzstan in the wake of the Soviet Union's collapse. When I returned to Kyrgyzstan in the summer of 1993, this time alone, the most visible change was the new national currency, the som, which had just entered circulation. The first Soviet republic outside the Baltic to break from the Russian ruble, Kyrgyzstan gave its citizens five days in May 1993 to hand in their rubles for new som notes, which began trading at four to the dollar. Not surprisingly, given the precariousness of the Kyrgyzstani economy—the country's national income had declined 26 percent over the preceding year—the som failed to hold its value, and by the time I arrived in June, a dollar was fetching over twenty soms.

The currency reform followed the script written for Kyrgyzstan by international financial institutions, which helped to support the separation from the ruble zone. But while the Kyrgyzstani government pleased Western advisers with this move, they angered several local constituencies. Consumers protested that merchants took advantage of the new currency to raise prices; manufacturers complained that the currency reform frightened away suppliers and buyers in other post-communist countries that were using rubles; and the neighboring countries of Kazakhstan and Uzbekistan, still in the ruble zone themselves, viewed it as an "irresponsible attempt to leapfrog over other Central Asian countries in economic development."[1]

Almost overnight small exchange booths emerged on the streets of Bishkek to compete with the country's few banks for the foreign exchange business. The day after arriving I walked to a nearby exchange kiosk, handed over $100, and received a wad of new som notes that bore colorful images of national landmarks and heroes, which are part of the branding of any new state. It was still a time when travelers to Kyrgyzstan had to bring cash to cover their expenses; even in the United States, debit cards and ATMs had yet to take off, and credit cards were not accepted by businesses in Kyrgyzstan. Before leaving the States, it was vital to obtain clean banknotes, without markings or heavy use, and preferably in $20 or $50 denominations. And whenever the American Treasury decided to introduce new versions of larger bills, traders in Kyrgyzstan insisted on getting the latest banknotes. Exchange booths or merchants who received currency that was soiled, ripped, marked on, or "out-of-date" would only give 70 cents on the dollar. As a result, preparing for trips to Kyrgyzstan always meant an awkward few minutes at a local bank in my hometown, rifling through bills with a teller who never quite understood the fetish for clean currency.

Unlike the previous summer, when I'd stayed in a small hotel, I lived this time with relatives of Roza Otunbaeva in a clean, modest apartment opposite Togolok Moldo Park, just a few blocks south of the center of town. I'd arranged the accommodation a few months earlier while visiting Roza in Washington, DC, where she had just become the first Kyrgyzstani ambassador to the United States. She and her family had moved into a comfortable home near the Maryland line, and when I stopped by for dinner one evening, she apologized that the furniture had not yet arrived. To make do, they had reverted to the traditions of their ancestors and spread Kyrgyz carpets that they'd brought from Bishkek across the floors. Operating on a modest budget, Roza settled into embassy offices that were clearly not Class A real estate. Located well away from Embassy Row, a few blocks north of the White House, the first Embassy of the Kyrgyz Republic in the western hemisphere was housed on an upper floor of a small, run-down office building. With only a handful of embassies scattered around the world in strategically important countries, Kyrgyzstan struggled to support a modern diplomatic infrastructure.

My apartment mates in Bishkek included several men and women, two from the capital and two from the provinces, the latter on a short-term teacher training course. The head of this household of close and distant kin, Edil', was an outgoing thirty-something who aspired to become a businessman. Not long after I moved in, he broached the subject of a partnership. The idea was to satisfy the rising demand for classic American cars among Chinese businessmen who lived just across the border. Although I'd rejected out of hand the deal-making overtures of the deputy minister the preceding summer, Edil' was a more sympathetic figure and the concept of supplying cars to the Chinese Far West seemed intriguing. The plans involved loading three cars in a 40-foot container from the port of Jacksonville, Florida, destined for St. Petersburg, Russia. The cars would then be off-loaded for the more than 3,000-mile trip across Russia and Kazakhstan to Bishkek. It was at this point that the scheme raised red flags for me. The image of a small convoy of Mustangs and Corvettes driving through provincial Russia, and then a Russian-Kazakh border post, was sufficiently surreal, and worrying, to put me off the plan.

Life in the apartment was instructive as well as enjoyable. It was there that I first became aware of regional differences among the Kyrgyz and the female modesty characteristic of some rural Kyrgyz women.[2] One of my female apartment mates, a cousin to Edil', was from the Naryn region, a remote, mountainous, and sparsely populated territory along the Chinese border. Raised in the most traditional part of the country—over 99 percent of the population there was ethnic Kyrgyz—she dressed conservatively but without a head scarf, which was rarely seen in Bishkek in those days. She seldom spoke, and then in passable but heavily accented Russian. Perhaps because of Muslim traditions, she tended not to venture out of her room when we were left alone in the apartment, but even when others were present, and she was speaking Kyrgyz, she exhibited a studied meekness that I had never encountered. The contrast with outgoing, confident Kyrgyz women of the cities, like Roza Otunbaeva and Zamira Sydykova, could not have been greater.

During one of my first nights in the apartment, the group prepared the signature Kyrgyz dish, *beshbarmak*, meaning five fingers, which is a simple stew with meat and noodles. As Edil' was pulling the mutton from the bone, another Kyrgyz present objected that he wasn't doing it properly. A spirited exchange ensued on the regional variations in Kyrgyz cuisine, which led to a broader discussion of the intra-ethnic differences in the Kyrgyz nation, on everything from dialect to carpets and clothing—all "cultural markers," in the language of contemporary social science. Living in valleys separated by mountains that were all but impassable in the winter, the Kyrgyz had developed local traditions and loyalties that continued into the Soviet era and beyond. It would not be long before I began to appreciate the important role that region of origin played in politics in Kyrgyzstan.

A few days before the introduction of the som, Kyrgyzstan had put in place another building block of a new state: a constitution. Like other Soviet republics, Kyrgyzstan exited the USSR not with a bang but a whimper. The currency, laws, constitution, and officials in place at the end of the Soviet era continued into the new regime, and so the initial months and years of post-communist rule were devoted to the gradual remaking of the political and economic order. As in other parts of the former USSR, the rewriting of the constitution threatened to redistribute political power—between executive and legislative branches, capital and the provinces, and government and the people.

The debates surrounding Kyrgyzstan's new fundamental law revealed deep divisions in the country's political elite, the most serious of which centered on the relative powers of the parliament and president. Although there was a consensus on the retention of a semi-presidential model of government, in which a president elected by the people shares executive responsibilities with a prime minister selected by parliament, many politicians in Kyrgyzstan sought to limit the powers of appointment and policy-making of the president. For his part, President Akaev argued that with the economy and society in disarray in the early 1990s, it was vital to entrust the president with enough authority to push through needed reforms and ensure political stability.

Objecting to constitutional drafts that denied the president decisive power atop the political system, Akaev asked in December 1992:

> Why did we introduce the institution of the presidency in the first place? So that it would turn the president into a figurehead like the Queen of England? We wanted to have an authoritative executive branch that could serve as a counterweight to the legislature. We see the consequences of such an amorphous, faceless system in neighboring Tajikistan [where a civil war was underway].[3]

Despite Akaev's protests, the parliament adopted a constitution that limited the prerogatives of the president. The president could appoint ministers as before, but only with the approval of the parliament. He also had to seek permission from parliament to change the structure of the executive branch or to dismiss the government before the end of a parliamentary term. To be sure, President Akaev and his allies got their way on many other provisions: the new constitution eliminated the office of vice president and dramatically reduced the size of the parliament, henceforth to be known by its Kyrgyz name, *Jogorku Kenesh* (Supreme Council), from 350 to 105 deputies. The smaller the parliament, the easier it was for a president to corral a majority. But dissatisfied with a constitution that balanced power among parliament, prime minister, and president, Akaev would devote considerable energy over the next few years to lessening the constraints on presidential power.

Six weeks after the adoption of the new constitution, I spent a hectic day interviewing government officials across the Chu Valley. I left Bishkek by car at 6:30 a.m. for Kara-Balta, a city an hour west of the capital that had the feel of a nineteenth-century industrial village. My first meeting, at 7:45 a.m., was with the leader of the Kalinin district government. Divided at that time into five regions and over fifty districts, Kyrgyzstan had a presidentially appointed *akim*, or administrative head, for each of these territorial subdivisions. The *akim* of the Kalinin district, Tologon Rakhmanov, was a brusque, middle-aged Kyrgyz man who had the air of an unreconstructed Soviet bureaucrat.

Dispensing with pleasantries, he launched immediately into an explanation—bordering on a diatribe—on how the local economy worked. It was not subtle levers like the market, he argued, but administrative measures that would ensure economic success in the transition from communism. Portraying himself as a victim of national policy over which he had no control, he noted that before the currency reform, his district, known for its machine-made rugs, had restored industrial production to 97 percent of pre-independence levels. The introduction of the som interrupted that revival, in his view. But for all his disillusionment with the national leadership, he admitted that the center gave him wide discretion in selecting personnel in the local government. He was every bit the local boss, and with over fifty such district leaders jealous of their personal power, the challenge of implementing a common national policy in this environment was formidable.

Following the interview in Kara-Balta, we drove further west to Kaiyndy, the last town before the border with Kazakhstan. Here I met with Gennadii Davidenko, the *akim* of Panfilov district. A pleasant, energetic man of Ukrainian background, he was the rare Slav living in Kyrgyzstan who spoke fluent Kyrgyz. Most Russians and Ukrainians saw little reason in the Soviet era to learn the local language, but Davidenko grew up in a Kyrgyz village where he picked up the language on the streets, playing with Kyrgyz boys. Like many local leaders in this period, when the Soviet Union collapsed he shed his former title as secretary of the district Communist Party committee for the new label of *akim*. When I asked him to compare the power of the *akim* to that of a party secretary under the communist regime, he replied without hesitation that he enjoyed greater autonomy as *akim*. Previously, Communist Party decrees were carried out, but this is not the case, he noted, with presidential decrees. As a result, he assured me, change would be very slow in coming in Kyrgyzstan. Unlike in Kara-Balta, where industry prevailed, his district was overwhelmingly rural, and the transition from Soviet collective farms to private farming was still in its infancy.

At 11:00 a.m., after we had spoken for about an hour, Davidenko ushered me into a meeting room where a long, festively decorated table was filled with bottles of cognac, vodka, and mineral water as well as *zakuski*—the appetizers that are the pride of Russian and Ukrainian cuisine. Joining us were a number of his colleagues in the small *akimiat*—the local government headquarters—and the traditional rounds of toasts cementing American-Kyrgyz friendship followed. It was a convivial group and I regretted not being able to stay longer, but we were on a tight schedule. Facing another lunch within an hour, I managed to extract myself from the generosity of my hosts in Kaiyndy without great offense and with some semblance of sobriety.

The next stop on my whirlwind tour of the Chu Valley was the home of the regional customs inspector. Even in the late Soviet period, high-ranking customs officials were known for their lavish lifestyle, supported by bribes that allowed goods to pass across the border without inspection or duties. My host was a welcoming and well-spoken Kyrgyz man whose home in a leafy village was expansive and tastefully furnished, without a hint of the ostentation that one associates with customs officials. He invited me into his large, shaded backyard, which sloped gently toward a creek. In the middle of the yard was a wood-roofed pavilion with a picnic table groaning under the weight of Kyrgyz dishes of every variety. Before we sat down, he pointed to the outhouse down the hill and, in need of the facilities, I approached the small wooden building with some reluctance. My father, brought up in rural Florida, liked to say that the house of his childhood had "three bedrooms and one path," but my generation looked upon outhouses as things to be gawked at instead of used. I needn't have worried, this was the most pristine and well-appointed privy I'd ever seen. Standing next to the outhouse was a portable metal wash basin that was common in rural parts of Kyrgyzstan. Fitted out with a faucet, a small water reservoir, and a towel rack, the stand-alone sink seemed like the kind of well-designed, retro picnic item that one might find in a Restoration Hardware catalog.

Taking our seats at the outdoor table, the customs inspector, his wife, and three children—one of whom was learning English—began to give me a mini-course in Kyrgyz cooking, explaining the names and ingredients of the dishes in front of us. Limiting myself to small tastes of several dishes so that I would emerge from the appetizer course intact, I was still not prepared for the pièce de résistance, which the customs inspector placed in front of me with a flourish. I looked down at my plate and saw a massive lamb's head staring at me, his long tongue protruding from the left side of his mouth. Lamb is my favorite meat, but I was not ready for the powerful smell emanating from the head or the life-like features. Cooking had done little to alter the look of the animal.

The slaughtering of a sheep is reserved for special guests, and so it was a great—if awkward—honor to be the person with the sheep's head in front of him. As I was to find out, it is the Kyrgyz tradition for the honored guest to eat the eyeball before others begin eating their lamb. When the host invited me to partake of the eyeball, I swallowed hard and began to peel away and eat the meat right under the eye, but the eyeball itself was a body part too far. I sheepishly confessed that as grateful as I was for the honor, I did not merit it and would not be able to down the eyeball. I learned later that Kyrgyz tradition provides an escape route at moments like this: the guest can transfer the honor to the oldest male in the group, in Kyrgyz the *aksakal*, or gray beard. Looking back, I wish I had had the courage to set aside my squeamishness and follow tradition.

After downing two massive lunches in less than two hours, we headed back to Bishkek. En route, the multi-ethnic and multi-confessional character of the Chu Valley was on full display. The collapse of communism had put people in motion, with rural Kyrgyz leaving the countryside for the cities while people of European backgrounds, including the Germans, left Kyrgyz-

Figure 5.1.   Sheep sausage (*chuchuk*) dressed as a snake. April 2009

stan for their homelands. Originally invited into the Russian Empire in the eighteenth century by Catherine the Great, Germans settled as farmers along the Volga River, but suspicions about their loyalty to the Soviet Union during WWII led to their resettlement to Central Asia. Pushed by their poorer prospects in an independent Kyrgyzstan dominated by the Kyrgyz, and pulled by the attraction of a recently reunified Germany, Kyrgyzstani Germans returned in large numbers to their native land after 1991. From a community of over 100,000, the German population dropped to under 20,000 by the beginning of the twenty-first century. Returning to Bishkek, we passed German villages with impressive brick houses, many of which were vacant. It's likely that these residences did not remain empty long because homes built and maintained by Germans enjoyed a reputation for high quality among Kyrgyzstanis.

On the edge of a Russian village, we passed an old, wooden Orthodox Church. Not far away was a building with a faded red wooden poster displaying a hammer and sickle, the symbols of communist rule. Draped across the poster was a new banner adorned in Arabic script with the Russian word "mechet'"—or mosque—beneath it. Until the end of the Soviet era, Bishkek had only a single Muslim place of worship, but there was now an explosion of mosque construction. Several were being built along our route back to the capital, and in the southern reaches of the city, a Turkish businessman was funding the construction of a large brick mosque that would serve the rural Kyrgyz migrants moving into squatter settlements nearby.

Although Islam in northern Kyrgyzstan was not as deeply rooted as in the south of the country, where the Uzbek minority had a long tradition of religious piety, it enjoyed a revival that surprised, and worried, the country's secular leadership. Recognizing the ideological and spiritual vacuum left by the collapse of communist ideals, President Akaev and other political leaders were willing to bring Islam out from the underground, where it had resided throughout the Soviet era, and grant it a respected place in public life. However, the political leadership sought to channel religious expression into forms that could be monitored and controlled by the state, a formidable challenge given the lack of a single organizational hierarchy in the Sunni branch of Islam that was indigenous to the region.

Returning from the western Chu Valley, I arrived in the capital just in time for a 3:00 p.m. interview with President Akaev. The setting was the Kyrgyzstani White House, a massive concrete structure that looks out onto the city's main commercial street, Chu Prospect. Built in 1985 as the headquarters of the Communist Party of Kirgizia, the White House is surrounded by imposing iron gates and well-kept grounds with small spruce trees. After

Figure 5.2.   Muslim cemetery overlooking the Chu Valley. July 2010

showing my passport to the uniformed guards manning the gatehouse for visitors, I crossed an empty plaza and climbed the stairs to one of four sets of tall wooden doors, only two of which ever seemed to be operational. Passing through a metal detector just inside the doors, I gave my passport to the uniformed guard, who placed it in a rack with other passports, each book-marked with a small handwritten form that noted the time of entrance and office to be visited. Met by an aide from the president's office, I took one of the diminutive elevators common in this part of the world to the presidential suite on the seventh floor.

Within a few minutes, a secretary showed me into Akaev's office, where he was working at his desk. I was struck immediately by his calmness. He slowly walked over to greet me, and then spoke deliberately and constructed his ideas with a kind of quiet confidence that seemed to betray his back-ground as a natural scientist. A physicist by training, Askar Akaev entered politics relatively late in life. After receiving his graduate training in Lenin-grad and working there for a decade, Akaev returned to Kirgizia to work in the republic's flagship university and then in the republican Academy of Sciences, rising at one point to the presidency of the organization. His first brush with politics came in 1986, when, at the age of forty-two, he was appointed secretary for education and science of the Communist Party of Kirgizia. His performance in that position was reportedly undistinguished by the standards of the day, and so he returned to work in the Academy of Sciences. A second opportunity in politics presented itself in 1989, when Gorbachev was looking for reform-minded figures in Kirgizia who could help to transform the republic's Communist Party, which was one of the most reactionary in the Soviet Union. Akaev was elected to a redesigned Soviet parliament in the spring of 1989, and in October of 1990 he emerged as the surprise winner of the presidency of the republic.

The fall of 1990 had been a period of turmoil in the Kirgiz Republic. The republic had just emerged from deadly inter-ethnic conflicts between Kyrgyz and Uzbeks living in the South, and the political leadership was split between moderate and hard-line communists. While most other Soviet republics had been moving away from an unbending, dogmatic interpretation of commu-nism, Kirgizia remained a bastion of ideological traditionalism, with Mos-cow continually racheting up its criticism of the Kirgiz leaders who refused to get with the new program.[4]

As the republican parliament was meeting in the White House to select its president—a newly created office at the federal and republican levels that was designed by Gorbachev and his team to wrest power away from the Communist Party bureaucracy—demonstrators surrounded the building, many drawn from the ranks of labor migrants demanding land and housing. In an unprecedented move, the republican Communist Party organization did not advance a single candidate, as had been the tradition for decades, but instead allowed three names to go forward as presidential contenders. When none of the candidates received a majority of the parliament's votes after two rounds, they were all eliminated from contention according to the rules of the republican constitution in place at the end of the Soviet era.[5]

At this moment, Gorbachev intervened personally and sought to convince Chingiz Aitmatov to allow his name to be placed in nomination for the presidency. Unwilling to assume the position, Aitmatov maneuvered behind the scenes to support the candidacy of Akaev, who won the vote in the next round.[6] A year later, in October 1991, Akaev stood unopposed in a direct election to the presidency. It was, to say the least, an unlikely road to power, and one that distinguished Kyrgyzstan from its neighboring post-communist countries, where the presidents had previously been leaders of the republican communist parties.

Sitting opposite Akaev on a couch in the presidential office, I reminded him that I was a former Sovietologist, adding that the label was something of a curse word in the Soviet lexicon. Akaev interjected immediately that he had always respected Sovietologists. He claimed to have been influenced by the work of Zbigniew Brzezinski—a Columbia University Sovietologist and later President Carter's National Security Adviser. In good Soviet fashion, he quickly added that Brzezinski, of course, "was not without his shortcomings." Throughout our forty-five-minute conversation, Akaev exuded an air of dignity, almost nobility—his grandfather, as Leonid Levitin, an Akaev aide, never tired of telling me, had been a local prince.[7] Akaev answered questions in long, often elegantly structured sentences and his attitude toward me was solicitous, almost to the point of being deferential. He was, in many respects, the antithesis of a traditional politician.

In response to my questions about the currency reform and language policy, Akaev provided formulaic, well-rehearsed answers. It was only when I urged him to talk about the challenges of getting executive officials in Bishkek and the provinces to work together on national policy that he became more animated and spontaneous. Expressing frustration about his leadership for the first time in our lengthy interview, he admitted that trying to impose discipline on ministers and *akims* was not easy. His comments suggested that it was one thing for members of parliament—as politicians—to insist on their independence, and something else again for officials in the executive branch to resist guidance from above. The tendency of officials to pursue their own interests to the detriment of the larger organization is, of course, a universal problem in government, but the reluctance to defer to authority based on an abstract concept like the state, instead of an organic unit like the family, clan, or tribe, was especially acute in countries like Kyrgyzstan, where statehood was in its infancy.

Because ethnic and regional loyalties were strong in Kyrgyzstan, Akaev was careful to speak of the country as the "common home" of an array of different ethnic, linguistic, and religious groups. In debates over divisive issues like land and language policy, Akaev always pursued a middle path to avoid alienating any of the country's diverse communities. On the crucial question of personnel policy, however, Kyrgyzstan's first president was insensitive to widespread perceptions of favoritism. Hailing from the small, rural district of Kemin, where the road to Issyk-Kul' begins to rise to the canyons, Akaev decided to surround himself with personnel from his home district as a way of ensuring the loyalty of his entourage. This appointment policy gave rise to accusations that he had replaced "Communism with Keminism." Along with this Kemin "mafia," Russians and northern Kyrgyz were well-represented in the halls of power, whereas those living in the South, whether Kyrgyz or Uzbek, saw few of their kin in positions of political power around Akaev. The subsequent rise in the influence of Akaev's immediate family members, including his wife, Mairam, his daughter, Bermet, and her husband, the Kazakh businessman, Adil Toiganbaev, only aggravated the perceptions of favoritism. Nepotism and the imbalance between North and South in Kyrgyzstan's political elite would return to haunt Askar Akaev.

As my circle of contacts in the country's leadership expanded, I realized that personal advisors to the president, whether formally on his staff or not, exercised greater political influence at times than the heads of prominent institutions, such as the prime minister or the speaker of the parliament. One such personal advisor was Leonid Levitin, who at the time of my visit in 1993 was the éminence grise of Kyrgyzstani politics. Born in the Soviet republic of Belarus to Jewish parents, he spent his entire career in Kyrgyzstan, working as a lawyer and then law professor before becoming Akaev's legal advisor on the eve of Kyrgyzstan's independence. He soon emerged as a jack-of-all-trades in the White House. Flaunting his overseas contacts, Levitin assumed responsibility for organizing many of Akaev's visits abroad; he claimed that he also served as his primary speechwriter for the trips. For the important mission of drafting a new set of laws to replace those inherited from the communist regime, Akaev relied heavily on Levitin, who in turn contracted out much of the work to academic lawyers in Moscow with whom he was close. There were suspicions that Levitin's reliance on Russian colleagues was explained as much by the money he stood to make from the deal as by the lack of competent legal draftsmen in Kyrgyzstan. Whatever his motivation, the decision to turn over the work to Moscow lawyers helped to ensure that Kyrgyzstan's post-communist civil code, which regulated business activity, followed the Russian model closely.

Besides his legal and diplomatic assignments, Levitin became involved in commercial matters, including one affair that scandalized the country. In circumstances that are still disputed, Kyrgyzstan transferred fourteen of its sixteen tons of gold reserves in 1992 to a firm in Switzerland, Siabeko, reportedly receiving less for the gold than it was worth. Leonid Levitin served as an intermediary in the transaction with Siabeko, which was run by a former Soviet citizen associated with Levitin, Boris Bernshtein. A few months before my return to Kyrgyzstan, under considerable public pressure Akaev had dismissed Levitin from his post of special advisor to the president and closed down the branch of Siabeko operating in Kyrgyzstan. As a Jew in a traditionally Muslim country, Levitin was an easy target for his many political enemies who resented his proximity to the president.

On my way to Kyrgyzstan in the summer of 1993, I ran into Levitin on the plane from Frankfurt to Almaty. He was accompanying a delegation of Kyrgyz military officers who had visited NATO headquarters in Brussels. Stripped of his formal title, Levitin nonetheless continued to serve Akaev as a close confidante and as a high-ranking administrator and professor at the newly created School of Management and Business in the center of Bishkek, which aspired to be a cross between the Wharton School and the Woodrow Wilson Center. Previously a training center for Communist Party officials, the institute passed into the hands of the presidency when the Soviet Union collapsed. It seems unusual in the West for an institution of higher education to be "attached to" (*pri*) the presidency, but this tradition of patronage of universities and research institutes had a long history in the Soviet era, which continued after communism's collapse in Kyrgyzstan, Russia, and other post-communist countries. Among the many other Communist Party properties that the presidency inherited was the stunning Ala-Archa National Park, a 5,000-acre reserve located in the mountains forty minutes south of Bishkek.

During conversations in his office in the School of Management, Levitin treated me to tales of his exploits in the White House and his characterizations of the leading players in Kyrgyzstani politics. He was a man of grand plans: for Kyrgyzstan, Akaev, and the School of Management. Aware that his information and contacts were valuable for an American researcher interested in his country, he expected me to reciprocate by presenting some lectures at his institute, which I was pleased to do. At the time, the School of Management enrolled some of the county's best and brightest students. Giving lectures there on American politics and the politics of ethnicity allowed me to interact with the first generation of Kyrgyzstani citizens to be educated in the post-communist era, a generation that was immensely curious about the world beyond Central Asia.

At the end of my first week back in Bishkek, I looked in at the offices of *Res Publica*, whose staff was enjoying the ritual of celebrating the completion of that week's edition. As the journalists shared shots of vodka with canned fish—the cheap tins that were the favorite of Soviet-era drunks—Zamira Sydykova brought me up to date on the state of the press in Kyrgyzstan. From my own conversations with politicians, it was evident that *Res Publica* continued to irritate the authorities; virtually every official I met volunteered criticism of the paper. One of *Res Publica*'s harshest critics was

Akaev's press secretary, Kabai Karabekov, a twenty-seven-year-old wunder-kind who had been a local correspondent for a Moscow newspaper before independence. Zamira believed that Karabekov had been responsible for excluding *Res Publica* journalists from a press conference held the previous week for Russian-language newspapers.

The relations between the White House and opposition-oriented newspapers like *Res Publica* were clearly strained, but Zamira and her staff still enjoyed virtually unlimited access to government officials. Early the next week, hearing that I wanted to interview several members of parliament, Zamira dropped what she was doing and accompanied me to the White House. I was expecting to deposit my passport as usual at the guard's station at the entrance, but Zamira waved us through, ignoring the demands of the security staff that I show my documents. Shouting dismissively "he's with me," Zamira hurried me into the White House and took me to the office of the parliamentary speaker, Medetkan Sherimkulov, who'd been a high-ranking official in the Kirgiz Communist Party apparatus in the Soviet era. Sherimkulov had just returned from an official visit to the Osh region in the South, where he had viewed the site of a devastating landslide and assessed the effects of the economic blockade that Uzbekistan had imposed in retaliation for Kyrgyzstan's introduction of its own currency. At Zamira's insistence, he made time in his busy schedule to speak with me for twenty minutes.

Of course, not all journalists were like Zamira, and not all papers were like *Res Publica*. Most Kyrgyzstanis read Russian or Kyrgyz-language editions of newspapers that were part of what might be called the semiofficial press—papers associated with and financed by government institutions. One such paper was *Svobodnye gory* (Free Mountains), the newspaper supported by the Kyrgyzstani parliament. A recent letter to the editor in *Svobodnye gory* illustrated the tenor of mainstream Kyrgyzstani journalism in this period. The editors were willing to publish a letter containing serious criticism of President Akaev and the country's government, but they insisted on including bracketed comments throughout that refuted the letter's accusations and apologized for the "harsh tone" of its author. In short, between the hypercritical media like *Res Publica* and the semiofficial press, readers had access to a wide range of information and opinions. The openness and pluralism of Kyrgyzstani society and politics stood in stark contrast to the conditions in most countries in the neighborhood, where repressive leaders had restricted the competition of ideas and the activities of organized groups. Kyrgyzstan was not immune, however, to the authoritarian impulse, as events the following year would reveal.

Chapter Six

The Power of Words

A country of less than five million people in the mid-1990s, Kyrgyzstan punched above its weight in international affairs. The reason was the perception in Western capitals that it was the best hope for democracy in a region where authoritarianism was quickly taking root. Employing the logic applied a decade later to Saddam Hussein's Iraq and the Middle East, many in the American foreign policy establishment believed that if democracy took hold in one country in the Central Asian region, it would spread to the remainder. On tours of Europe and North America in the early 1990s, President Akaev exploited these assumptions by carefully cultivating the image of Kyrgyzstan as an "island of democracy" in a sea of authoritarianism. The results were loans and grants from Western governments and international financial institutions that totaled over a billion dollars by the end of the 1990s.

In a whirlwind tour of the American East Coast in May 1993, his first visit to the United States, Akaev told his audiences what they wanted to hear in elegant speeches that invoked the names and ideas of Jefferson, Franklin, and other American founders. At a meeting with business and financial leaders in Manhattan, he began his speech with these words:

> I have always had the greatest respect for the entrepreneurial class of any country. All of world history has shown that it is the most energetic social group in any nation. Your energy . . . has transformed the world around us. [1]

Contrary to some misgivings before his arrival in the United States, President Akaev had a very successful American tour, obtaining a last-minute meeting with President Clinton and Vice President Gore in the White House and giving presentations to an impressive range of institutions, from Harvard to the Carnegie Foundation. The day after his speech to business leaders in Manhattan, I attended a dinner given in President Akaev's honor by Freedom

House at their offices in Rosslyn, Virginia, across the river from Washington, DC. As the only American Russian-speaker seated at the president's table, I was able to talk at some length over the meal with Akaev and found him again to be forthcoming, gracious, and hospitable. It was something of a shock, therefore, to hear his after-dinner speech, perhaps the only discordant note on his tour. After lauding the range of media outlets in his own country and recognizing the role of free expression in bringing an end to communism, Akaev suggested that his patience with certain elements of the press at home was growing thin.

> [The press in Kyrgyzstan] doesn't always maintain a necessary level of [professional] culture, and that violates basic ethical norms. However, we, the representatives of governmental authority, are restraining ourselves and have not allowed any limitations on the freedom of the press.

He continued by warning about the dangers of a press that exercised what he called an immature freedom, which in a new country like Kyrgyzstan could lead to anarchy and mob rule.

In a room full of American activists dedicated to the expansion of a free press around the world, he concluded his remarks with a quote from Thomas Jefferson, which he offered as a pleasantry but quickly noted that "in every joke is an element of truth."

> The man who reads nothing at all is better educated than the man who reads nothing but newspapers.[2]

The organizers of the event from Freedom House appeared stunned, and the evening came to what seemed an abrupt end. On his way out of the room, much to my surprise, he handed me a folder with the original typed version of that night's speech along with all the other speeches he gave in the United States on this visit.

I thought of this evening a year later when Akaev began to clamp down on the press. The campaign against his critics in the media began with the formation of a Committee to Defend the Honor and Dignity of the President. Then in June 1994, with the broadcast media already under the influence of the president and his allies, Akaev sanctioned the closing of two newspapers that strayed beyond the bounds of what he considered to be acceptable journalism. The first was *Svobodnye gory* (Free Mountains), which had published a photomontage on an inside page of Akaev in a Star of David, surrounded by six Jewish advisors, including Leonid Levitin. The other paper shuttered was *Politika*, which had distorted a speech of the president. Instead of printing "the prevention of the exodus of Russians is a condition of democratization," the newspaper reported Akaev's words as "the exodus of Russians is a condition of democratization."[3] These actions of Akaev prompted a sharp response by Strobe Talbott, President Clinton's envoy to the former Soviet republics, who reminded the Kyrgyzstani president that American financial support remained contingent on the Central Asian country maintaining its reputation as a democratic outpost in the region. [4]

Despite this American warning, Kyrgyzstan's parliament passed a law that made certain forms of libel a criminal offense, which granted the president an additional weapon in his battle against his harshest critics in the press. The first journalists prosecuted under this legislation were Zamira Sydykova and Tamara Slashcheva from *Res Publica*, who were convicted and sentenced to eighteen months for publishing an article claiming that the president had an overseas bank account. Although the sentences were suspended, Sydykova and Slashcheva lost their right to work in journalism for a year and eighteen months, respectively.

After Sydykova returned to work at *Res Publica* in 1997, she quickly became the subject of another criminal complaint, this one arising from an article written by *Res Publica* journalist Alexander Al'ianchikov, an article that described corruption in a gold mining company in Kyrgyzstan. Again, both journalists were convicted and sentenced to jail, and this time Sydykova served four months of an eighteen-month sentence before being released when the Supreme Court intervened. [5] Fearing for her twelve-year-old son's safety in Bishkek—her older son had already been beaten up by unknown assailants—she sent him to school in the small town in Central Florida where I lived. When I next saw Zamira, in Florida in 2000, she was stopping off on her way to receive the Courage in Journalism Award in Hollywood from the International Women's Media Foundation.

The International Women's Media Foundation was one of a large number of Western nongovernmental organizations that sought to assist those who were working to liberalize developing societies like Kyrgyzstan. Among the NGOs that had a presence on the ground in Kyrgyzstan, the most influential was the Open Society Institute (OSI, now Open Society Foundations), which was funded by the billionaire financier, George Soros. Recognizing the importance of education in shaping the new post-communist generation, the Open Society Institute supported numerous initiatives directed at the country's youth, including a contest for the best high school history textbook. As Soros well understood, having been educated in his youth in communist Hungary, the heroes and events and values woven into the national narratives taught in schools help to mold the worldview of a country's citizens. Besides offering alternative textbooks to those published under communism, Soros' group sought to reteach the teachers inherited from the old regime, and for one such effort the Open Society Institute invited me to Kyrgyzstan in September 1995.

Traveling for the first time to Central Asia as a consultant rather than a researcher, I was at the mercy of the OSI staff for travel arrangements.

Leaving Orlando in the afternoon, I arrived in Frankfurt early the following morning, with an eight-hour layover before my next flight, to Almaty, then the capital of Kazakhstan. Because the Frankfurt Airport was under construction, seating in the terminal was extremely limited, so I spent the layover stretched out on the floor trying to rest, as announcements in German and English seemed to play on a loop above me. Flying overnight for a second time, I arrived in Almaty the next morning as the sun was rising over the mountains east of the city. Taxiing to the terminal, I looked to my left to find a new Boeing 747 with the aqua flag of Kazakhstan glimmering in the early morning light. It was the personal aircraft of the country's president, Nursultan Nazarbaev, a luxury made possible by Kazakhstan's vast oil and gas reserves, which attracted the interest and investments of the world's great energy companies. For his part, President Akaev of Kyrgyzstan had to make do with a mid-sized Soviet-era hand-me-down.

At the Almaty airport, a representative of the Open Society Institute was waiting to drive me the three-and-a-half hours to Bishkek. The two cities are connected by a well-maintained two-lane road built just a few miles from the border on the Kazakhstani side. To the south are the high mountains of Kyrgyzstan; looking north one finds the beginning of the Kazakh steppe, which extends without break or trees to the horizon. Nodding off for parts of the drive, I was jolted awake occasionally by the driver swerving to allow a car approaching from the rear to pass. Impatient motorists, who always seemed to be behind the wheel of large Mercedes, would drive at speed on the center line, forcing slower vehicles to veer onto the shoulder. As I would learn after several trips to Kyrgyzstan, Central Asia was where old German cars came to die. High-mileage Audis, VWs, and Mercedes, most spewing visible pollutants from their aging engines, were all the rage in a region that had been restricted for decades to Soviet-produced Volgas, Ladas, and Zhigulis.

Turning south on the final leg of the trip, we passed through the low canyon lands around the border town of Kordai before crossing the frontier, which is located just ten miles from Bishkek. Desperate for a bed to recover from the two-day trip, I began to relax in anticipation of checking in to the hotel. Much to my chagrin, we headed instead to the headquarters of the Open Society Institute, where an 11:00 a.m. meeting had been arranged with the director, Chinara Jakypova. After only a few minutes with her, I realized that she was a woman of limitless energy and drive, and so the idea of having to rest after spending two nights in a row in economy seats on a plane would never have occurred to her.

One of Jakypova's childhood friends, later a prominent professor, explained that Chinara possessed an encyclopedic memory and an insatiable curiosity. In his words, she was "always the best at whatever she did."[6] Like many of the best and the brightest in the early years of post-communist

Kyrgyzstan, Jakypova studied in Russia, at Moscow State University, where she received a doctorate before returning to Kyrgyzstan to teach at a local university. In the early 1990s, President Akaev appointed her to the post of minister of education, but as her popularity began to approach that of the president, Akaev distanced himself from her and she decided to resign from the government.

The story of Chinara Jakypova is emblematic of a generation of immensely talented young women who entered public life in Kyrgyzstan in the 1990s. Where a handful, such as Roza Otunbaeva, made a successful career in government, most turned to work in NGOs, where there were no barriers to entry or glass ceilings. In addition, the "third sector," as it is sometimes called, allowed a freedom of thought and expression that was unavailable in officialdom. By the second half of the 1990s, the NGO community in Bishkek, funded largely by money from abroad, represented a kind of female-dominated alternative government that constantly held workshops and hearings and lobbied for progressive changes to public policies. In interviews over the succeeding years with the heads of NGOs, who dealt with issues ranging from environmental affairs and women and children's welfare to penal policy and electoral administration, I was in almost every case meeting with a woman.

The training course for which the Open Society Institute brought me to Kyrgyzstan in September 1995 enrolled about twenty participants, most of them young men, who were teaching what might be called social studies courses in local universities. All had received their education in the Soviet era and most were trained in subjects infused with a dogmatic approach to Marxism, like dialectical materialism and the history of the working class. With the interest in Western-style social sciences increasing in Kyrgyzstan, the Open Society Institute seized the opportunity to offer a one-week intensive course on contemporary approaches to political science. My assignment was to introduce the participants to the central concepts in the field of comparative politics. What was already an intimidating prospect—teaching other professors an entirely new literature for them, and doing so in Russian—became even more unsettling on the first morning when I looked over the group and saw a familiar face in the front row. It was that of Medetkan Sherimkulov, the fifty-five-year-old speaker of the country's first post-communist parliament and a former secretary of the Communist Party of the Kirgiz Republic.

It was not an easy week. The problem was not teaching but sleeping. Plunging into work after two days of sleepless travel from the United States had thrown off my internal clock, and the unforgiving schedule of meals, lectures, and meetings with co-teachers prevented me from shutting down my system. As a result, I worked on lectures till 11:00 p.m. and then went to bed, but invariably woke up around one o'clock each morning, after fitful sleep. What made the week bearable was the curiosity of the students and the comradeship of my teaching colleagues. One was a very dignified, just-retired Russian diplomat, Anatolii Sliusar', who spoke on international relations. The other was Mikhail Guboglo—Misha to his friends—who was one of Russia's leading specialists on the politics of ethnicity. An infectiously optimistic and humorous member of a small Turkic Christian group from the Black Sea region, the Gagauz, Misha had been a fellow-in-residence at Duke and part of Jerry Hough's workshop. Just two months earlier, we had spent a memorable week together at the annual conference of Russian anthropologists and ethnographers, which was held in a remote Russian village in the Riazan province. With a background as a Soviet scholar and a collaborator on Western social science projects, Misha served as an invaluable bridge between the old and new worlds intersecting at this week-long training course.

Figure 6.1. Students in a lecture hall at the Academy of Tourism, Bishkek. September 1995

Our handler from the Open Society Institute approached me one day with an invitation to speak at a newly opened Academy of Tourism in Bishkek. My credentials in this field were as thin as those on Kyrgyzstan a few years earlier. I had, it's true, been raised in Florida, and I had visited Disney World nine times in its first three years of operation, occasionally as a guest of a cousin who worked there. I knew nothing, however, about the professional training of persons in the tourism industry. As I discovered when I arrived at the "Academy," a series of rented rooms in the center of the capital, my hosts did not appear to be much better informed than I was about the subject. Ushered into a large, stuffy lecture hall that held over seventy students, I gazed out on a sea of young Kyrgyz women and men, most of whom did not appear as well-dressed or privileged as the students at the elite institutions in the city. They were a keen, attentive audience who were desperate to learn a trade and make their way in an economy that was touted by the country's leadership as a market-based system. Unfortunately, the capitalism in Kyrgyzstan in this period was the Wild West variety, and educational institutions such as the Academy of Tourism were opening left and right with little prospect of placing graduates in related fields. As I left the lecture hall that afternoon, I thought of the painful reckoning that was coming for these students, and for the country.

Chapter Seven

Kyrgyzstan Goes to the Polls

My visit to Kyrgyzstan in 1995 fell between the first parliamentary and presidential elections of the post-communist era. The country was just emerging from a series of political crises that had begun with the premature dissolution of Kyrgyzstan's parliament a year earlier. Elected in 1990, while Kirgizia was still part of the USSR, the parliament continued to function with the same members, organization, and rules in the post-communist era. Although its members—known as deputies—were largely traditionalists who did not wish to see the Soviet Union come to an end, most adapted to changing times and ultimately embraced their role as the legislative framers of a new state. This "legendary parliament," as it was called, adopted Kyrgyzstan's declaration of independence, its constitution, many foundational legal codes, and legislation that established the symbols of the nation, such as the flag and the national anthem. In short, it had acquired a mission and a sense of self-confidence that established it as a competitor to President Akaev.

After the enactment of a new constitution in 1993, however, this relationship moved from healthy political competition to a destabilizing confrontation with the president. Each institution had its own weapons in this struggle. The president, along with the prime minister, ministers, and regional *akims*, governed the country on a daily basis, but the parliament had the ability to embarrass the president with critical speeches from the floor of the chamber. They could also reject his nominees to vital government posts and block his legislative initiatives. In September 1994, the parliament was preparing to appoint new members to the Central Election Commission, which would oversee legislative elections in early 1995. Intent on blocking this move, the president successfully conspired to dissolve the parliament by convincing a group of sympathetic deputies to boycott the session, thus denying it a quorum. Unable to meet, the parliament effectively ceased to function until after the legislative elections, during which time the president governed the country without the oversight of the *Jogorku Kenesh*.

The first elections in independent Kyrgyzstan took place in February 1995, when candidates competed for 105 seats in the parliament. Trying to prevent the formation of strong political parties that he felt might constrain his power, President Akaev helped to craft electoral rules that favored the election of individuals with strong local ties rather than national appeal. Because voters cast their ballots for their individual deputy rather than for a national slate of candidates, which is common in many European countries, territorially based *akims* and powerful local businessmen had an outsized role in determining the outcome of the election. In fact, the largest single group of deputies in the lower house, which had seventy members, was made up of executive officials. In the even smaller upper house, with thirty-five members, businessmen gained over half the seats. Businessmen-deputies had a powerful incentive to seek a spot in parliament because it granted them immunity from prosecution at a time when many men and women of commerce were like vultures picking over the carcass of the old Soviet economy or benefitting from special deals arranged through their contacts in government. The chair of the fledgling Social Democratic Party, Almazbek Atambaev, commented during the parliamentary election campaign that the greatest danger facing Kyrgyzstan was no longer "socialism but Sicily-ism."

Not only did crony capitalism and more crude forms of corruption create economic winners—and of course losers—they also gave those in law enforcement, and their political overseers, the ability to strip the newly wealthy of their gains, and their freedom, if they fell afoul of powerful officeholders. In an era where virtually everyone with money was guilty of violating the country's shifting and often onerous commercial and tax laws, those in high office were tempted to use selective prosecution to remove, or extort money from, their political enemies. According to one report, "nearly 30 percent of the new deputies were being investigated by the State Prosecutor's Office for illegal financial dealings."[1] It would not be long before President Akaev resorted to this tool in his struggle against highly placed political adversaries.

Voters everywhere like to think that they decide elections, but politicians put in place the electoral rules that shape the choices available to voters. In mature democracies like the United States, electoral rule changes are generally infrequent and incremental.[2] In Kyrgyzstan, on the other hand, politicians didn't let an electoral cycle go by without making fundamental changes to the size and structure of parliament or the voting method. Those in power in Kyrgyzstan weren't just a restless lot, they were trying to throw the opposition off balance and to structure institutions and elections in ways that would perpetuate or strengthen their political advantage. In so doing, they created unintended consequences that rippled throughout the political and social system.

The composition of the parliament elected in February 1995 was one such unintended consequence. By forcing voters to elect deputies in large constituencies where they could only choose a single candidate, the rules made it difficult for ethnic minorities to gain seats in parliament. In large electoral districts, pockets of minority settlements tend to be overwhelmed by the majority population, a phenomenon known as "minority vote dilution." As a result, ethnic Kyrgyz deputies made up 83 percent of the new parliament, at a time when they accounted for less than 60 percent of the country's population.[3] This indigenization of the political class had its parallels in law enforcement and other areas of government, where hiring practices favored the Kyrgyz. By the second half of the 1990s, minorities were virtually absent in several state institutions, including the police.

Behind the creation of Kyrgyz-only enclaves in the workforce was not official or even conscious discrimination but an informal preference for hiring one's own, whether they were persons from one's family, clan or tribe, home district, or ethnic group. President Akaev's own press secretary, Kamil' Baialinov, admitted as much to me in an interview.

> It is no secret that responsible officials of the very highest rank come primarily from this or that kinship group. That's reality. In our small republic, no matter where you turn, everyone is someone's man.[4]

As a former presidential chief of staff explained to me, in a country like Kyrgyzstan, where everyone knows their forefathers to the seventh generation, unacquainted Kyrgyz meet and "immediately begin to look for kin seven, even ten times removed, and soon we find that we're related."[5]

Electoral campaigns are never fought on a completely level playing field, and in Kyrgyzstan in 1995 the advantages of incumbency, money, and connections tilted the contest decisively. Wealthy candidates sought to buy their way into office, occasionally using imaginative campaign tactics. One businessman gave out left-footed boots to the population in his district, promising to supply the right boot if he won. In the Jalal-Abad region in the South, another candidate, the director of an agricultural equipment factory, distributed plows to local leaders and vodka and freshly slaughtered horses to the voters. One observer noted that in some districts, "vodka flowed like a river."[6] It was not uncommon to see drunken voters sprawled around the voting booths, and in one precinct, an old woman died of overconsumption near the polling station. It would clearly take time for a population schooled for decades in Soviet elections, which were little more than rituals of subservience to the existing order, to see voting as a means of holding political leaders accountable.

Because President Akaev had rejected the idea of creating a presidential party—the disgrace of the Communist Party cast a pall on the very idea of parties for many years—he could not rely on a stable majority of deputies in the new parliament to support his initiatives. Because they were elected in local constituencies, the new deputies understandably responded first to the needs of their districts rather than to the needs of the president. Frustrated by the limits of his resources and authority, Akaev launched two gambits that he hoped would strengthen the office of the president and his hold on it.

A year before the expiration of his five-year term in the fall of 1996, Akaev sought to hold a referendum that would have granted him a second term without having to face opposition in a presidential election. This end run around democracy, which had already been employed by the presidents of neighboring countries in Central Asia, was presented as the idea of the Kyrgyzstani people, whose 1.2 million signatures adorned a petition demanding a referendum. No doubt some citizens signed the petition willingly, amid a media campaign that sought to create a cult of personality around Akaev. Villagers wove rugs with Akaev's image to present to the president, and Kyrgyz elders extolled the virtues of Akaev daily on television and radio.[7] But the signature drive also had a darker side. In several interviews I conducted in Bishkek in this period, several informed commentators stated that in some areas the authorities required a signature on a referendum petition before distributing pension or wage payments.

Usually the observer, I was drawn in as a participant in the debate on the referendum during a TV interview in Bishkek on September 14, 1995. The correspondent conducting the interview was Alexandra Cheremushkina, one of the country's best-known journalists, who enjoyed a reputation as a liberal. At one point in the broadcast, she asked my view of the proposed referendum. I responded that it was a terrible idea and an affront to democracy. Her broad smile on set turned quickly into an icy scowl as we walked off the stage at the end of the program. Glaring at me, she said, "You are completely naive to think that the people should be given a choice for the presidency." Just as in Russia, where journalists a year later were willing to do anything to get President Yeltsin elected, many in the media in Kyrgyzstan regarded the alternatives to Akaev as so unpalatable that they were unwilling to risk holding a competitive election. Suspicion of the average citizen's ability to make sound political choices extended to the president himself. In a speech in Paris a few months earlier, Akaev had argued that his people were not yet ready for Western forms of democracy, owing to their "historical traditions, way of life, and ethnopsychology."[8]

Despite the pressure to fall in line with the president, the parliament in late September refused to approve the holding of a referendum designed to grant Akaev a second presidential term by acclamation. It did, however, accede to Akaev's wish to push up the election by ten months, to December

1995. Desperate to go to the people while he was still reveling in the after-glow of the carefully staged celebrations of the one-thousand-year anniversary of the Kyrgyz national hero Manas, and before a projected decline in the economy, Akaev understood well the importance of timing in politics. He won the election handily, with 71.5 percent of the vote. His closest rival, the head of the Communist Party of Kyrgyzstan, Absamat Masaliev, received just under a quarter of the vote, and Medetkan Sherimkulov, who four months earlier had been my student in the political science training course, won just under 2 percent of the vote.

Immediately following his electoral victory, Akaev launched his second gambit: a referendum in February 1996 to alter the constitution. Strengthened by his landslide victory, Akaev was able to convince the parliament to approve the holding of this referendum. On the ballot was a proposal to significantly expand the powers of the presidency. With a 95 percent turnout and a 98 percent yes vote, the population granted the president broad appointment powers over judges, ministers, and other officials and made it more difficult for the parliament to reject the president's nominee for prime minister. After successfully expanding the formal powers of his office, Akaev then moved to replace independent-minded *akim*s in the provinces with individuals who were more oriented toward the center and toward Akaev personally.[9] These younger "yes-men" succeeded a generation of regional elites who had helped to give birth to post-communist Kyrgyzstan.

My hotel room in the fall of 1995 was in Bishkek's southern suburbs and looked out onto the newly opened Manas Village. Dedicated to the legendary founder of the Kyrgyz nation, this small theme park contained a bizarre collection of towers, spires, and monuments that was supposed to invoke the valor and unifying spirit of Manas. Set in a forest, behind which were the high mountains of the Ala-Too Range, Manas Village inspired confusion rather than awe. It was like an outdoor museum of unlabeled oddities that allowed visitors to make what they would of the exhibits on display. Perhaps for the Kyrgyz the ensemble sent the imagination soaring, and placed them in touch with the spirit of their legendary ancestor, but for a visitor from afar it had the air of a hastily conceived and unfinished tribute to one of the world's great oral epics.

Tracing the life of Manas from his birth in the Enisei—the historic homeland of the Kyrgyz people in Western Siberia—to the Altai region and finally to the land that is present-day Kyrgyzstan, the epic came down through the ages in verses that were recited and occasionally revised and embellished by *manaschi* (narrators). With some versions running to 500,000 verses, twice the length of the world's next longest epic, it took *manaschi* several days to recite the entire legend from memory. Because Kyrgyz was traditionally an oral culture, it was only in the late nineteenth century that the epic was written down.

The opening of Manas Village coincided with the national celebration of the one thousandth anniversary of the Manas legend. For President Akaev, memorializing Manas had become a centerpiece of his efforts to construct a unifying national identity for Kyrgyzstan. To win the support of both the titular population and minority groups, Akaev emphasized the ethnic diversity of Manas' entourage as well as the role of Manas in forging a single Kyrgyz people.[10] Soviet authorities had been well aware of the political uses of the Manas legend. Fearful that reviving a cult of Manas might contribute to unhealthy nationalist sentiments, officials in Moscow in the Soviet era had rejected calls by Kyrgyz to mark the one thousandth anniversary. For a president of the new Kyrgyzstani state, on the other hand, the celebrations were not just a rallying point for the population of a new state that was uncertain of its identity, they were also a chance for Akaev to present himself as a latter-day Manas. Where Manas was the founder of the Kyrgyz people, Akaev could claim to be the founder of the first state for the Kyrgyz.

Figure 7.1. Manas Village on the outskirts of Bishkek. September 1995

The evening before my departure for home, I took one last walk in Manas Village. The crowds had thinned and only a few scattered groups remained in the park. As I approached the statue of Manas, I noticed a lone man in uniform standing in front of the monument. Pulling a half-finished bottle of Kyrgyz cognac from his jacket, he approached me and started baring his soul. He was taking his first overseas trip the following morning and he wanted to pay his respects to the spirit of Manas before leaving. Learning that I was a foreigner, he insisted that I join him in a drink. I dutifully took a small sip and passed the bottle back. Over the next few minutes he finished the cognac by himself. Struggling to remain upright, the middle-aged officer seemed to grow ever more fearful of the journey that awaited him. The Russians had passed along to the Kyrgyz the tradition of "bathing oneself in liquor" (*obmyvat'*) on important—and in some cases, not so important—occasions; however, this man, alone in the fading light, did not appear to be celebrating his good fortune but steeling himself against a journey into the unknown. I wonder to this day whether he reached his destination: NATO headquarters in Brussels.

Chapter Eight

Central Asia through Students' Eyes

During the 1990s, I began teaching an undergraduate course devoted to the five former Soviet "Stans"—Kazakhstan, Kyrgyzstan, Tajikistan, Turkmenistan, and Uzbekistan. Entitled "The Unknown Asia: Politics and Society in the Russian, Chinese, and Middle Eastern Borderlands," the class inspired some of the more adventurous students to suggest that I lead a trip to the region. Teaching at small colleges, I was all too aware of the work of many of my selfless colleagues who regularly organized student tours to various parts of the country and the world. My single experience as tour leader, while teaching at Bowdoin College in the 1980s, had been a cautionary tale. A sorting machine at the FedEx distribution center in Memphis managed to rip apart a packet with twenty-five checks from parents, which was destined for a travel company in College Station, Texas. The morning after our arrival in Leningrad from the United States, an embarrassed young male student confessed to me that he had been with a Russian prostitute a few hours earlier. Feeling discomfort in his loins, he confided, "I think I've caught something," and asked to see a doctor. Serving as recruiter, travel agent, lecturer, and overseas chaperone hardly seemed worth the free passage for my wife and me to the Soviet Union.

It was with some reluctance, then, that I agreed to organize a study-tour to Kyrgyzstan in May 2000, this time for only three students who would shadow me as I conducted research in the country. The first stop on the tour was London, where a visit to the British Museum and a seminar led by a scholar from the School of Oriental and African Studies revealed to students the porousness and fluidity of borders in Inner Asia. Surrounded by high mountains on the south and east, the Caspian Sea on the west, and the seemingly endless steppe to the north, Central Asia's permanent settlements were widely scattered along the foothills of the mountains and the region's two great rivers, the Syr Darya and the Amu Darya. As the students learned in London, the interplay of nomadic and sedentary peoples and Turkic and Iranian languages and cultures had long been at the heart of political and social developments in the region, where empires and khanates formed and re-formed with ill-defined frontiers.

Even the gradual expansion northward of Islam from the eighth century, and the movement southward of Russian and Soviet civilizations in the nineteenth and twentieth centuries, did not eliminate entirely the tensions between nomads and settled peoples or Turkic and Iranian cultures. Where these groups were in regular contact, contending traditions often melded into new cultural forms, though not without residual resentment from the people that felt their way of life had suffered the greater loss. None of us discussing these patterns of Central Asian history in London in the late spring of 2000 could have predicted, however, the violence that would erupt in a few years in southern Kyrgyzstan between the long-sedentary Uzbeks and the traditionally nomadic Kyrgyz living there.

At the end of our first full day in London we were waiting outside our hotel in Bloomsbury to be picked up for dinner when a large black Mercedes pulled to the curb. Jumping out of the back seat to greet us was Roza Otunbaeva, who had recently moved from Washington to London to serve as Kyrgyzstani ambassador to the Court of St. James. Insisting that I sit in the front next to the driver, Roza seemed amused as the three students piled into the back seat, trying to avoid sitting on the ambassador's lap. Driving west a few miles to a smart but affordable neighborhood—inasmuch as anything can be affordable in the heart of London—we arrived at Roza's flat, where her son and daughter, just a few years younger than the students, met us with warm smiles that one rarely sees on teenagers, especially those welcoming strangers brought home by their mother.

Over an informal dinner that Roza had ordered in, we talked about what the students might expect on their arrival in Kyrgyzstan. The country was just emerging from a financial crisis that had shaken the foundations of all post-communist states in the summer of 1998. The fallout from Russia's default on its debt and the collapse of its currency had serious ripple effects in Kyrgyzstan, where the government found it increasingly difficult to service the massive debt that it had accumulated during the free-spending days of the early 1990s. As a result, President Akaev was increasingly vulnerable to a serious challenge in the presidential election that would be held that October 2000. From February to December 1999, his positive rating among the country's elite had fallen dramatically, from 3.6 to 2.6 points on the 5-point scale used in reputational polling in Kyrgyzstan.[1]

What Roza Otunbaeva could not speak about openly with the students was the just-concluded parliamentary election campaign. Using the careful language common to large international organizations, the monitoring team of the Organization for Security and Co-operation in Europe (OSCE) noted that the election was "characterised by a series of negative trends that ultimately prevented a number of political parties and candidates from competing in the election on a fair and equal basis."[2] The details of their report left no doubt about the efforts by political forces close to President Akaev to prevent the president's most prominent opponents from winning a seat in parliament, which would have positioned them for a run for the presidency in the fall. Some of the most egregious violations of voting procedure occurred in the Talas region, where the country's second most popular politician, Felix Kulov, who had recently had a falling out with Akaev, was seeking election. As the OSCE report revealed, in this contest pre-marked ballots were found in the safe of the local election commission; some voters were paid 150 soms ($3) for their vote, while others, especially students, were forced to show their ballots to the authorities before depositing them in the voting urn; the number of absentee ballots increased dramatically in the second round of voting; and in one precinct, the 647 votes registered for Kulov by the local election commission turned into 147 votes on the protocol of the regional election commission, whose tallies were used to determine the outcome. Manipulating elections assures the regime the results that it favors but it also throws into doubt the legitimacy of the political system and the mandates enjoyed by elected officials. By the next electoral cycle, in 2005, the declining public confidence in the voting process would have dramatic consequences.

Kyrgyzstan's political and economic problems may have been mounting, but the country was gradually integrating into the world economy. One indication of these linkages was the opening of direct flights to Bishkek from Europe, which broke Moscow's monopoly on air travel into Kyrgyzstan. Not all of these new choices were attractive, however, especially for someone with responsibility for a student group. Seeking to take advantage of its close proximity to the Indian subcontinent, Kyrgyzstan Airlines had begun to offer direct flights from Birmingham, England, to Bishkek and then on to Delhi. A cheap alternative for the many residents of Indian origin living in the British Midlands, the flight enjoyed a less-than-stellar reputation. Emblematic of the problems facing the airline was a flight that left Birmingham in January 1999 and arrived in Delhi three days later, forty-eight hours behind schedule. After an eighteen-hour delay in Birmingham due to mechanical issues, the flight took off for Omsk in Russia, its scheduled refueling stop. Unfortunately, the pilot landed at the military airbase instead of the civilian airport in the city, and Russian troops immediately surrounded the plane. While the pilots and the Kyrgyzstani government negotiated with the local Russian authorities for needed fuel over the next twenty-four hours, the passengers remained on the plane, as toilets ceased working and food ran out. The additional litany of passenger complaints was long: broken seats and seat belts; luggage blocking the emergency exits; no life jackets under the seat; no safety demonstration before takeoff; and a crew that spoke little English. Within months, word of this "nightmare flight" had doomed one of the few direct flights connecting Europe and Kyrgyzstan.[3]

Our airline choice from England to Kyrgyzstan was British Mediterranean Airways, a discount carrier franchised by British Airways that served less-popular destinations in Africa, the Middle East, and Central Asia. Making a brief stop in the republic of Georgia on the way, using older, smaller aircraft than those normally servicing long-haul flights, British Mediterranean had opened the London-Bishkek route in response to demand from the gold mining industry in Kyrgyzstan, specifically the large Canadian-owned mine known as Kumtor. Located at an elevation of 14,000 feet in a remote region south of Lake Issyk-Kul' and only forty miles from the Chinese border, Kumtor was the second-highest gold mine in the world. Work at this altitude required management to take numerous precautions with their personnel, who included many professional miners and engineers brought in from Canada. As one Canadian miner explained to me on the flight, those suffering from altitude sickness had access to a hyperbaric oxygen chamber on site, and the hitches of workers lasted no more than a couple of weeks, after which the Canadian staff returned home or to Europe to recuperate before their next shift.

Kumtor kept the Kyrgyzstani economy afloat and British Mediterranean Airways in business. The mine had begun production in 1997 and soon accounted for over 10 percent of the country's GDP and 50 percent of its export earnings. As the country's golden goose, Kumtor was in constant disputes with national politicians, especially those in the opposition ranks, who sought to claim a greater ownership share of the mine for the state. For their part, officials in the Issyk-Kul' region pushed the Canadian owners, Cameco, to hire more locals and increase spending on social needs in surrounding communities, though how much of the money allocated by Cameco for these purposes actually reached the local population, rather than the pockets of local politicians, has always been in dispute.[4]

Not long after taking off from Tbilisi, the capital of Georgia, we flew over the Caucasus Mountains and then the Caspian Sea, beyond which lay the deserts of western Central Asia. Looking toward the south, we spotted what was left of the Aral Sea, once the world's fourth largest inland lake. In only forty years, the Aral Sea had shrunk to a third of its original size, largely due to the Soviet government's overfarming of cotton and poor irrigation practices. The coastline around the original oval-shaped sea had receded, leaving ships beached and port towns and cities separated from the water by dozens of miles. Dust storms picked up salt and pesticides left behind on the expanding seabed and deposited them across fields and settlements for hundreds of miles around the shrinking lake. The effects on the health of the surrounding population were chilling, with some areas registering an infant mortality rate of 100 babies per 100,000 births, a figure four times that observed in the region in 1950.[5] The children who survived suffered unusually high rates of respiratory diseases and developmental disorders, creating a public health crisis in an area that was ill-equipped to face these challenges.

After the inhospitable and foreboding landscape around the Aral Sea, the sight of Kyrgyzstan's greenery was all the more welcome as we deplaned following the almost ten-hour flight from London. Meeting us at the airport was a colleague in charge of local arrangements, Gulnara Iskakova, a professor of law at the American University of Central Asia. As we headed out to place the students in home stays around the capital, Gulnara informed us that we had arrived just in time for "prophylaxis," an announcement that gave the students a start. In Bishkek, as in most post-Soviet cities of its size, a single electric plant was the source of the hot air and water that coursed through underground pipes to radiators and faucets in homes and office buildings. "Prophylaxis" referred to the three to four weeks at the end of the spring when the local authorities cut off hot water to the city in order to clean and repair the pipes, though one always suspected that the length of the down time, usually a month in the case of Bishkek, was designed to save money for the local budget as well as to make the necessary repairs. Like other residents of the city, most of us used a small electric immersion heater to boil water when needed, not wishing to shower and shave in the cold mountain water that fed the faucets. The one student who escaped the consequences of the dreaded period of "prophylaxis" lived with a Russian family in a village-type settlement at the northern edge of town, where the better-off homeowners had their own boilers.

My housing for this stay was a spare bedroom in the apartment of a Kyrgyz family. Coming out of the elevator on my way to the apartment for the first time, I was surprised to see a set of locked steel gates several feet in front of the apartment's door, which created a caged anteroom to the residence. It was a respectable, but not luxurious, apartment, and the security measures reflected the rising burglary rates in the capital. The rhythm of daily life in the building, one of several late-Soviet midrise structures that formed part of a small housing complex, began at dawn with cries in Russian of "moloko," or milk, echoing off the buildings and across the large courtyard. A middle-aged Kyrgyz man peddled dairy products daily to hundreds of residents in these and surrounding buildings. The days ended with the sound of young children playing on rusting gym sets in the courtyard that were legacies from the Soviet era.

The day after our arrival, we walked along Chu Prospect to the city's central plaza, Ala-Too Square. Bounded at one end by a U-shaped ensemble, with decorative arches gracing the two detached wings and golden domes atop all of the buildings, the plaza had at its opposite end a square structure built of white stone, which had the air of a large mausoleum. It was a fitting home for the country's Historical Museum, most of whose exhibits during our stay in 2000 were devoted to Soviet history. Neither the historical arti- facts nor the accompanying explanations had changed since the collapse of communism, which allowed the students to step back into an unmolested tomb of Soviet history. Only a part of one floor housed exhibits devoted to the independence period. Quick to change the place names inherited from the Soviet era, the Kyrgyzstani government and people were in less of a hurry to remove the physical evidence of their Soviet past.

As we exited the Historical Museum on this unusually hot day in mid- May, a massive statue of Lenin loomed in front of us. It was the iconic pose that had graced squares across the Soviet Union, but in this case Lenin's outstretched right hand was pointing toward the snow-capped mountains that rose above the golden domes on Bishkek's central plaza. The government finally removed Lenin's statue three years later, well over a decade after the collapse of communism, but instead of discarding it—or transferring it to a special park devoted to Soviet-era relics as the Russians did in Moscow—the authorities gave it a new home right behind the Historical Museum, facing a prominent building of state.

Figure 8.1.   Ala-Too Square, Bishkek. May 2000

Figure 8.2.   Lenin Statue, Bishkek. May 2000

In the ensuing years, the battle over monuments and memory on this plaza continued. Lenin's replacement was a Kyrgyz version of Marianne holding a *tunduk*, with the word Erkindik (Freedom) displayed prominently on the plinth. It did not enjoy Lenin's longevity in this location. After her installation in 2003, critics began claiming that men, rather than women, traditionally carried the *tunduk*; moreover, some said the image of the woman bore an uncanny resemblance to President Akaev's wife, Mairam, whose popularity had fallen faster than that of her husband. The most recent monument to occupy this symbolically sacred space appeared in 2011.[6] It was a courageous-looking Manas on horseback, which gave credence to the claims of some that Kyrgyzstan's leaders were seeking to replace Marxism with Manasism.

My students' first encounter with academic life in Kyrgyzstan came at the American University of Central Asia (AUCA), which had opened its doors less than three years earlier. Funded by the American government and George Soros' Open Society Foundations, AUCA occupied the former headquarters of the Communist Party of Kirgizia, a Stalinist-era structure in the heart of Bishkek that had friezes of Marx and Engels in the main lecture hall and the emblem of the Kirgiz Soviet Republic carved into the stone facade above the entrance to the building. Although the long-neglected interior of the building had the feel and smell of an American elementary school from the 1950s, the academic program—an American-style liberal arts curriculum taught in English—was rigorous, and the university attracted some of the country's most talented and ambitious high school graduates.

The intellectual energy and acumen of AUCA students was apparent at a well-attended late-afternoon seminar where I presented a paper on identity politics in independent Kyrgyzstan. AUCA students jumped in without prompting to offer comments and criticisms that revealed a knowledge of the Western literature on comparative politics that matched, or exceeded, that of the curious American students accompanying me. AUCA undergraduates were of course living the post-communist transition that Western scholars were writing about, and so these students approached the literature on democratization and economic development with an unusual level of interest and insight. In fact, many of the twenty-something AUCA students attending this seminar were more astute analysts of comparative politics than the university-level instructors that I had helped to train five years earlier.

The paper I presented that day focused on the tensions in Kyrgyzstan created by ethnic and linguistic differences among the country's citizens. Several students around the large seminar table who hailed from the country's South agreed with my general conclusions but insisted that I had paid insufficient attention to a critical cleavage—that between northern and southern Kyrgyz. As southerners studying at an institution in the North, these students were far more aware than their northern peers of the widening gap in political power and economic prosperity between the two halves of the country, which were separated by high mountains and difficult to cross even in the best weather. Although the country's two major cities—Bishkek in the North and Osh in the South—were less than two hundred miles apart as the crow flies, there was no rail connection between them and the treacherous journey by road took twelve hours, passing through long, narrow, and poorly ventilated mountain tunnels. Living in a region with a lower living standard and many fewer institutions of higher education, the southern students attending the seminar expressed their discontent with current policies, which prompted rebuttals from some students from the North. Judging by the mounting tension in the room, the exchange was unusual for AUCA and Kyrgyzstan at the time. Within two years, this tension between North and South would spill onto the public square and begin to destabilize the Akaev regime.

Shattering the stereotype of the southern Kyrgyz as more backward than their northern peers, the most prominent and articulate voice among the AUCA students that afternoon belonged to Kadyr Toktogulov, who came from Osh. A member of AUCA's first graduating class, Kadyr became press secretary to the president of Kyrgyzstan in 2011, at the age of thirty-one, and his country's ambassador to the United States four years later. Kadyr represented a new generation of Kyrgyz whose values, education, and life experiences differed dramatically from those of their parents. Yet many of the graduates of AUCA—or the new Manas University, supported by the Turkish government—found it difficult to adapt to the traditional workplace in Kyrgyzstan, where many of the skills and values inculcated by institutions like AUCA were suspect. The vast majority of university students attended state-supported institutions, where corruption permeated the educational enterprise, with students commonly paying administrators for admittance and faculty members for grades. Both students and faculty in these institutions were expected to turn out for the campaign rallies of political incumbents and to vote for them on election day. Unfortunately, this kind of training prepared graduates well for the economy of favors and cronyism that dominated post-communist Kyrgyzstan.[7] Rather than play by rules that constrained their advancement or violated their principles, many of the country's brightest and most idealistic youth, whether graduates of AUCA, Kyrgyz State University, the Kyrgyz-Russian Slavic University, or other institutions of higher learning, chose to leave Kyrgyzstan to pursue careers abroad.

Chapter Nine

Falsification and Conciliation

Bishkek had the feel of a village compared to Moscow, which meant that having three American undergraduates in tow on a research trip was far easier in Kyrgyzstan than it would have been in the Russian capital. Most government buildings were within a few blocks of each other, and government officials and party leaders had not yet wearied of questions from visiting scholars and journalists. In the first decade of the post-communist era, it was always useful to have a local facilitator who could arrange the initial interviews, though by the early 2000s the widespread use of cell phones, and the surprising ease with which one could obtain the phone numbers of key political figures, made it possible to arrange interviews on the fly. On this visit with students, Professor Gulnara Iskakova from AUCA had organized meetings for us with leaders of five political parties and several government officials, including a leader of a key department in the presidential apparatus, which was the nerve center of government in the country.

Although interviews offered revealing detail about the course of the parliamentary election campaign, field research also required the collection of material, most already in existence, such as books and articles, but some generated on the ground in response to my requests. One such artifact was a large map of Kyrgyzstan that showed the country divided by electoral districts. Unable to find the map anywhere, even at the Central Election Commission, which oversaw electoral administration in the country, I turned to Kyrgyzstan's National Cartographic Agency. For $40, an enormous sum in those days, I was able to procure a three-by-five foot color map on a day's notice from a staffer at the agency, who almost certainly took on the assignment *nalevo*. When I arrived with the students to pick up the map, we entered a large room filled with modern computers and oversized screens. Behind each was an ethnic Russian, or at least someone of European descent. The absence of Kyrgyz faces in this specialized agency testified to the continuing balkanization of the labor force in the country, where high-tech jobs remained largely the province of non-Kyrgyz peoples.

Arriving between the parliamentary and presidential elections of 2000, most of our discussions in Bishkek centered on the barriers facing opposition candidates for elective office. Our meeting with Daniiar Usenov, a successful businessman turned parliamentarian, was a vivid reminder of the tactics employed by the political authorities against troublesome opponents.[1] Leading his parliamentary district race by a wide margin in the first round of legislative elections in February 2000, Usenov never made it to the run-off balloting in March. Between the two rounds, the prosecutor's office charged him with tax fraud and also reopened a case from the mid-1990s of his alleged assault against a fellow businessman. These charges disqualified Usenov from the final round of voting. In the interview with us, Usenov revealed another tactic employed by presidents in Kyrgyzstan and other parts of Central Asia. To distance Usenov gracefully from competitive politics in Kyrgyzstan, Akaev offered him the ambassadorship to Iran, which Usenov refused.

Two of our interviewees, Omurbek Tekebaev and Melis Eshimkanov, were preparing to mount campaigns for the presidency, though neither their modest offices nor their skeletal staffs suggested to the visiting American students that they were in the presence of contenders for the Kyrgyzstani White House.[2] Like other prominent politicians who had their eyes on the presidency, Tekebaev and Eshimkanov had hoped that the constitutional limitation of two presidential terms would prevent President Akaev from seeking reelection in October 2000. Unlike in Russia, however, where the Constitutional Court ruled that a similar provision disqualified Yeltsin from seeking a third term, Kyrgyzstan's Constitutional Court—filled with supporters of Akaev—decided that because the president's first term began before the Constitution of 1993 came into effect, it would not count toward the two-term maximum.

With evidence all around of the growing threat to competitive politics in Kyrgyzstan, it was remarkable during our interviews to see the equanimity with which some opposition politicians, like Tekebaev and Eshimkanov, greeted the barriers placed in their way by the president. One explanation may be that these two candidates were among the few who would actually make it onto the ballot for the October 2000 presidential election. Akaev's most serious adversary, Felix Kulov, was arrested on trumped-up charges in March 2000, only weeks after he announced his candidacy for the presidency. Temporarily freed at the end of the summer, he was rearrested in September. For many years Akaev's closest comrade-in-arms, Kulov had supported Akaev in his controversial decision in August 1991 to resist the coup against Gorbachev.[3] He later served his country as vice president, head of the State Committee for National Security, mayor of Bishkek, and governor of the

Chu region, before falling out with Akaev in 1999, when he created his own party, Ar-Namys (Fatherland), whose slogan was "Down with Akaev." Kulov's relations with Akaev had begun to deteriorate a year earlier when, as minister of national security, he investigated the questionable business practices of members of the president's family and entourage.

An ethnic Kyrgyz from the North who spoke Russian in his youth, Kulov withdrew his candidacy for president rather than subject himself to an examination of his knowledge of the Kyrgyz language by a presidential language commission. Article 62 of the 1993 Constitution required candidates for president to be between thirty-five and seventy years old, to have lived in the country for at least fifteen years, and to have a "command of the state language." Operating for the first time in the 2000 presidential contest, a language commission appointed by President Akaev determined what "command" of the Kyrgyz language meant. Predictably, the members of that commission applied standards reminiscent of the literacy tests in the Jim Crow South that disenfranchised black voters. Kulov and one other candidate refused to participate in the proceedings, while four other potential candidates—all apparently competent Kyrgyz speakers—failed the test. In all, the selective prosecution of political enemies and the work of the language commission disqualified eight candidates for the presidency.[4]

Not satisfied with restricting the field of candidates, Akaev's team used the many administrative resources at its disposal to ensure a first-round victory for the sitting president. Although winners in run-off elections are common in the West, they are rare in the post-communist world, where a failure to beat all comers in the first-round is seen as a sign of political weakness and vulnerability. With Kulov out of the race, Akaev won the October 2000 presidential election handily in the first round, with 76 percent of the vote. Tekebaev came in second, with 14 percent vote, while Eshimkanov received just over 1 percent of the ballots.

Akaev's easy victory was due in no small part to his dominance of the media. He silenced those outlets he could not co-opt by subjecting them to buyouts, tax inspections, or lawsuits. The result was a virtual monopoly of media coverage for President Akaev during the presidential campaign and an "information blockade" for his opponents. On the national channel, KTR, Akaev received 34,920 seconds of coverage, only 490 seconds of which were negative. Tekebaev got only 292 seconds of coverage, about half of which had a negative slant.[5]

For Western observers, the graciousness of the losers in Kyrgyzstani politics may have been the most extraordinary feature of the 2000 presidential election. After criticizing the arrests of his campaign aides and what he called "the massive falsification that took place during the elections," presidential candidate Eshimkanov adopted a conciliatory tone:

> I have sufficient courage to congratulate Askar Akaev on his victory, achieved
> even at such a price. We must now think about the country. What will happen
> to the people, to the economy, to the exchange rate? I think he [Akaev] has
> sufficient intellect, conscience, and humanity to understand that we can't live
> like this any longer.[6]

It is difficult to explain such generosity. Did it reflect a recognition of
how much less open and competitive life had been in the Soviet era? Or did it
acknowledge how much worse things were in the neighboring countries of
Central Asia, where presidents brooked little or no opposition? Or, less generously, was it a tactical surrender in the face of insurmountable odds? Even
his political enemies in this period recognized that, for all his faults, Akaev
was not a ruthless politician and that he employed a Machiavellian economy
of violence, that is, just enough force to maintain himself in office and no
more. While he did what it took to keep himself in power, and to expand the
role of his family and friends in the country's economy, he allowed all but
the most implacable and popular opponents to organize parties, contest elections, and complain about the shortcomings of his rule. Resisting pressures
from neighboring presidents—especially from Islam Karimov of Uzbekistan—to tighten the screws on his political adversaries and his society,
Akaev governed as a moderate in foreign and domestic policy, which meant,
among other things, permitting businessmen and women to expand their
commercial interests to the point where they represented a social force capable of serving as a check on governmental power.

For most, then, the cost of losing in politics in Akaev's Kyrgyzstan was
tolerable, which is one of the preconditions for the rise of democracy. When
the stakes of elections or policy choices become too high, democracy suffers
because those participating in politics are tempted use extreme measures to
prevent an unfavorable outcome. Ironically, that was the position Akaev
found himself in. For a sitting president in a country like Kyrgyzstan, electoral defeat did not just entail a loss of political power and a return to civilian
life, it threatened to strip the president of his ill-gotten property gains and
even his freedom or his life—and not just the president himself, but his
family and his entourage. Once a president sanctions—even on a small
scale—selective prosecution of his enemies or schemes for personal enrichment, he crosses a political Rubicon, which exposes him to retribution on his
departure from office. The only exit strategy for such a leader is to find a
replacement who is sure to win and sure to remain loyal, which means a
willingness to protect the property and personal security of the former ruler.
But unlike in Russia, where Yeltsin found such a dauphin in Putin, Akaev
saw no immediate need for a replacement. He was, after all, a younger man
than Yeltsin and he had the prospect of a five-year term, or perhaps more,
ahead of him.

From a shy scholar who entered politics reluctantly at the end of the Soviet era, Akaev had developed by the turn of the millennium into a leader willing to exact a high price for disloyalty on the handful of persons who were capable of threatening his hold on power. Akaev's relentless pursuit of Kulov led to the latter's conviction in early 2001 for abuse of office, for which he was stripped of his property and General's rank and sentenced to seven years in solitary confinement. In 2002, in a separate trial, a court found Kulov guilty of misuse of state funds while he was governor of the Chu region in the mid-1990s, which added another ten years to his sentence. Much to Akaev's dismay, as Kyrgyzstan's first political prisoner, Kulov continued to pose a challenge to the president's authority, this time from his jail cell, where his incarceration was a constant reminder to the population of the precariousness of Akaev's hold on power.

The intense political life in Bishkek seemed a world apart as our group approached Lake Issyk-Kul' for a weekend of sightseeing before departing the country. Driving along the north shore of the lake in a VW mini-bus with our Russian driver and Gulnara and her husband and young son, we stopped for the night at the Kyrgyz Shore, one of the two large Soviet-era hotels in the small tourist town of Cholpon-Ata. Perhaps nowhere in the world is the built environment more of an assault on the natural environment surrounding it than at Issyk-Kul'. Rising incongruously from the shore of a pristine mountain lake, beyond which loom breathtaking mountains, our hotel offered the tasteless architecture, indifferent service, and neglected grounds for which communist tourist destinations were famous. On my way to dinner that evening, I stopped by the room of the two young women in our group to see if they were ready. One poked her head out of the door sheepishly and said that there had been an accident in the bathroom. The sink, it turned out, had come loose from the wall and lay cracked in two on the bathroom floor. When the maintenance man arrived a few minutes later, he immediately put the students at ease, noting that such occurrences were common in the hotel.

The lake in late May was still too cold for a swim, so we walked over the next morning to a makeshift dock on a lagoon near the hotel in search of a boat to take us out on the water. Finding the owner of a small, seemingly seaworthy old vessel, we settled on a price of $20 for an hour-long boat ride for six of us. As the owner steered the boat into the open lake, the water turned from light green to a rich turquoise. The further we got from shore, the more dramatic the surrounding landscape appeared and the more conscious we were of being the only human beings in sight on this vast lake, which was more than 110 miles long and 40 miles wide. Just as we were preparing to turn around, we noticed that the boat was taking on water. Looking around for something to use to bail out the boat, we urged the captain, who did not seem terribly bothered by the leak, to head back to the dock as quickly as he could. With few expectations about things working as advertised, whether in politics or everyday life, many citizens of Kyrgyzstan confronted broken sinks, leaking boats, and flawed elections with an acceptance that bordered on fatalism.

Before leaving Cholpon-Ata, we paid a short visit to an open-air museum of more than four hundred granite boulders whose carvings of animals and other natural symbols date back to the first millennium BCE. As a horse and her foal scampered among the rocks nearby, we tried our hand at decoding these petroglyphs, which were scattered across a 60-acre plain at the base of the mountains. Containing images of hunters and snow leopards, among other fauna, this massive collection of seemingly randomly distributed rocks has thus far resisted decryption, and we left the site puzzled by the role of these rocks and their symbols in the lives of the Issyk-Kul' peoples who predated the Kyrgyz.

Driving east from Cholpon-Ata we quickly left behind the cafes and small guest houses serving the tourist industry and entered flatter, more verdant terrain, where farmlands and traditional Kyrgyz villages dominated the landscape. As we turned south at the end of the lake, we passed wheat fields that stretched all the way to Kyrgyzstan's easternmost city, Karakol. Our first stop in the city was the central market, whose facade sported a prominent banner with the words, "President Akaev is the Guarantor of Stability and Prosperity." Standing in front of the market was a large, two-humped camel, fitted out with a brightly colored carpet that ran almost the length of his body, with cut-outs for the two prominent humps. Although the Bactrian camel is native to the steppes of Central Asia, its role here was not as beast of burden but attention-grabber, rather like the large American flags that grace car lots in the United States. The gimmick worked, and we stopped to tour the market and taste the Kyrgyz fast food on offer at the small stands along the street.

Known as Przheval'sk in the Soviet era—after the Russian geographer of Central Asia, N. M. Przheval'skii, who died here in 1888—Karakol had been home until recently to a large Russian population, many of whom traced their roots to the late tsarist era. In the center of the small city was an imposing Russian Orthodox Church, the Holy Trinity Cathedral, which dates to 1895. After touring the church, with its large gold-framed icons standing improbably in a traditional wooden structure, we descended the stairs, at the bottom of which sat an old Russian woman who was asking for alms. When we inquired about the Russian community in the city, she replied that the young and able had left for Russia, and those remaining were either too old or too poor to think about emigrating. Noting that she had relatives in Cheliabinsk, a city in the Russian Urals, she said that if she could scrounge up the money for the flight she would consider departing as well, which may have been an appeal for charity rather than a real indication of interest in leaving a city where she had spent her entire life.

Karakol was also home to a sizeable community of Dungans, the name for the Han Chinese who had converted to Islam. Their striking wooden mosque, located just a few streets away from the Holy Trinity Cathedral, bore the distinctive architectural markers of Chinese temples, with their sweeping curvatures at the corners of the roof. Extending well beyond the building, the eaves were supported by round wooden columns, which created the effect of a loggia around the entire mosque. Similar columns appeared in the prayer room inside, whose ceiling sported intricate wooden designs. The mixture of Islamic and Chinese design in the mosque was a reminder that Karakol, like Kyrgyzstan itself, lay at the meeting point of two great world cultures.

Traveling southwest from Karakol, we arrived at our turnoff within twenty minutes and headed south into the mountains and away from Lake Issyk-Kul'. As we drove up a ravine, a small village and well-tended fields gave way to the seven prominent red stone outcroppings that gave the settlement its name, Jeti-Oguz, meaning "seven bulls" in Kyrgyz. Often compared to the Garden of the Gods in Colorado Springs, the massive red rock formation, which juts unexpectedly out of a hillside, is an incongruous sight amid the green mountains and fields that surround it. Continuing up the mountain, the paved road turned into a narrow, unimproved trail, and at one point our VW mini-bus had to cross a small stream that threatened to block our ascent. As the trail flattened out, we entered a lush, high-mountain valley—the *jailoo* that Bolot had described in our conversations in Moscow two decades earlier. It was an idyllic setting for our picnic, with sheep grazing on lush grass near a yurt.

At the end of a lazy afternoon in the *jailoo*, we drove back down the mountain to the Jeti-Oguz Sanatorium, where we spent the night. Touted as a health resort, the sanatorium offered radon baths and geothermal treatments for patients with various maladies, and a place of rest for those wishing to escape the pressures of city life. Entering the facility, we didn't know if we'd stepped back in time or onto the set of a horror movie. Unsmiling women in white coats and high white chef hats walked the dimly lit hallways, past treatment rooms containing unfamiliar medical equipment. As in Cholpon-Ata, the soulless built environment inherited from the Soviet era was an affront to the natural marvels around it. After settling in our bedrooms, which were in various states of disrepair, we headed to dinner, served in a small, windowless room nearby. Fortunately, we had eaten a healthy and plentiful lunch in the open air; the food at the sanatorium—mystery meat and porridge—was institutional fare at its most challenging. The absence of a TV and other modern distractions that evening was welcome, and we spent the time playing cards and reflecting on our trip. Retiring to my room for the night, I felt a cold wind blowing through cracks in the glass of the window, a reminder that even in the late spring, the air at 7,000 feet could seem wintry.

In the morning light, the sanatorium appeared less eerie and foreboding. As I stepped outside to survey the dramatic scenery, I ran into a group of Kyrgyz WWII veterans dressed in dark outfits that were adorned with military medals. Seemingly a head shorter than the current generation of Kyrgyz men, these veterans were enjoying a month's stay at the sanatorium, with all expenses paid by the state. For them, the annual retreat was a welcome chance to discuss with a rapidly dwindling group of comrades-in-arms the defining experience of their lives. Not all spoke Russian confidently, but those who did volunteered their reflections on the harsh conditions they endured during the Great Patriotic War, as WWII was known in the USSR. There was little talk of combat itself.

As in other post-Soviet countries, the government of Kyrgyzstan sought to distance itself from most of the symbolic legacy of the communist era, but not the Great Patriotic War. Just two weeks earlier at the sanatorium, this group of Kyrgyz veterans had celebrated the fifty-fifth anniversary of the victory over fascism. Although their generation may not have many more opportunities to remember the glory of victory, their children and grandchildren are likely to retain a sense of national pride that Soviet soldiers, sailors, and airmen from Kirgizia had helped to defeat the Nazis in the 1940s. On this issue, Kyrgyzstan's political class was united.

Our return journey to Bishkek took us along the little-explored southern shore of Lake Issyk-Kul', where a two-lane road hugged the shoreline. Less than an hour after departing we passed through the village of Barskoon, which had been the site of a much-publicized environmental disaster two years earlier. On May 20, 1998, a truck hauling cyanide to the Kumtor gold mine lost its load several miles south of Barskoon. Two packets of granular cyanide, weighing one ton each, spilled into the Barskoon River, which flows into Lake Issyk-Kul'. Widely used in the mining industry to separate gold from ore, cyanide as well as other hazardous materials were regularly transported by truck up to Kumtor, and this was the first significant accident along the route.

There were conflicting reports on the number of local residents who were harmed by the spill, but as many as four villagers may have died from drinking contaminated water. Because the small river was the sole source of water and irrigation in the community, the local population expressed understandable alarm at the health consequences, and more than a thousand persons visited medical facilities in the first month after the spill. For their part, Dutch scientists employed by the World Health Organization issued an official report in the wake of the accident stating that the danger of cyanide poisoning passed within a few hours of the spill, and there were no residual effects on the river, the lake, or the surrounding fields and the crops grown there.[7]

Figure 9.1.   Kyrgyz WWII veterans, Jeti-Oguz Sanatorium. May 2000

Despite these assurances, the Barskoon accident became a cause célèbre in local and national politics. The Canadian owners of Kumtor paid restitution, but not in amounts that satisfied the local population or their representatives. Politicians at the national level sought to use the disaster to extract further concessions from Kumtor on ownership issues and also to advance their own reputations as populist defenders of the victims of unscrupulous foreign owners. Periodic protests against Kumtor broke out in the years that followed, and well over a decade after the accident, a group of opposition politicians seeking to launch an uprising against the government rode into Barskoon on horseback and stirred up the still raw emotions surrounding the cyanide spill at a massive rally of local residents. Barskoon became the first of many locales around Kyrgyzstan whose names came to symbolize events that would challenge the political and social order in the new millennium.

Chapter Ten

Borders and Regions
Bedevil a President

The next place to attract the attention of the nation was the Aksy district of southern Kyrgyzstan. In March 2002, local police from Aksy fired on unarmed demonstrators, killing six and wounding ninety at a rally to protest the jailing of a fiery local judge turned national politician, Azimbek Beknazarov. It was a watershed moment in the country's short political history. Never before had the authorities fired on political protesters, never mind killed them. The fact that it happened in a small town in the increasingly restive South was all the more damaging for the reputation of President Akaev, who had never enjoyed broad-based support in the region. In the months and years that followed, Aksy would become a rallying cry for those opposed to the president, especially southerners, who managed to block the main road between Bishkek and Osh for more than a week in May 2002.[1]

The nation closely followed the case of Beknazarov, a member of parliament who had been arrested in January 2002 on charges that he had released a murder suspect in his custody while working as a prosecutor in the mid-1990s. The man was later convicted of the crime. Whatever the extent of Beknazarov's culpability in that long-forgotten case, the decision in early 2002 to bring charges against him had all the hallmarks of a selective prosecution engineered by law enforcement officials working on the instructions of President Akaev. As informed citizens understood, Beknazarov's real crime was using his position as parliamentary deputy to criticize Akaev relentlessly for his decision to cede 120,000 hectares—almost 500 square miles—of Kyrgyzstan's borderlands to China. Along these borderlands were some of the tallest mountains in the world, including Victory Peak, at 24,406 feet, which remained in Kyrgyzstani possession.

Originally demarcated in the 1860s and 1880s between the Tsarist and Chinese governments, the disputed frontier between the two countries was the subject of lengthy negotiations through the 1990s. President Akaev signed, and parliament ratified, the first stage in the new delimitation of the borders in 1996, which granted China 30,000 hectares of territory previously controlled by Kyrgyzstan. A 1999 addendum, negotiated by President Akaev but never submitted to the parliament, only came to light in the spring of 2001, prompting a furious reaction by many parliamentary deputies, including Beknazarov. The addendum ceded another 90,000 hectares to China, including the headwaters of two rivers and territory with significant mineral reserves, including tungsten. The government's reaction to the criticism was swift and forceful: one of Akaev's closest advisors warned that those objecting to treaties on border demarcation could be subject to criminal prosecution.[2]

Akaev's justifications for the concessions, based in part on what he described as thinly veiled military threats from the Chinese side, were unconvincing to many deputies, and some launched an unsuccessful attempt to impeach the president. Whether or not Akaev and persons in his entourage received personal bribes from the Chinese to seal the deal, as several well-placed officials indicated in conversations with me, his 2000 campaign for the presidency reportedly received millions of soms in contributions from the Chinese government.[3] The parliament itself was not above suspicion in the ultimate ratification of the border treaty in 2002. Shortly before the successful vote on ratification, a large group of Kyrgyzstani deputies who supported the treaty visited China on an all-expenses-paid trip covered by the Chinese government.

The Chinese border dispute was one of several territorial issues facing Kyrgyzstan when it gained its independence from the Soviet Union. On its southern border with Tajikistan, uncertainties about the frontier led to periodic conflicts between Tajik and Kyrgyz farmers over water rights in the remote Batken region of the country. Just a few miles away, at the intersection of the borders of Kyrgyzstan, Tajikistan, and Uzbekistan, the Soviet government under Stalin had granted Tajikistan and Uzbekistan several small enclaves inside Kyrgyzstani territory. During the Soviet era this geographical oddity posed few problems, but once the former republics gained statehood, the erection of border posts complicated the lives of residents and travelers alike, and Uzbekistan has repeatedly pushed Kyrgyzstan to cede territory that would serve as access corridors connecting these enclaves with Uzbekistan to the north. Because the main east-west road in southwestern Kyrgyzstan passed through the town of Sokh—located within a salamander-shaped 135-square-mile enclave belonging to Uzbekistan—those traveling from one point in Kyrgyzstan to another were subject to Uzbekistani border checks and customs inspection.

For the residents of Sokh, this geographical anomaly was even more disruptive. If the predominantly ethnic Tajik population living there wished to visit relatives in Tajikistan, whose border was less than twenty miles away, they could do so legally only by traveling almost two hundred miles each way to the capital of Uzbekistan, Tashkent, in order to obtain a visa. Because this was impractical, those traveling to Tajikistan took their chances at the Kyrgyzstani-Tajikistani frontier, which often meant bribing the border guards to let them through. Accompanying one young Tajik woman from Sokh on this short but nerve-wracking journey to her childhood home, the British anthropologist Madeleine Reeves described in sobering detail the consequences of communism's collapse for the everyday lives of those trapped on the wrong side of a border. Lamenting the erection of hard borders, the Tajik woman complained to Reeves: "I become a criminal every time I want to visit my mother. What kind of freedom is that?"[4]

At the end of the 1990s, this sparsely populated corner of Kyrgyzstan began to attract the attention of Western defense experts as well as anthropologists. Only seventy-five miles of Tajikistani territory separated Kyrgyzstan from Afghanistan, where the Taliban had emerged as an incubator for terrorist groups, including not only Al-Qaeda but the Islamic Movement of Uzbekistan (IMU). On an early morning in February 1999, I was in Washington, DC, at a small conference organized by the Swiss Peace Foundation, which sought to produce a handbook designed to predict—and thereby forestall—outbreaks of violence in Central Asia. The member of our group responsible for producing the chapter on Uzbekistan, a regional expert from the State Department, arrived late and in an excited state. Cable traffic from Tashkent had just reported a series of explosions in the Uzbekistani capital. The IMU claimed responsibility for targeting President Karimov, who emerged unhurt from the incident. We had obviously missed our first chance at prediction.

The same summer a small group of heavily armed members of the IMU left their forward base in a remote, mountainous region of Tajikistan and crossed the poorly defended southwestern border of Kyrgyzstan, where they took the *akim* of the Batken district, several Kyrgyzstani military officers, and four Japanese geologists hostage. All were ultimately released unharmed, the latter in exchange for a ransom. With an army of only 12,000 men, Kyrgyzstan struggled to expel the invaders from an area of the country where ravines and mountain passes gave cover to guerrilla fighters, whose most potent adversary was the onset of winter. The IMU repeated this small-scale invasion of the Batken region of Kyrgyzstan the following summer, again taking hostages, including four young American mountain climbers who had come to scale the 2,500-foot Yellow Wall in Kyrgyzstan's picturesque Kara-Su Valley. If their story can be believed, these adventure seekers escaped by pushing one of their captors off a mountain to his death.[5]

With its limited military capacity and unfavorable geography, Kyrgyzstan found it difficult to protect its borders, not just from the IMU but from the government of neighboring Uzbekistan. Intent on using all means necessary to defeat the avowed enemies of the Karimov regime, the Uzbekistani government unleashed air strikes against IMU positions on Kyrgyzstani territory without seeking permission from Bishkek. They also planted land mines along portions of the poorly demarcated Kyrgyzstan-Uzbekistan border, which would kill and maim scores of innocent local residents over the next decade.

Al-Qaeda's attack on the United States on September 11, 2001, brought these localized skirmishes in a little-known region of Asia into the sights of the West's new "War on Terror." The American government's earlier, and largely symbolic, labeling of the IMU as a terrorist organization now acquired real teeth. In November 2001, within weeks of the American intervention in Afghanistan, US airstrikes killed one of IMU's two main leaders, Juma Namangani, in northern Afghanistan. Western military forces ultimately drove the remnants of the IMU into the tribal regions of northwestern Pakistan where, in 2009, the other founder of the movement, Tahir Yuldash, died in a drone strike.

Despite its small population and limited resources, Kyrgyzstan began to play an outsized role in the Afghan War. With the blessing of Moscow, with whom Bishkek had maintained close relations through the 1990s, the Akaev government invited the United States, and later NATO forces, to use the country's major airport as a staging point for Western troops arriving and departing from Afghanistan. Later restyled the Transit Center at Manas, Bishkek's main airport was transformed in December 2001 from a sleepy civilian terminal into a bustling center of logistics and transport on what the Pentagon called the Northern Supply Route into Afghanistan.[6] Arriving in the early morning hours on subsequent trips to Bishkek, I always awoke to the improbable and oddly reassuring sight of military-gray KC-135 refueling tankers lined up on the tarmac opposite the main civilian terminal.

As the reliability of the Southern Supply Route through Pakistan declined in subsequent years, and Western forces lost their access to an Uzbekistani airbase near the Afghan border, the Transit Center at Manas assumed an increasingly vital role in the West's ability to wage war in Afghanistan. Predictably, as the West became more dependent on the cooperation of Kyrgyzstan, the US government became more reticent to criticize the shortcomings of the Akaev regime. However, in the wake of the Aksy incident, an emboldened and growing opposition needed little encouragement or support from the outside to push for an end to Akaev's leadership. Their opportunity came in the next election cycle, which kicked off with parliamentary elections in February 2005.

Besides the backlash from the Aksy events, and the increasing frustration of southerners with northern dominance in political and economic affairs, there were broader developments in the post-communist world that signaled the vulnerability of Akaev and his political allies in the upcoming elections. Opposition forces in post-Soviet Georgia had exploited popular discontent with a flawed parliamentary election in their country in November 2003 to topple the sitting president, Eduard Shevardnadze, and hold new elections, including a presidential contest that was won by a young political maverick, Mikheil Saakashvili. A similar uprising against an unpopular leader followed parliamentary elections in Ukraine, where voting results, as in Georgia, did not correspond with exit polls. These popular rebellions in Georgia and Ukraine—labeled the Rose and Orange Revolutions, respectively—sent shock waves throughout the former Soviet Union, and Putin and his supporters in the Russian political establishment introduced a series of measures designed to inoculate their country against the scourge of so-called color revolutions.

Protecting himself from rising popular discontent in the forthcoming parliamentary campaign proved more difficult for Askar Akaev, in part because of the precariousness of his position as a president serving out his last constitutionally mandated term. Akaev never openly ruled out the possibility of changing the constitution to extend his time in office, but he made statements in the fall of 2004 that led many to conclude that he was a lame duck. Believing that Akaev would not maintain his hold on power, many former political allies of the president formed a kind of "establishment opposition" to the Akaev regime and prepared to challenge the parliamentary candidates aligned with the president. Joining this mass betrayal of the sitting president were former foreign ministers, a former head of the country's Security Council, and four diplomats who abandoned their positions overseas to contest the parliamentary election. Among these diplomats was Roza Otunbaeva, who in December 2004 returned from her post as UN envoy to the conflict in Georgia's breakaway republics to help form a new anti-Akaev party called Ata-Jurt (Fatherland). Kurmanbek Bakiev, the former prime minister whom Akaev had tossed aside as a scapegoat in 2002 in the wake of the Aksy events, established another opposition-oriented electoral alliance, the People's Movement of Kyrgyzstan. The growing number of defectors from Akaev's camp also included prominent businessmen and women who had tired of the relentless demands of Akaev's inner circle for bribes or favors. One leading northern businessman, Kubatbek Baibolov, told me that the worst offender was the country's First Lady, Mairam Akaeva, who was a master of the shakedown, which was used to benefit her favorite "charities."

Leading the president's team in the parliamentary election campaign was Akaev's daughter, Bermet. When I first met her over a decade earlier, at a breakfast for her father at the National Academy of Sciences in Washington, she was a fetching and somewhat demure student at a Swiss business school who had a deep curiosity about the West. Now in her early thirties, she was the founder and leader of a new pro-presidential party known as Alga, Kyrgyzstan! (Forward, Kyrgyzstan!). The presidential chief of staff led another new pro-Akaev political party, Adilet (Justice). Based on the model of party development that Putin had used successfully in Russia, and that President Nazarbaev had likewise employed in neighboring Kazakhstan, these "parties of power" were responsible for nominating two-thirds of the party-backed candidates in the 2005 parliamentary election. In keeping with Kyrgyzstan's penchant for constantly changing the electoral rules to keep the opposition off balance, the new parliament would have only a single chamber with 75 seats filled in single-member district elections.

Numerous parliamentary races pitted prominent members of the "establishment opposition" against pro-Akaev candidates, but none was more visible than the contest in Bishkek's electoral district No. 1, where Roza Otunbaeva squared off against Bermet Akaeva. The campaign had barely begun when the Central Election Commission, whose members were beholden to President Akaev, ruled that Otunbaeva and the other returning diplomats were not eligible to stand for office because they had not lived in the country for the preceding five years, one of many obscure provisions of the country's electoral law. Opposition lawyers argued that the diplomats' permanent residences had remained in Kyrgyzstan, and that the provision had never been applied in earlier contests, but the diplomats' names were stricken from the ballot, as were those of several other opposition candidates.

On January 20, 2005, a little over a month before the first round of parliamentary voting, I published an article in the *Moscow Times* entitled, "The Next Colored Revolution?" The piece argued that:

> if lawsuits in the courts and negotiations with the government fail to restore the opposition leaders' rights to run for office, they will have little choice but to mobilize the population against the regime. At that point, a yellow revolution will become a possibility in Kyrgyzstan. Although Kyrgyzstan may lack some of the features present in the Georgian and Ukrainian revolutions, such as a dominant opposition leader with ties to the West and a well-organized following, it does have an important regional divide and a politically active population, at least by Central Asian standards.
>
> [In addition,] pro-presidential forces must face the election without many of the country's most popular and experienced politicians on their side. In such a contest, the Akaev Family has no choice but to blatantly manipulate the election to assure victory. These tactics may guarantee victory, but they would also guarantee the illegitimacy of the election and risk launching a colored revolution in a deeply divided society with a vigorous and visible opposition.

Events played out as predicted. President Akaev and his allies used their considerable resources to ensure a sympathetic and decisive majority in the parliament. The size of the majority was important because with two-thirds of the seats in the hands of his supporters, Akaev could have changed the constitution to run for another term. Besides disqualifying prominent opposition candidates, Akaev's team restricted the ability of their adversaries to get their message out by closing the country's only independent printing press, intimidating newspapers that were not aligned with the president, and, four days before the first round of the election, shutting down local transmissions of Radio Azattyk, the US-funded Kyrgyz-language service of Radio Liberty that broadcast from Central Europe. With opposition media outlets hobbled, government-backed news dominated the final stages of the campaign, which fed the population a steady diet of positive news stories about President Akaev and his achievements. Combined with other tactics designed to stifle the opposition, including vote buying and voter intimidation, these methods assured almost a complete sweep of the parliament's 75 seats by pro-government politicians, including Akaev's daughter and son. Six opposition candidates managed to win seats, among them Azimbek Beknazarov, but the emerging leader of the "establishment opposition," Kurmanbek Bakiev, lost his contest in his home region of Jalal-Abad in the second round, which helped to trigger massive protests against the results in the South.

In no other country in Central Asia—and perhaps the world—was public protest such a frequent and accepted part of political life. As the Aksy incident illustrated, ethnic Kyrgyz turned out with alacrity to defend their local "Big Man" against the central authorities. Protests took numerous forms, from the pitching of "yurt cities" in public parks to lengthy marches to the capital. During the 2005 parliamentary elections, attempts to disqualify a popular politician from the Issyk-Kul' region led to demonstrations around the election commission that temporarily prevented the ballots from being distributed to voting precincts. When the election finally took place in that constituency—minus the disqualified local candidate—voters cast two-thirds of their ballots "Against All."

Reacting angrily to the defeat of their candidates in the second round of parliamentary voting in March, many voters in the South took to the streets, blocking the single artery connecting North and South and seizing control of district and regional *akimiats*, the seats of local governmental power. Forces sympathetic to Akaev regained control of the buildings temporarily, but were later ejected by the crowds. Without enough loyal law enforcement officials in the South or well-trained and reliable crowd control units from Bishkek that could be dispatched to the scene, Akaev and his supporters watched helplessly as disgruntled southerners began a trek to Bishkek.

Chapter Eleven

The Tulip Revolution

On March 24, 2005, a week after the second round of the parliamentary elections, protesters from around the country gathered at rallies in Bishkek that were organized by opposition leaders from the North and South.[1] Because each leader had his or her own following, and cooperation among the politicians was limited, the demonstrators were spread out across the city in separate rallies, including one led by the controversial physician turned substance abuse healer, Jenishbek Nazaraliev. As the crowds left these events to converge on the central square in front of the White House, the number of demonstrators there swelled to over five thousand, and the initial contingent of one hundred presidential guards was no match for the protesters.

In the middle of the afternoon, a large group of uniformed personnel suddenly appeared from behind the White House and marched into the crowd, hoping to disperse it. After a series of melees involving demonstrators and the police, groups of protesters began to scale the fence around the White House grounds and enter the building. In the disorder that followed, the police defending the White House exhibited remarkable restraint, in part because President Akaev refused to give the order to fire on the crowds. However one assesses Akaev's decade-and-a-half in power, it did not end with the bloodbath that often accompanies such scenes in the developing world.

Opposition leaders were effective at mobilizing but not controlling the protests, whether in the earlier takeovers of government buildings in the South or around the White House in Bishkek. Despite calls for calm by opposition leaders, many protesters entering the White House helped themselves to computers, printers, and memorabilia from government offices there. The looting spread to commercial establishments along Chu Prospect, with the upscale Turkish-owned shopping mall, Mega Stores, particularly hard hit. As Roza Otunbaeva explained to me in the wake of the events,

> Those of us in the opposition tried to lead this uprising, but we were often left in its wake. We didn't appreciate the degree of anger of the population, and the people passed us by. They decided to act, and we only appeared on the scene later.[2]

When Otunbaeva, Bakiev, and other opposition leaders entered the White House in the late afternoon of March 24, Akaev, his family, and his entourage had already fled the building, and the country. Traveling to Kazakhstan and then on to Moscow, where he was taken in by the Russian government, Akaev insisted that he was still the lawfully elected leader of the country, but opposition leaders in Bishkek moved quickly to create a new political order.

Joining the other opposition leaders in Bishkek was Felix Kulov, whom the crowds had freed from a local prison the morning of the revolt. That same evening, a *kurultai*—the name for a traditional meeting of elders in the Turkic world—entrusted Kulov with responsibility for the country's uniformed services. As a much-decorated general and former head of law enforcement agencies, Kulov used his considerable popular authority and organizational skills to help bring order to the streets of the capital. Assisting in this effort were self-defense committees established by business owners and ordinary citizens, many of whom patrolled the capital wearing red armbands that recalled the old Soviet volunteer brigades of *druzhinniki*, a kind of informal people's guard.

As the population began to repair the damage to Bishkek's looted buildings, the "establishment opposition" met to mend political institutions that had been disrupted by what the Kyrgyzstanis called the Tulip Revolution, named after the spring flowers in bloom at the time of the uprising. As traditional politicians rather than revolutionaries, most opposition leaders were intent on putting the country on firm constitutional footing as quickly as possible. The question was how to do that. Having criticized for weeks the flaws in the parliamentary election, they were reluctant to recognize the newly elected legislative body as the legitimate representative of the Kyrgyzstani people. And yet failing to accept the electoral results would have required a new election, which would have postponed for weeks the parliament's ability to grant executive authority to a new leadership team.

With various interests and institutions competing for political advantage in this constitutional vacuum, governing institutions were in disarray for days after the Tulip Revolution. The Supreme Court initially annulled the results of the election, but the new parliament ignored the ruling and assembled anyway, which meant that for a time the country had an old and new parliament meeting separately but simultaneously. In the provinces, several losing candidates mobilized protests against the new parliament in their home districts, and as late as April 6, several thousand demonstrators seized the *akimiat* and court building in the regional capital of Talas, in western Kyrgyzstan, in support of a favorite son who failed to win a parliamentary seat. In parts of the South, competing crowds sought to promote their own Big Man as *akim*, which resulted in one city having four *akims* at the same time.[3]

A framework for new political arrangements finally emerged in early April, two weeks after the popular revolt. After the Supreme Court reversed its earlier decision annulling the elections, the old parliament reluctantly ceded power to the new assembly, several of whose members traveled to Moscow to obtain the signature of Askar Akaev on a document offering his resignation from the office of the presidency. The new parliament confirmed Kurmanbek Bakiev as the country's new prime minister, and with the presidency now vacant, Bakiev also served, according to the Constitution, as the acting president. New presidential elections were set for July 10.

Recognizing the fragility of the country's political institutions and the risks of a divisive presidential election campaign, the politicians who helped make the revolution forged a power-sharing arrangement designed to avoid the winner-take-all outcomes of traditional presidential contests. Because Kyrgyzstan's two most prominent politicians at this moment—Kurmanbek Bakiev and Felix Kulov—had their political bases in the South and North, respectively, an electoral battle between these two leaders could have split the country apart on regional lines. To ensure that both northern and southern elites had a seat at the table—arrangements that political scientists call consociationalism—Kulov agreed to support Bakiev for the presidency, in return for Bakiev's promise to appoint Kulov prime minister immediately after the election.

As a result of this agreement among the country's key political elites, Bakiev anticipated facing only second-tier candidates in the presidential election. However, an unexpected challenger emerged in the person of Urmat Baryktabasov, an oligarch from Issyk-Kul'. Like numerous Kyrgyzstani businessmen, Baryktabasov held both Kazakhstani and Kyrgyzstani passports. Not surprisingly, the authorities used his status as the citizen of a foreign country to disqualify him from the presidential race. Angered by this move, Baryktabasov organized a rally of two thousand supporters outside the White House, though whether the demonstrators were in fact loyalists or members of a rent-a-crowd is not known—a new business called "Picketer!" had formed to supply needed bodies to demonstrations. Outfitted with professionally made banners labeling Baryktabasov a "real patriot," the demonstrators surged past guards into the White House and for a short time occupied the president's office. After the crowd was removed, Bakiev responded angrily that next time he'd defend the White House with an automatic weapon.[4]

With Baryktabasov out of the way, Bakiev went on to win the presidential election handily, with 89 percent of the vote. As promised, he then named Kulov prime minister and the parliament confirmed the nomination. In the wake of the elections, relations at the top of the Kyrgyzstani political system seemed to stabilize. However, the increasingly brazen involvement of criminal groups in public affairs had the nation on edge. Some in the Russian press referred to the revolt in March as the Poppy, rather than Tulip, Revolution, attributing the upheavals to money originating from opium shipments that transited Kyrgyzstan on its way from Afghanistan to Europe.[5] Several members of parliament were widely suspected of having close ties to the criminal underworld. One of these, Jyrgalbek Surabaldiev, had been a close ally of President Akaev and allegedly unleashed his personal retinue of "sportsmen" on demonstrators during the Tulip Revolution—"sportsmen" was the euphemism for fit young men, often dressed in track suits, who served as "muscle" for the Big Men in Kyrgyzstan. On June 10, Surabaldiev was gunned down in broad daylight in central Bishkek. A few weeks earlier, shortly after announcing that he was considering a run for the presidency, parliamentary deputy Bayaman Erkinbaev had been injured in an assassination attempt outside the parliament. He would die at the hands of an assassin in September. In October, another member of the *Jogorku Kenesh*, Tynychbek Akmatbaev, was murdered while visiting a prison on a parliamentary fact-finding mission. He was the younger brother of one of Kyrgyzstan's most notorious criminal figures, Ryspek Akmataliev, who was murdered the following year while leaving a mosque in the city of Osh.

The removal of Akaev had destabilized relations between criminal groups and their patrons in the government, and so some of the violence was related to the turf wars that always follow the demise of powerful individuals or families in the criminal underworld. The weakness of the new government also emboldened criminal kingpins, as did the significant popular support that many of them enjoyed. One such kingpin, Bayaman Erkinbaev, won his seat in parliament in the 2005 elections with 95 percent of the vote from his constituents in the remote southern district of Kadamjai. A constituent's comments to an interviewer from the International Crisis Group revealed one of the reasons for popular support of figures like Erkinbaev.

> He will always help out, in any case; he can even physically defend you. So what if some people say he broke the law, he is the best deputy and many residents in other constituencies envy us.[6]

In countries like Kyrgyzstan, where the government can't be relied on to provide either economic or physical security, and institutions like the market and courts are immature, it is understandable that voters will turn to Big Men who appear able and willing to provide for the well-being of their constituents.

Beside an array of domestic challenges, President Bakiev confronted an unenviable legacy left by Askar Akaev in foreign policy. To his credit, President Akaev had shaped an imaginative formal foreign policy doctrine that he called Diplomacy of the Silk Road, which viewed Kyrgyzstan as a crossroads country that should be open to influences from other countries.[7] But the efforts to sustain what was called a multivector foreign policy became increasingly difficult as relations between the United States and Russia deteriorated over the early 2000s. The agreement reached after 9/11 between the United States and Russia on the use of Kyrgyzstan as a supply route to Afghanistan had started to fray in the wake of the American invasion of Iraq and Russia's suspicions about US involvement in the color revolutions. Kyrgyzstan was subject, therefore, to increasing pressure from Moscow to limit its role in the West's war effort in Afghanistan, and in order to balance American influence in Kyrgyzstan, Russia gained basing rights of its own in October 2003 at a military airfield in Kant, a small city just seventeen miles east of Bishkek. For the next decade, Kyrgyzstan was the only country in the world that hosted both American and Russian military bases. Sandwiched between military contingents from two of the world's Great Powers on either side of its capital, Kyrgyzstan served as a barometer of tensions between Moscow and Washington.

Bakiev's first major appearance on the international stage was at the United Nations in New York in September 2005, five months after the Tulip Revolution. Accompanying him on this trip was Roza Otunbaeva, who had assumed the position of acting foreign minister after the Tulip Revolution. Another prominent opposition figure who assumed a key diplomatic post was Zamira Sydykova, the former newspaper editor, who became Kyrgyzstan's ambassador to the United States and Canada in the summer of 2005. At Zamira's invitation, I flew to New York to meet Bakiev, who, along with dozens of other presidents and heads of state, gave a short talk at the opening session of the General Assembly. Bakiev's speech reminded delegates that Kyrgyzstan was deep in debt, which prevented the country's budget from covering needed expenditures on human development. He noted, however, that Kyrgyzstan was a donor as well as a recipient nation. It may have taken money from other countries and international organizations but it also gave back: its melting glaciers and snow-fed rivers were a vital source of free water for its region and, on a planet that was suffering from an increasingly polluted atmosphere, his country served as a rare zone of ecological purity.[8] This thinly veiled appeal for financial support from the world community recalled the diplomatic efforts of President Akaev in the early 1990s: with little to offer in the way of goods or services, he tried to sell the West the idea of his country as an island of democracy. Bakiev was now packaging Kyr-

gyzstan as a selfless source of natural resources and environmental regenera-
tion.

Arranging a personal meeting for me with Bakiev turned out to be harder
than Zamira had expected. Even getting him to agree to see key governmental and financial figures turned out to be a challenge. Frustrated by President
Bush's unwillingness to schedule him in, Bakiev had to be dragged kicking
and screaming to other important appointments, including a visit to the New
York Stock Exchange and meetings with the financier, George Soros, and a
high-ranking State Department official, William Burns. With Bakiev accompanied by only a small group of assistants from the presidential administration, the remainder of the Kyrgyzstani delegation was left to fend for themselves on the street opposite the UN with me and a woman seeking an
interview with Bakiev for *The New York Review of Books*.

When it became clear that Bakiev was not entertaining any more meetings that day, Roza Otunbaeva asked me to accompany her to JFK airport,
where the presidential delegation was scheduled to depart for Kyrgyzstan
that evening. As we joined a police escort for the thirty-minute drive to the
far reaches of Queens, Roza and I discussed the consequences of the Tulip
Revolution on foreign and domestic policy. She highlighted the popular fear
that the gains of the revolution would be lost. As a result, she said, citizens
had "formed revolutionary committees everywhere, especially in the South,
which monitor the situation to this day."[9]

Roza insisted that the course of the country's foreign policy had changed
little as a result of the Tulip Revolution, but there were broader developments
in the region, especially the rise of China as an economic powerhouse, that
were inevitably reshaping what she called Kyrgyzstan's Eurasian-oriented
foreign policy. As the foreign minister of a small, poor state, Roza placed her
hopes in the ability of a new regional security organization, the Shanghai
Cooperation Organization, to protect Kyrgyzstan's interests in an increasingly unstable part of the world. Consisting of Russia, China, and Kyrgyzstan
and other states of former Soviet Central Asia, the Shanghai Cooperation
Organization provided a forum that allowed small members like Kyrgyzstan
to deal with the regional behemoths in a structured and relatively public
setting.

Just before reaching the main entrance to JFK, our driver exited the Van
Wyck Expressway and drove down a little-used service road to a remote part
of the airfield. The cortege of vehicles carrying Kyrgyzstani dignitaries and
support staff came to a halt in front of a guardhouse, the only visible break in
the high chain-link fence around this part of the airport. Waved through the
opening, the convoy turned right and within 100 yards pulled up to the lone
aircraft in this abandoned and distant corner of JFK. As we got out of the
cars, two uniformed Kyrgyz flight attendants came out of the aircraft and
stood on the landing at the top of the mobile airstairs that led to the plane. It

was a Tupolev 154, a narrow-bodied Soviet-made aircraft that would soon be banned from West European airports because of its excessive noise pollution.

Shortly thereafter, a car bearing President Bakiev arrived on the tarmac. In a ritual that recalled the airport send-offs of Soviet leaders traveling overseas, those not boarding the plane lined up parallel to the aircraft, about ten yards beyond the steps, and shook the hands of the dignitaries making the trip. I dutifully took my place in line with the members of the entourage that were remaining in the United States and awaited my turn to shake hands with the president. Making his way down the receiving line, Bakiev didn't utter a word. When he reached me, he shook my hand perfunctorily and gave me a quizzical look, apparently wondering what this American face was doing among the Kyrgyz. A hard, cold stare followed, and then he moved quickly down the receiving line and boarded the plane. We waved while the aircraft headed toward the runway, and then a deafening blast from the jet engines less than 100 yards away forced us to steady ourselves as the president headed for home.

Chapter Twelve

The Revolution Betrayed

President Bakiev returned to a country where the spirit of cooperation among members of the victorious "establishment opposition" was flagging. The short-lived mood of political harmony had given way to increasingly public and ill-tempered disputes over the division of the spoils, whether they related to government offices or the property that had been controlled by the Akaev family and its business allies. The day after Bakiev's arrival from New York, he signed an order dismissing Azimbek Beknazarov, the main figure in the Aksy events of 2002. Beknazarov had assumed the critical post of Procurator General immediately after the Tulip Revolution, and as the country's chief law enforcement official, he became embroiled in attempts to strip former Akaev supporters of their property. Predictably, his dismissal created a firestorm. In good Kyrgyz fashion, twelve thousand of Beknazarov's supporters gathered in Aksy a few days later to protest his removal from office, and eight of his Cabinet colleagues threatened to resign in protest. In response to the latter move, Bakiev reminded the ministers that they were his subordinates and not his partners in an opposition movement. He warned them against coming to him in the future as a group to protest: "We're not the Popular Movement of Kyrgyzstan anymore–you're ministers, and I'm the president."[1]

President Bakiev's frustration was understandable. Kyrgyz politicians found it very difficult to serve as subordinates in an executive hierarchy. Whether because of the collective decision-making imbedded in nomadic cultural traditions or the unchecked personal ambition that I saw in virtually all the Kyrgyzstani leaders I met, politicians were reluctant to accept direction from those above them. Beknazarov himself commented to me that "deep inside, every Kyrgyz sees himself being President."[2]

Instead of trying to build institutions like cohesive parties that could harness the talents of the political class behind common projects, politicians constantly advanced their own narrow agendas. The parties that did emerge in Kyrgyzstani politics were little more than vehicles for furthering the career of one—or on rarer occasions, several—politicians. As a result, electoral alliances came and went with the political wind, and each new electoral cycle seemed to give birth to a new crop of parties.[3] Even a longstanding party like Ata-Meken struggled to develop a professional staff in the center and an effective network of regional offices. When I stopped by Ata-Meken's head-quarters in Bishkek for an interview during the Bakiev presidency, I found a bevy of men playing ping pong, watching TV, and chatting in the courtyard of a sprawling house in a residential neighborhood. There were children underfoot, running in and out of the office of the party leader, Omurbek Tekebaev.[4]

The absence of disciplined and well-organized parliamentary parties in this period meant that there was no easy mechanism for pulling together a majority of deputies on parliamentary votes for legislation or cabinet nominees. Instead, the president and his staff—and to a lesser extent the prime minister's office—had to cobble together majorities on an ad hoc basis, using whatever tools of encouragement or intimidation were at their disposal. Unwilling to expend scarce political capital on several of the Cabinet nominees, Bakiev effectively assured the defeat of Roza Otunbaeva and several of her ministerial colleagues when their nominations came before parliament for a vote. Left hanging out to dry, Roza and other ministerial nominees were easy pickings for a parliament intent on asserting its authority vis-à-vis the executive. The rejection of Roza and another female minister, Irina Pronenko, left only one woman in the Cabinet and virtually an all-male *Jogorku Kenesh*.

Lifelong politicians like Roza had no "emergency landing strip"—as the Russians liked to call it—when they lost their government posts. Lacking personal wealth or a traditional profession that they could readily return to, those cut loose by the authorities struggled to make ends meet. Many turned to well-off patrons for material support until they could regain their foothold in power. The personal vulnerability of most Kyrgyzstani politicians helps to explain why the stakes of the political conflicts in the country were so high for them as individuals. For some, of course, politics was a means of enrichment, but for many others it was a means of survival.[5] Especially for those without wealth, a position in government or a prominent political party was also a way of maintaining one's status in the capital city as a respected leader of a kinship or local group.[6]

By the end of 2005, the power-sharing arrangements emerging from the Tulip Revolution were in tatters. Initially, the major political fault line was not between the offices of the president and prime minister, in part because Prime Minister Kulov by temperament and by virtue of his inferior position was not keen to challenge Bakiev directly. The most serious confrontation was between the president and his largely southern support base, on the one hand, and a growing political opposition with its primary roots in the North, on the other. In this struggle, the parliament was the primary battleground, with most of the deputies sympathetic at first to the demands of the opposition to limit the powers of the presidency. Once again, the standoff in high politics occurred against a backdrop of provincial protests, triggered as always by politicians seeking to place public pressure on their adversaries in Bishkek. In late May, 2006, four thousand persons came together in a *kurultai* in the South to call for the dissolution of the parliament, which only confirmed the view of many in an expanding political opposition that Bakiev was fomenting a political crisis in order to close down the parliament and hold new elections that would give him a submissive assembly.[7]

Kyrgyzstan lurched from one mini-crisis to another until the confrontation between president and parliament came to a head at the beginning of November 2006 in what one journalist called "a seven-day revolution."[8] Worried that the opposition would follow through with its threats to call a Constitutional Convention in order to reduce the powers of the presidency, Bakiev finally relented to his critics' demands and supported the adoption by parliament of a revised constitution. Because adopting an entirely new constitution would have forced Bakiev to run in another presidential election, merely amending the constitution had the advantage for Bakiev of diffusing an increasingly dangerous constitutional crisis and keeping him on track to complete his five-year term.

To strengthen his hand in negotiations over the terms of the revised constitution, the president's team organized a rally of over 20,000 of his supporters in the major city of the South, Osh.[9] Opposition politicians mobilized their own allies on the streets of Bishkek and other northern cities. In early November, citizens critical of President Bakiev pitched yurts and tents in the capital, and at any one time 15,000 to 20,000 people were protesting on the street, which led one opposition leader to claim that because their supporters came and went during the day, as many as 100,000 persons cycled through the crowds in a 24-hour period.

The adoption of a compromise constitution on November 9, 2006, temporarily quieted the crowds and calmed the tension between President Bakiev and his critics, who had united in an opposition group called "For Reforms" (*Za reformy*). But no sooner had the ink dried on the president's signature than several prominent politicians and jurists pointed out technical flaws in the hastily prepared document, whose final version had passed without debate. The result was the adoption of yet another constitutional revision, this one signed by President Bakiev on January 7, 2007.

These battles over the Constitution exposed two important features of Kyrgyzstani politics in the post-Akaev era. The first was a deeply held belief

by the opposition to Bakiev that better rules of political engagement represented an antidote to the country's political instability and the dangers of
what was called "family rule." The new Constitution went a long way toward
cutting the presidency down to size, at least in terms of the formal rules of
the game. It stripped the president of his right to unilaterally appoint court
chairs and regional and local *akims*, and it shifted control over the formation
of a government—meaning the selection of the prime minister and the cabinet—from the president to the parliament. As Beknazarov proclaimed proudly, if naively, the constitutional changes promised to introduce in Kyrgyzstan
a parliamentary system similar to that found in Great Britain, which would
put an end to "family rule."[10]

The second notable feature of Kyrgyzstani politics in this period was that
without politicians of good will who were committed to respecting constitutional norms, the letter of the law meant little. As the Russians like to say,
"paper will stand anything" (*bumaga vse sterpit*). Instead of adapting his
style of rule to the demands of the new Constitution, Bakiev continued to
exercise the formal powers laid out in the old Constitution while accumulat-
ing ever greater informal authority for his team of loyalists in the presidential
apparatus.

Bakiev's ability to flout the law and the agreements he had made with his
opponents rested on several tactical advantages attendant to his office and his
character. First, unlike the opposition, he could act quickly, decisively, and
ruthlessly. Although there were certainly byzantine intrigues on the seventh
floor of the White House, the presidency presented a united front to the
opposition and the public. For its part, the opposition was deeply divided
over even the most basic tactical questions, such as whether they should seize
power immediately, insist on early presidential elections, or allow the president to serve out his term. Where some of Bakiev's opponents wanted to
engage him in dialogue, others viewed that step as an unacceptable compromise. Facing what social scientists call a collective action problem, the opposition was never able to exhibit the solidarity that would have limited Bakiev's room to maneuver.

Crucial to Bakiev's success in maintaining, and ultimately tightening, his
grip on power was the willingness of key opposition-leaning politicians to
work with him, largely on his terms. At several critical junctures in late 2006,
Prime Minister Kulov was on the verge of defecting from the tandem and
throwing his weight behind opposition demands. Each time he held back,
worried about the chaos that might ensue and confident that only he had the
capacity to serve as a check on President Bakiev's ambitions. In early November 2006, one of the leaders of the opposition group, "For Reforms,"
threatened to exclude Kulov from any new government if he didn't give his
support to the anti-Bakiev forces on the street, who were clamoring for
action. Justifying his refusal to seize this rare opportunity to halt Bakiev's

consolidation of power, Kulov stated: "For me the most important thing is maintaining stability through the tandem."[11] That same week, he rejected the overtures of another opposition leader, insisting that:

> I know Bakiev better than any of you, and I know what he is capable of because I've worked with him and was alongside him. Only I can counter him. I have sufficient power [to confront him], while others don't."[12]

In January 2007, Bakiev repaid Kulov's loyalty to the tandem by scheming with members of the parliament to unseat the prime minister. Once removed from office, Kulov finally went over to the opposition, angrily accusing Bakiev of a "usurpation of power by a narrow circle [of officials] who are bound by family and regional ties."[13] But instead of joining the already-existing anti-Bakiev organization, "For Reforms," which was governed by a collective leadership, Kulov formed his own opposition group, the "United Front."

Just as these two groups were trying to coordinate their strategy, Bakiev shocked the opposition by appointing one of its most vocal leaders, Almazbek Atambaev, to the post of prime minister. This was the same politician who only weeks earlier had rounded on the sitting president, when the opposition had Bakiev on the ropes. In Atambaev's memorable words:

> Bakiev is a political corpse. Why should we revive him? I don't see any reason to hold talks with him, he's mired in lies and hypocrisy.[14]

Like Kulov, Atambaev was another political heavyweight who believed that he could single-handedly use the feeble post of prime minister to contain Bakiev's concentration of authority. Atambaev may have overseen a few positive changes in economic policy—the primary portfolio of the prime minister—but he was unable to check the advance of authoritarian politics in Kyrgyzstan. In fact, it was on Atambaev's watch that Bakiev engineered changes in the political system that laid the groundwork for a family dictatorship.

Atambaev's betrayal of the opposition came back to haunt him two years later when he launched a bid for the presidency as the standard-bearer of the anti-Bakiev forces. When I met him in his office in the summer of 2009, he opened our conversation by presenting me with a small pamphlet, having just published several thousand copies. The subject of the brochure: a justification of his decision to work with Bakiev as prime minister from March to November 2007. The pamphlet included claims that certain members of the opposition knew and approved of his plans. Whatever the truth of those assertions—and all politicians with whom I spoke denied them vigorously—Atambaev's assumption of the prime minister's post only seemed to energize the opposition against Bakiev. Less than two weeks into his tenure as prime minister, crowds began to gather in the capital for yet another round of demonstrations.

Political protests in Kyrgyzstan could happen at any time of year, but there were two favorite seasons—in the early spring, when the weather was warming up, and in the early fall, when the political class had returned from their holidays on Issyk-Kul'. The spring 2007 edition of anti-government protests began on April 10 with the pitching of thirty yurts and sixty tents in the center of the capital. With Felix Kulov now at the forefront of the rallies, the size of the crowds and the pressure on the country's political leadership built for more than a week, until on April 19 the Bakiev regime took decisive action to still the protests. After forcibly clearing away the yurts and tents, armed personnel from the special forces, known as OMON, and the Internal Security division of the Interior Ministry dispersed the crowds with stun grenades and tear gas. They then ringed the central government district to keep the protesters away from the White House.[15] It was a decisive defeat for the opposition, and a signal to Bakiev and his entourage that force worked.

In these confrontations between the Bakiev regime and the opposition, neither side sought to mobilize support using the kinds of policy appeals that are common in political competition in the West. In a word, the fundamental disagreements weren't over policy but power. Power was not seen, then, as a means to achieve a particular set of policies but as a means of rewarding one's own group. This group might be the immediate family, as was the case with Bakiev; or a broader kinship group, like a clan or tribe, into which the Kyrgyz had been divided for centuries; or individuals from one's village, district, or region of the country, such as North versus South.[16] Politicians might occasionally nod in the direction of political ideals like social justice or limited government, but it was geographic and kinship ties—real or imagined—that bound supporters most tightly to their leaders.

Having one's kin or classmate or hometown hero in office brought more than a psychological reward. It also made it more likely that you or your relatives or neighbors would benefit directly from the protection and patronage of those in power, which might mean more access to government jobs or licenses or funding. Many Kyrgyzstani politicians, especially from the North, were loathe to admit to foreigners or to themselves, at least in public, that kinship or other ascriptive ties mattered very much in their country. When asked by a Russian journalist in March 2007 about tensions between kinship groups in the country, Felix Kulov insisted that there is "no confrontation between clans." And yet he went on to tell the same journalist that Kyrgyzstan needed a greater balance between branches of government in order to eliminate "nepotism, clan loyalty [*klanovost'*], and corruption."[17] He also admitted that Bakiev had been playing the regional card, stoking North-South tensions, as a means of defending himself against the opposition. Kulov further noted that his enemies were afraid to kill him because suspicion would fall on Bakiev, and in that case his own supporters "wouldn't allow [Bakiev's] kin to live on this earth."[18] Like it or not, appeals to supporters based on kinship or region of origin were tools available to politicians on all sides.

Another weapon employed by Bakiev in his struggle with the opposition was the court system, over which he exercised decisive influence in this period. In a complex and unexpected maneuver that opened the way for Bakiev to reshape the political system to his advantage, Melis Eshimkanov, a longstanding member of the opposition, brought a lawsuit before the Constitutional Court in August 2007. It asked that body to annul the constitutions of November 2006 and January 2007 because the parliament did not follow proper procedures in enacting them. In September, the court ruled in his favor, which vacated both constitutions and restored the Constitution of 2003, essentially undoing the institutional reforms that had been introduced after the Tulip Revolution. The following day, Bakiev rewarded Eshimkanov's treachery to the opposition cause by appointing him head of the national television and radio network. Like Kulov, Atambaev, and others, Eshimkanov chose the protection and rewards of power over the vulnerability and uncertainty of life in the opposition.

In the immediate aftermath of the Constitutional Court ruling, President Bakiev submitted a new constitutional draft to the nation, which approved it by a wide margin in a referendum held on October 21, 2007. Just as in the Akaev era, a Kyrgyzstani president had used a popular referendum to circumvent parliament and strengthen his hold on power. While the new constitution restored many of the presidency's formal powers, it did not assure the country's leader of a stable and loyal majority in the parliament. The *Jogorku Kenesh* still had the potential to make life uncomfortable for Bakiev. To eliminate this obstruction, Bakiev had included on the October 21 ballot, alongside the constitutional draft, a new electoral law designed to eliminate the independent-minded parliamentary deputies elected in single-member districts. Adopted overwhelmingly by voters, this law provided for the election of deputies by party lists in a single national vote.

When voters went to the polls in these proportional representation contests, they cast their ballot for a slate of candidates that had been filtered by party leaders for their loyalty as well as their prominence. The percentage of the votes received by each party gave that party a corresponding percentage of seats in the parliament, as long as the party reached a minimum threshold, which was five percent of the national vote and one-half percent of the vote in each of the seven regions of the country. This double threshold was specifically intended to exclude parties from the parliament that lacked a base of support in the South. With this carefully designed array of legislative pieces in place, Bakiev dissolved the existing parliament and called new parliamentary elections for December 16.

Only two more steps separated President Bakiev from the attainment of an unassailable position atop the Kyrgyzstani political system. The first was the creation in late October of a new "party of power" that could serve in the parliament as a disciplined and decisive bloc of votes for the president and his initiatives. Called Ak Jol, the Kyrgyz words for Bright Path, the new pro-Bakiev party united several small, existing parties and a range of prominent politicians without party affiliation. Heading the party list for the upcoming election was none other than the chair of the country's Constitutional Court, Cholpon Baekova, who had just helped to advance the president's agenda by annulling the previous constitutions. She joined a long list of powerful executive officials on the Ak Jol slate, ensuring that it was not a party of ideas but a party of officeholders intent on protecting their sinecures.

The final hurdle in Bakiev's elimination of an institutional opposition was a favorable electoral outcome for Ak Jol in the December 2007 parliamentary elections. As in the previous parliamentary elections, pro-presidential forces, in this case Ak Jol, dominated the media, buying three times the airtime of its closest rival and receiving the lion's share of free publicity, virtually all of it positive in tone. The Bakiev regime also used the existence of new technologies in this electoral cycle, namely cell phones, to police the voting behavior of university students. Many of those enrolled in Kyrgyzstani higher educational institutions were required to take pictures of their cast ballots and show them to the authorities. [19]

The intrusive hand of those administering the election was most apparent, however, in the vote counting. Serving as a magnet in this period for numerous anti-Bakiev forces was the Ata-Meken, or Motherland, Party, which received more than 11 percent of the vote according to the official results, an obvious undercounting of its support. In fact, a scholar who worked for the Ak Jol Party claimed in an interview with me several months after the election that he had seen the undoctored results and they showed Ata-Meken winning a majority of the votes. Even an 11 percent result would have entitled Ata-Meken to approximately 15 percent of the seats, given that votes cast for parties failing to cross the five-percent threshold would have been "redistributed" to the successful parties. Yet Ata-Meken received no seats in the new parliament. The Central Election Commission claimed that its support in southern regions fell below one-half percent of the votes there, which disqualified it from parliamentary representation.

Equally suspicious was the dramatic difference in the preliminary electoral results published the day after the election—when over 95 percent of the results had been tabulated—and the final results announced three days later. At first glance, the divergence in results is puzzling. The tally for the party of power, Ak Jol, declined by more than fifteen thousand votes, while two opposition parties, the Social Democrats and the Communists, saw their vote totals almost double. As a result, the Social Democrats received eleven seats in the new parliament and the Communists eight.

In effect, the original manipulation of the election had gone too well. If the preliminary results had held, the Social Democrats and the Communists would have fallen short of the five-percent national threshold required for representation in parliament. With Ata-Meken excluded for not crossing the regional threshold, Ak Jol would have been awarded all 90 seats in the new parliament if the results had not been revised. In short, Ak Jol's officially reported 61 percent of the popular votes would have turned into 100 percent of the seats, an outcome that would have delegitimized the election in the eyes of the country and the world. Instead of uniting opposition parties and their supporters by excluding them altogether from parliament, the last-minute boost to the Social Democrats and Communists divided the opposition and left Bakiev's more formidable and irreconcilable opponent, Ata-Meken, politically isolated. [20]

Having fought the election as the leading opposition party, Ata-Meken was understandably outraged by the results. It formed a new social movement to challenge the Bakiev regime, "For Justice," which consisted of twelve small parties and twenty-one nongovernmental organizations, and it filed suit against the results in the Supreme Court, though to no avail. In an effort to undermine the legitimacy of the newly elected parliament, it helped to found a parallel parliament, known as the Public Chamber, which served for a time as a forum for monitoring the actions of those in power and discussing alternatives to policies pursued by the Bakiev regime. Predictably, Ata-Meken also announced that it would lead public protests in the wake of the electoral results. Yet despite the shabby treatment it received at the hands of the authorities, the party was unable to sustain street demonstrations.

Obviously frustrated at his inability to rally his supporters, Ata-Meken's leader, Omurbek Tekebaev, later explained to me that they were at the mercy of forces beyond their control. It was the dead of winter, and the party's treasury had been depleted after an expensive election campaign. The electoral injustice may have aroused indignation in many of Ata-Meken's supporters, but protesters in Kyrgyzstan expected to be fed and in some cases housed at the massive rallies. The party's funders and rank-and-file alike were exhausted and pessimistic because of the failure of political protests and elections to contain the consolidation of authoritarian rule by Bakiev. It was at this moment that Kyrgyzstan began to take on the features of the more repressive "Stans" that surrounded it. By the beginning of 2008, the long revolution that began in March 2005 had come to an inglorious end.

Chapter Thirteen

Fear Stalks the Land

Arriving in Kyrgyzstan in July 2008, I found a climate of fear that was out of keeping with the unmuzzled, freewheeling country that I had watched develop for a decade and a half. Even the daily rituals of the Bakiev regime began to assume a sinister tone. Walking along Manas Avenue during one of my first afternoons back in Bishkek, I turned around to see an unusual motorcade zooming past me toward the mountains. Behind a marked police car was President Bakiev's large black Mercedes with heavily tinted windows that obscured the faces of its occupants. Trailing the president were two black Cadillac Escalades that swerved menacingly across each other's paths, hurtling forward in figure-eight fashion. Looking more like attack dogs than professional security personnel, athletic young men with balaclava-covered faces and automatic weapons at the ready glared through the Escalades' open windows. An ambulance brought up the rear of the cortege, ready to tend to a president who had been taking lengthy trips to Germany for treatment of an undisclosed ailment. Shortly after the motorcade sped past it drove under a railroad trestle where a massive portrait of a faintly smiling Bakiev looked down on the multitude of drivers and pedestrians along Manas. The president followed this or a parallel route daily to and from his official residence, a former Communist Party property located in a densely forested compound in the foothills south of Bishkek.

Like many countries in the developing world, Kyrgyzstan was increasingly governed not as a modern state but as the personal domain of the ruler and his family. On a walk down a mountain trail in the Ala-Archa National Park south of Bishkek, I came upon dark-uniformed security personnel peering at the surrounding gorge through handheld scopes. When shots rang out in the distance, I assumed they were on the trail of a poacher. They were instead part of the president's security detail. Bakiev had come to the park from his

Figure 13.1.   Poster of President Kurmanbek Bakiev. August 2008

residential compound a few miles away to enjoy an afternoon of hunting, a privilege denied to other Kyrgyz citizens in this nature sanctuary.

If the gap between the political leadership and the citizenry had become starker, so had the social distance between the haves and have-nots in the country. While migrants to the city—many from rural communities in the South—were living in deteriorating conditions on the city's periphery, nouveau riche families were moving into newly built "elite" apartments in Bishkek's center and frequenting the growing number of smart cafes and restaurants that gave parts of the Kyrgyzstani capital a Western feel. When I asked one of the developers of the new high-end apartment buildings who could afford such luxury, she answered "government officials." Money to support such a lifestyle did not come, of course, from their meager state salaries but from the side deals they made with prominent local businessmen and domestic and foreign companies seeking licenses and contracts from the state.

The newfound wealth was especially evident on the streets of Bishkek, where the adolescent sons of Kyrgyzstan's parvenus drove at breakneck speed in black Mercedes or Jeeps. While this Kyrgyz jeunesse dorée was joyriding during working hours, unemployed and underemployed youth looked on jealously along the roadside. Huddled on their haunches in small groups, this growing underclass of young Kyrgyz men with few marketable skills found work when they could in the ubiquitous car washes that dotted the often dusty capital. These establishments were so plentiful that one suspected that their primary reason for being was not washing cars but laundering money or providing employment to the city's youth.

With a modest research grant from an American funding agency, I sought accommodation on this stay in one of the inexpensive guest houses that had recently opened in Bishkek. I settled on the Radison—not the international hotel chain, the Radisson, but a guest house run by a welcoming Tatar couple that was located on a dirt street near the city's Philharmonic Hall. With no external markings to indicate that it offered accommodations, the Radison had seven small guest rooms in a low, L-shaped block building separated from the proprietors' house by a small courtyard, in the middle of which was a carefully tended rose garden. Before heading out each day, I ate breakfast on the elevated patio with flowering vines along trellises and a fascinating assortment of young European and American adventure tourists speaking in a Babel of languages around small tables. One Italian man, on his first visit to Central Asia, had just bicycled in from two weeks on the treacherous roads of Tajikistan and southern Kyrgyzstan, all without knowledge of Russian or any local language.

Taking breakfast on the patio each morning was a relief from my dark and Spartan bedroom, where a hard mattress and a continually barking dog made sleeping all but impossible. Apparently hungry, the large German shepherd that was the security system for the abandoned property next door did not cease barking for more than three or four minutes at a stretch. It was a plaintive wail that seemed to emanate from a spot directly under my window. It finally stopped in the early morning when the property owner threw food over the wall from the street. It was only then that I got to sleep, and so my days did not usually begin before 9:00 a.m.

Leaving the guest house and turning left on Abdumamunova Street toward the city center took me past a row of industrial-looking buildings in various states of decay and disrepair. Less than fifteen minutes' walk from the White House and the city's central square, this stretch of road—more reminiscent of a war zone than an urban landscape—was testimony to Bishkek's uneven development, as was the presence of gaping potholes on city streets lined by chic boutiques and trendy restaurants. Deferred maintenance from the Soviet era had caught up with independent Kyrgyzstan, whose economy under Bakiev was struggling to deal with rising energy costs. Drivers had to weave carefully through the capital's poorly maintained thoroughfares to avoid breaking an axle, and pedestrians were constantly on the lookout for sidewalk sinkholes where collapsed asphalt could seriously injure an inattentive passerby, especially at night, when portions of the city were often thrown into complete darkness.

During the daytime, Bishkek residents used the deep recesses in the sidewalks as trash receptacles, which was jarring to Westerners unused to open littering. It was also contrary to the expectations of Kyrgyz nationalists, who believed that their ethnic kin would be more respectful of their motherland than the Russians and other Europeans who had dominated the capital in the Soviet era. In a memorable article published in *Literaturnyi Kirgizstan* a few months before the collapse of the Soviet Union, nationalist Kyrgyz authors attacked the habits of local Russians who, they claimed, despoiled the pristine Kyrgyz countryside by leaving trash at picnic sites when they ventured out of the city.[1] Predictably, the Kyrgyz proved no better at cleaning up after themselves. On a visit to the Ala-Archa National Park with a Kyrgyz family, I was troubled to see them leave all of the refuse from our lunch in the woods. When I tried to inquire gently as to why they didn't take the trash with them, they responded that we had paid for admission to the park and it was the responsibility of park personnel to clean up after us.

The purpose of this visit was to launch a major research project with Professor Gulnara Iskakova to investigate the reasons why the leaders of the Kyrgyzstani opposition found it so difficult to cooperate with each other in their struggle with Bakiev. Much of the evidence for this project came from lengthy interviews that we would conduct with three dozen members of the current or former opposition during three stays in Kyrgyzstan in 2008 and 2009. But as is often the case with field research in places like Kyrgyzstan, there was as much to be learned from observations and conversations about broader political conditions in the country as from the narrowly focused surveys and structured interviews that we administered to politicians and government officials.

One striking feature of the new political environment under Bakiev was the concern for physical security exhibited by those in opposition to the Kyrgyzstani president. An incident a few months earlier, on December 31, 2007, had put the entire Kyrgyzstani political class on alert. On this most festive evening of the year for citizens of Kyrgyzstan, a package arrived at the home of Bakiev's chief of staff, Medet Sadyrkulov. It contained a severed human finger and ear. A Talleyrand-like ethnic Kazakh who had served as both Akaev's and Bakiev's right-hand man, Sadyrkulov was the rare official at the heights of Kyrgyzstani politics in this period who appeared to enjoy the respect of the president as well as leading members of the opposition. He had aroused, however, the suspicion and envy of ambitious figures in the president's entourage, most notably Bakiev's brother, Janysh, who was in the process of consolidating his grip on the country's security services.[2] The New Year's gift was clearly a warning to Sadyrkulov that was not lost on lesser figures in government and opposition, including Omurbek Tekebaev, the head of Ata-Meken, the opposition party that had been denied representation in parliament a few months earlier because of their alleged failure to receive sufficient votes in the South.

After an initial round of interviews in Bishkek, I traveled to Cholpon-Ata, on Lake Issyk-Kul', to speak with Tekebaev. He arrived at my guest house in the tourist zone of Cholpon-Ata at mid-morning, shook my hand quickly, and asked where I proposed to conduct the interview. When I suggested the common room of the guest house, he surveyed the ground floor space and then went outside and cased the entire building. Looking glummer and more concerned by the minute, he finally told me to get into his car, an aging, light-colored Mercedes, and we drove a few miles west to his rented apartment in a gated compound on the lake. Once inside his residence, this avuncular former parliamentary speaker pulled a pistol from his pocket and laid it on the coffee table in front of me. He then pointed to a Kalashnikov on a table in the corner of the room, noting that unlike other, wealthier leaders in the opposition, he had to provide his own security. "In the Akaev era," Tekebaev told me, "I was the leader of the opposition, and yet I could sit in restaurants, drink beer, get up and walk home late at night, not fearing anything. Now look, I've got an automatic weapon lying there, and you see that I pack a pistol."[3]

Tekebaev had every reason to be concerned about his safety and reputation under the Bakiev regime. In early September 2007, several months before Sadyrkulov received the severed body parts, Tekebaev had been arrested in Warsaw, where customs agents found more than a half kilo of heroin in his suitcase. Part of a small delegation of deputies from the Kyrgyzstani parliament, Tekebaev had been scheduled to speak to an international economic forum in Poland on the subject, "Can a Democratic State Be Established in Central Asia?" He was released by Polish authorities after it was discovered that an official from the Kyrgyzstani security services, headed at that time by Janysh Bakiev, had taken Tekebaev's bag into a room at the Bishkek airport beyond the view of surveillance cameras for a "special operation," as the head of security described it to a subordinate. Those responsible for the plant had "tipped off" Interpol representatives in Almaty, who forwarded information to their colleagues in Warsaw that the parliamentary deputies were suspected members of the banned Islamist organization, Hizb ut-Tahrir, who had heroin in their bags.[4]

Toward the end of our conversation in Tekebaev's apartment on Lake Issyk-Kul', a friend and wealthy patron of the leader of Ata-Meken came downstairs to join us. He was Kubatbek Baibolov, a prominent politician and businessman who had grown up in a village on the outskirts of Bishkek. The owner of a bazaar in the capital, he had spent the early part of his career in the Soviet KGB, including a lengthy stay in Afghanistan in the 1980s during the Soviet occupation of that country. When the USSR collapsed, this Soviet patriot fell into a deep depression, and for two months he was housebound.[5]

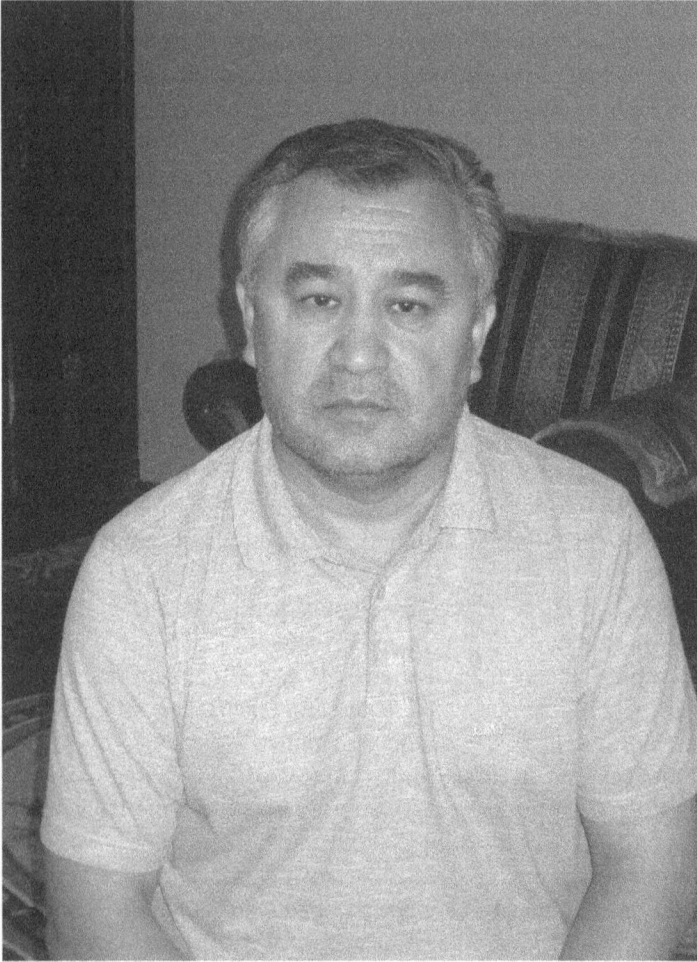

Figure 13.2.   Omurbek Tekebaev. July 2008

But like many "KaGeBeshniki" of his generation, Baibolov was a talented and curious man who ultimately used his connections and entrepreneurial skills to take advantage of the Wild East capitalism that was emerging in the post-communist world in the early 1990s. Anxious like many other success-ful businessmen to use his fortune as a springboard to political office, Baibo-lov won election to parliament in 1995. He served for a time as deputy speaker, and he retained a parliamentary seat until the December 2007 elec-tion when, as the number two candidate on the Ata-Meken Party list, he was denied a place in the new assembly along with other members of the party.

Figure 13.3.   Kubatbek Baibolov (with the author). October 2011

In a meeting later the same week, I toured Baibolov's elegant company headquarters on the outskirts of the capital, where he told me of the ultimatum he had recently received from the Bakiev regime: either quit politics or give up his business. It was a Hobson's choice facing a number of Kyrgyzstani businessmen and women in this period. With several small children whom he did not wish to expose to the political crossfire, Baibolov left the business in charge of his son-in-law and fled to the United States, where he bought a home in McLean, Virginia, in the Washington suburbs. It would be a difficult, but relatively short-lived, exile for Kubatbek Baibolov.

Although his livelihood came from his business dealings, especially his ownership of the Dordoi Bazaar, one of Kyrgyzstan's largest, Baibolov's passion was politics. He fancied himself an amateur political philosopher, and he read widely in American political history and the classics of Western political thought. In this he was not alone. Numerous Kyrgyzstani politicians prided themselves on being the framers of a new order, the Founding Fathers of a post-communist state that had ambitions to chart a different path from that of their authoritarian neighbors. But for Baibolov and a surprising number of his peers, politics either involved lofty musings about political philosophy or down-and-dirty talk about political tactics and the weaknesses of fellow politicians. Very few public figures plowed the middle ground, where matters of policy lay. In scores of discussions with Kyrgyzstani politicians, I could count on one hand the number of times they mentioned their own, or their party's, platform. If politics is about choice, in Kyrgyzstan the political class tended to frame the options in terms of persons or institutions and not policy.

Chapter Fourteen

Talk of Kinship, Gender, and Islam

In a country full of outsized political characters, few were as colorful as Kyrgyzstan's Ombudsman, Tursunbek Akun, whom I interviewed on my return to Bishkek. I often began my sit-downs with Kyrgyzstani politicians with the self-effacing comment that my limited knowledge of the country was based largely on newspapers and books read from afar, and I had come to hear their insider's view of how things really worked. Akun took the bait.

> I don't want to engage in self-praise, but you don't need to spend a year reading literature, or newspapers, or journals. You don't need to listen to radio or watch television. Just sit down with Tursunbek Akun and you can learn everything.

No sooner had I entered his massive office than he spotted the new miniature recording device that allowed me to tape conversations and download them directly to a computer. "Are those sold in Bishkek?" he asked. "I need one of them." Hearing that I had bought it in Florida for $70, he quickly added, "Send me one and I'll pay you back." When I returned a few months later with a new device for him, he quickly pocketed the "gift" and launched into his usual survey of the Kyrgyzstani political landscape, where he appeared without fail as the centerpiece.[1]

Akun's accounts of political life in Kyrgyzstan were often embellished and always self-serving, but they revealed important truths about political dynamics in the country. He recognized that for all the attention given to the dramatic and highly visible conflicts in parliament, the media, and the streets, what went on behind the scenes, especially in the corridors of the White House, was at the heart of governance. In this internal bureaucratic game, Chief of Staff Sadyrkulov played a decisive role as consigliere, refereeing disputes among various relatives and subordinates of President Bakiev. Like other members of the political elite, Akun seemed incapable of pronouncing Sadyrkulov's name without immediately adding that he was an ethnic Kazakh, but he expressed a deep admiration for his ability to manage the conflicts among the diverse factions surrounding the president and between the president and the opposition. It was clear that for Akun and all but the most radical members of the opposition, Sadyrkulov enjoyed a reputation as a moderating influence on hard-line officials in Bakiev's entourage.

At a time when many members of the opposition were demonizing Bakiev as the source of all that was wrong in the country, Akun offered a more nuanced and, in some respects, more compelling portrait of the president. Instead of a Machiavellian schemer intent on eliminating all of his enemies, Akun presented Bakiev as a Soviet-style industrial manager (*khoziaistvennik*), who lacked the skills of a natural politician. Recognizing this weakness, Bakiev granted considerable latitude to Sadyrkulov, who was responsible, in Akun's view, for the few positive reforms introduced in this period. Bakiev's main political mistakes at this time, Akun suggested, were acts of omission rather than commission, most notably allowing his vast network of relatives to acquire control over important sectors of the economy and the state.[2] Where his brother Janysh brought law enforcement and security agencies under his wing, his son, Maxim, was allowed to create a business empire that operated as an extension of the state. In this assessment, President Bakiev, like Akaev before him, was at the apex of a system of family rule in which the president may have had the last word but he didn't call all the shots in daily matters of governance.[3]

Proud of his position as the country's monitor of citizens' rights, Akun stressed to me his unique position as a kind of mediator between state and society and government and opposition. Appointed as the head of the presidential Committee for Human Rights, which was established in the wake of the Tulip Revolution, Akun was named to the newly created post of ombudsman of the Kyrgyz Republic a few months before our meeting. Operating from a large, run-down building in the center of Bishkek, his bureau received a steady stream of complaints of violations of citizens' rights by government agencies, and Akun used the authority of his office to intervene with state officials on behalf of individuals. He clearly relished his role as champion of the little guy who was at the mercy of the large state bureaucracy, but he also knew how to pick his battles so that he did not embarrass the president and his key allies. It was a job that required a deft touch and a deep knowledge of the leading personalities in Kyrgyzstani officialdom, both of which Akun possessed.

Although Akun could be deferential and diplomatic when dealing with more powerful figures, he—like most of my interlocutors—spoke with stunning frankness about the strengths, but especially the weaknesses, of fellow politicians. At times I felt like a gossip columnist collecting dirt on Kyrgyzstan's ruling class. Akun relayed a conversation he'd just had with the young, charismatic Adakhan Madumarov, state secretary to Bakiev. "You've become arrogant and a fool," he told Madumarov. "You're not normal." My Kyrgyz interviewees often rendered harsh judgments as well on the attributes of their own ethnic group. Akun noted at the end of our interview that "we Kyrgyz are slackers [*lodyri*]. We're not decisive, and we live for the moment instead of thinking about the future."[4] Another politician called his fellow Kyrgyz "the most insubordinate, rebellious, and mutinous nation" in Central Asia.[5]

But for every negative stereotype I heard from the Kyrgyz about their ethnos there was, predictably, a laudatory comment about the exceptional qualities of their ethnic kin. Speaking of the Kyrgyz as a people, Akun noted that "we are a quick study and we master things quickly. The Kyrgyz are as talented as the Japanese. No other nation in Central Asia is equal to the Kyrgyz." Even the best-educated politicians tended to fall back on "the Kyrgyz mentality" as the explanation for why their "Stan" stood out from the others. In their view, it wasn't so much leaders, or circumstances, or structures of government but the distinct cultural values of the traditionally nomadic Kyrgyz that were held out as the secret to understanding the country's travails and successes. As another member of the elite told me, "it's easier to govern 300 Uzbeks than 3 Kyrgyz."[6]

Educated in a Western social science tradition that gave little credence to such cultural explanations of political behavior, I tended at first to be dismissive of comments asking me to accept that the answers to my questions lay in piercing the mysterious Kyrgyz mindset. Yet there were elements of Kyrgyz traditions that did shape contemporary values and behavior. Kyrgyz women were generally less restrained than their counterparts in sedentary Central Asian societies, in part because of the nomadic tradition. As one Kyrgyz woman commented to me suggestively, because they knew how to ride horses, women could be out of sight of their husbands and fathers in a flash in the mountainous terrain that covered 95 percent of the country. Islam had also come late to Kyrgyzstan and it penetrated the culture less fully than in some other Central Asian societies, in part because of the legacies of the Kyrgyz traditional mountain beliefs known as Tengrism. Expressions of female modesty were relatively uncommon among the Kyrgyz, especially in the towns and cities, and there were many examples of outspoken women in the front ranks of public protest. After the Tulip Revolution, political leaders wishing to intimidate their opponents would often mobilize groups of aggressive, middle-aged women to employ aural and physical muscle in street confrontations. These hired bands of women were known as OBON—a Russian acronym for Women's Brigade on Special Assignment, a take-off on the special police crowd-control units, OMON. As Bakiev was beginning his consolidation of power in 2006, the presidential chief of staff, Usen Sydykov, warned the parliamentary speaker, Omurbek Tekebaev, that if he didn't relinquish his post Sydykov would send in 200–300 women from OBON to drag him out of his office.[7]

Alongside the image of the strong, independent Kyrgyz woman, however, is the gruesome reality of bride kidnapping—*ala kachuu* in Kyrgyz. A long-standing tradition in Kyrgyz society, kidnappings are at times consensual, a form of elopement that allows a couple to avoid parental involvement in the selection of a mate or the payment of a bride price by a family of a groom that lacks means. Such benign bride kidnapping does not represent the majority of cases, however. Especially in rural areas, where there is no dating culture and few opportunities for courtship, young men often seize acquaintances or even strangers against their will and transport them to their home, where the future mother-in-law and other female relatives subject the kidnapped woman to excruciating psychological pressure to break her will. Although reliable figures on this practice do not exist at the national level, a careful study of one large village in northeastern Kyrgyzstan revealed that well over half the young married women were kidnapped without their consent, a figure far higher than that among older women in the village.[8] At least for many Kyrgyz women, then, the collapse of communism has removed norms and institutions that could help to protect them from a fate that most women and men would find unimaginable.

Other features of Kyrgyz culture have aroused considerable interest, and controversy, in journalistic and academic circles. Many Western scholars, for example, have been dismissive of the influence of clan and tribal loyalties on political and social behavior, and most of the Kyrgyz public figures and political activists we interviewed agreed with them. Steeped in a communist tradition that emphasized the importance of a single Soviet identity—and the backwardness of persons who still clung to their clan, tribal, or ethnic associations—almost all the persons we talked to for our research project on the opposition ranked clan or tribal identities as inconsequential factors in shaping political behavior. And yet no sooner would an interviewee give "clan identity" a 1 or 2 on a 5-point scale than he or she would recount an experience that highlighted the importance of kinship groups. Immediately after denying a role for clan identity in the country's political and social system, a young businessman and political activist introduced me to his father in the next room. The father, the young businessman explained, was holding a meeting with other northern clan leaders to discuss possible means of resistance to what they considered to be a southern takeover of the country by the Bakiev family.[9]

In the absence of serious debates over policy or ideas, dense networks of personal and kinship relations were the lifeblood of Kyrgyzstani politics. To cultivate these relations, politicians spent an inordinate amount of time traveling the country's back roads to attend weddings, milestone birthdays, and funerals, which were usually celebrated in the home village of the honorees or deceased. The accompanying feasts often brought out hundreds of people and cost the organizers a hefty share of their annual income. It was in these settings that politicians reconnected to extended family and local networks, which would bring out votes in elections and protesters to defend the honor or security of their patron in Bishkek. In exchange, the Big Man from the capital was expected to use his connections to advance the careers and interests of his kin or neighbors. As an unusually gregarious public figure, Akun clearly enjoyed these life-stage events, and at one point he expressed his great disappointment that Sadyrkulov did not attend his father's eightieth birthday celebration in his remote hometown of Naryn. Akun also lamented, however, the time that such events took from his work. No doubt some of the politicians who later pushed a bill to limit the expenditures that families could devote to celebrations of these rites of passage were thinking of their own well-being as well as the budgets of their constituents.

As I was taking my leave of Akun, this short, wiry man, ever brimming with energy, asked me to step into his private antechamber. There he presented me with a signed copy of his recently published memoirs, and then picked up a traditional Kyrgyz musical instrument, the komuz, a three-stringed fretless lute akin to the mountain dulcimer from the Appalachians. He began strumming it, and then sang several full-throated minutes of a traditional Kyrgyz tune. Having grown up with a father who always kept a harmonica in his pocket, ready to impress all comers, I couldn't help but feel a certain kinship with Kyrgyzstan's expansive ombudsman.

The following morning, with the quickly rising temperature promising a scorchingly hot day, I walked across town with Gulnara Iskakova to the apartment of Myktybek Abdyldaev, who served Bakiev as chief of staff immediately before Sadyrkulov's tenure. In stark contrast to the ebullient Tursunbek Akun, Abdyldaev was a reserved technocrat who had worked for many years in law enforcement, including a stint as the country's procurator general in the last years of the Akaev regime. We entered Abdyldaev's well-appointed study to find the shutters closed and the room dark and stuffy—a power outage in this section of town had cut electricity to thousands of homes, a relatively frequent occurrence in Kyrgyzstan.

A few minutes into our conversation, Abdyldaev settled a question that he knew was on our minds: why had he left the chief of staff position after only a year. Emphasizing that he had departed of his own volition, Abdyldaev insisted: "I told Mr. Bakiev that as a patriot of my country, I could not personally accept Kazakhstani expansion, which was fleecing our entire economy."[10] His concern related to the significant privileges granted to Kazakhstani businessmen working in Kyrgyzstan and to the transfer of several important tourist sites on the northern shore of Lake Issyk-Kul' to the Kazakhstani government in exchange for the forgiveness of bilateral debt. In

**Figure 14.1.   Tursunbek Akun, Kyrgyzstan's ombudsman, playing the komuz.
July 2008**

effect, this property concession created new mini-enclaves of Kazakhstan dozens of miles inside Kyrgyzstani territory. Abdyldaev also criticized the willingness of President Bakiev to deplete the vast reservoir behind the Toktogul Dam, the country's major source of electric power, in order to release water to irrigate fields in the neighboring downstream countries of Kazakhstan and Uzbekistan. Throughout the post-communist period, water politics had been a source of tension in Kyrgyzstan's relations with its neighbors. Where the downstream countries wanted water released in the spring and summer, to irrigate crops, Kyrgyzstan needed the water to flow through the turbines in the winter, when electricity for home heating was most needed.

Abdyldaev also broached a subject of growing importance in Kyrgyzstan: the rise of Islamic fundamentalist groups. He began by repeating the received wisdom about the Kyrgyz, that "they are not by their nature very religious." Referring to the recent death of Chingiz Aitmatov, Abdyldaev observed that if his funeral had taken place in other Turkic countries, such as Uzbekistan, Azerbaijan, or Turkey, there would have been the obligatory respect for traditional Islamic rites, but Aitmatov's ceremony commingled nomadic rituals with Muslim prayers.[11] Yet Abdyldaev admitted that "the more the population's living standards erode, the more likely they are to succumb to religious proselytizing." For that reason, he said, he had supported a ban on the Islamic party, Hizb ut-Tahrir, when he was procurator general, a ban that was upheld by the country's Supreme Court. As he recognized, the effect of this ruling was to send the group underground, where they have been able to develop a considerable following in the more traditional southern districts of Kyrgyzstan, especially among ethnic Uzbeks. Espousing an unusual blend of nonviolent and gradualist tactics and an intolerant, chiliastic reading of Islam, Hizb ut-Tahrir—Arabic for "Party of Liberation"—has continued to spread its message through private study groups and the clandestine circulation of religious literature.[12]

A prominent ethnic Uzbek journalist I interviewed later that week, Ulugbek Babakulov, considered Hizb ut-Tahrir to be an even more potent force in Kyrgyzstan than Abdyldaev was willing to concede.[13] At Babakulov's suggestion, we met over lunch in a restaurant I had been trying to avoid, Fat Boy's, a British-owned hangout for Westerners whose only saving grace was its patio dining overlooking Chu Prospect. While downing an overpriced American-style sandwich, I listened to Babakulov challenge my assumptions about the real political opposition in Kyrgyzstan. This astute observer of Central Asian politics, who worked for the Kyrgyzstani version of a Moscow-based newspaper, *Moskovskii Komsomolets*, insisted that while the same small political elite circulated in and out of government positions, Hizb ut-Tahrir was slowly and imperceptibly building a formidable underground opposition movement to the established secular order. "Only one thing unites all the opposition figures [that you are studying]," Babakulov argued, "their lack of a clear, unifying idea or doctrine about what kind of country they'd like to create. . . . They see only themselves in the future." The leaders of Hizb ut-Tahrir, in contrast, "do not think of themselves or their party somehow at the helm, but instead they have a vision of the country's place in the theological world." This invitation to become part of a universal calling, Babakulov noted, had a particular resonance with a rising generation of Central Asians who, unlike their parents and grandparents, had no Communist Party or Young Communist League to join and no grander idea to inspire them. Put simply, the current crop of politicians was doing nothing to fill the ideological or spiritual void left by the collapse of communism, and in that regard they operated at a distinct disadvantage to the selfless and transcendent appeals of organizations like Hizb ut-Tahrir. [14]

Clandestine groups like Hizb ut-Tahrir were not the only Muslim voices seeking to win over the hearts and minds of religiously oriented Kyrgyzstani citizens. Among the handful of openly religious politicians competing in the traditional political game was Tursunbai Bakir uulu, whom the young political activist Edil' Baisalov called the country's "most Muslim friendly politician." [15] The dearth of competitors to Bakir uulu, who had served as ombudsman before Tursunbek Akun, was one reason that Hizb ut-Tahrir enjoyed such popularity: traditional politicians accorded little attention in this period to the interests of the significant minority of religiously devout Muslims in Kyrgyzstan.

When I called Bakir uulu to arrange an interview, he suggested that we meet for dinner at a restaurant with a traditional Central Asian menu and ambiance, the Arzu. Entering the Arzu early one evening, I spotted Bakir uulu and an aide sitting at one of the outside tables whose partitions on two sides offered patrons semiprivate dining. Sporting a closely cropped salt-and-pepper beard and dapper clothing that gave him the air of an Iranian diplomat, Bakir uulu refrained from his usual criticisms of the questionable mores of Kyrgyz youth, including the miniskirts worn by Kyrgyz women during the hot summer months. He spoke instead of his long-simmering disappointment with his treatment by the United States government which, he claimed, had considered him a nonperson since his criticism of the American invasion of Iraq several years earlier. Clearly not a fan of the ascetic lifestyle, as one might expect in a devout Muslim, Bakir uulu missed the occasional junkets to the United States that the American government had paid for in earlier years. Perhaps his only consolation on this evening was that the check for the lavish dinner for himself and his parliamentary aide was being picked up by an American scholar.

For all his criticisms of American policy, it was the growing influence of China in Kyrgyzstan that most alarmed Bakir uulu that evening. When he raised similar concerns with Zbigniew Brzezinski in an earlier meeting, the former national security advisor to President Carter wisely encouraged him and his countrymen to make their peace with China, which was, after all, their permanent neighbor and a Great Power. For Bakir uulu, however, like many other Kyrgyzstani politicians, the solution to the country's security dilemma lay in balancing Great Power interests in this small country. Whatever misgivings he had about American foreign and domestic policies, especially as they affected the Muslim world, he was enough of a pragmatist, or a cynic, to fear a complete American withdrawal from the country. Playing Great Powers off each other was, of course, a dangerous game, and one that would soon prove difficult for the Bakiev regime to manage.

Chapter Fifteen

Taking the Lonely Road Home

After two weeks of interviewing in Bishkek and Issyk-Kul', I traveled to Karakol on my way out of the country to attend the wedding of two former students. The bride, Uliana, was an ethnic Russian brought up in Karakol. In her teens she had made her way to the Florida Panhandle to attend high school with an American host family before enrolling at Stetson University as an undergraduate. Her parents in Kyrgyzstan owned several apartments in a nondescript, Soviet-era building on the edge of Karakol, which they rented out to Russian and West European skiers and trekkers. Less than five miles from town was one of Central Asia's most modern lifts, which took skiers and hikers up past majestic fir trees to a drop-off point at an altitude of 7,500 feet, more than 2,000 feet above Lake Issyk-Kul'.

After the small wedding party settled in these apartments on the afternoon before the ceremony, several of us gathered in the tiny kitchen of Uliana's parents to chat and begin preparing the evening meal, whose main dish was *golubtsy*, stuffed cabbage. Talking to the relatives and friends of the bride and groom while cutting up vegetables, I could not have felt more removed from the political machinations in the Kyrgyzstani capital. With the dishes on the stove, a few of us wandered across the dirt road behind the apartment, through untended fields and toward a small footbridge that spanned a turbulent stream flowing from the Tien Shan Mountains toward Lake Issyk-Kul'. The air was lighter and fresher than in Bishkek, and as I stood on the bridge talking to Thomas, the groom, I marveled at the simplicity of the arrangements, which were a welcome change from the choreographed and over-planned weddings that had become the norm in the United States.

There was, however, one would-be wedding planner in the group, Yulia, an ethnic Tatar friend of Uliana from Kazakhstan who had been an exchange student at Stetson. Shortly before dinner, Yulia came calling for Thomas in the room that he shared with me in a neighboring apartment. After blindfolding him, she led Thomas up the stairs toward Uliana's parents' place. While twirling him around as they climbed the stairs, she peppered Thomas with riddles about his bride-to-be. Physically and emotionally disoriented by the time he reached the apartment, poor Thomas had nonetheless passed the most grueling test of his marital rites.

Wedding day was August 8, 2008—8/8/8—chosen by Uliana for the good luck that such rare alignments in the calendar were supposed to bring. Although the shrinking population of Russian youth in Karakol meant that weddings in the picturesque local Russian Orthodox Church were a rarity, another young couple had also chosen to exchange their vows on this special day, and so the priest greeted two wedding parties at the entrance to the church that uncomfortably warm morning. Filing into the same old wooden church that I had visited with students eight years earlier, the scene was now very different—the church was alive with the sights and smells of an Orthodox wedding. Incense wafted from a thurible waved back and forth by the golden-robed priest, and well-wishers stood in groups behind each wedding couple, who were facing the priest on either side of the nave. When it came time for Uliana and Thomas to exchange their vows, they observed the traditional ritual in which close friends or family members held crowns above the bride and groom as they circled around the sanctuary. This was no mean feat for Yulia, who had the difficult task of holding the crown above the head of Thomas, by far the tallest person in the room.

After the short ceremony, family and friends gathered at the base of the church steps for pictures before heading to the food, drink, and dancing at the reception. Unfortunately, I could not join them. With a flight home scheduled for 3:00 a.m. the next day, and the international airport at Almaty, Kazakhstan, a seven-hour drive away, I could only wish the newly betrothed well and jump into a waiting car for the long journey. The Tatar driver, an acquaintance of Uliana's family, came recommended as a teetotaler who was not in a hurry to get anywhere, the two essential qualities to look for in drivers in this part of the world. His car was another matter—a worn-out old VW with no air conditioning and what seemed to be no springs cushioning the ride. Ditching my jacket, I settled in the front passenger seat for the marathon journey that lay ahead.

Instead of taking the main road to Almaty, which skirted the northern suburbs of Bishkek, I chose the shorter and less-traveled route, which took us closer to the Chinese border. Heading north from Karakol, we took a right at Tiup and began a gradual ascent through the gaps in the mountains that formed the eastern end of the Issyk-Kul' Valley. Within twenty minutes of the Tiup cutoff, the well-paved two-lane highway gave way to a gravel road that skirted the Kazakhstani border. It was a beautiful and isolated corner of the country, where cars appeared rarely on the roads and the only signs of human settlement were the occasional light-colored yurts positioned a short distance above the road. Traveling along this stretch at an unhurried pace due to the rough gravel underneath, we had time to observe the varied forms of animal life: large magpies, small flocks of sheep, the occasional dog, and hobbled horses. With their front legs tied together by rope just above the ankles in order to prevent them from straying, the hobbled horses were a pathetic sight as they struggled to move forward in short hops.

We had traveled less than two hours from Karakol when the car's engine started to overheat. At first, the driver didn't seem overly concerned. He stopped from time to time at a stream, filled a Coke bottle with mountain water, poured it in the radiator, and drove on. As these stops became more frequent, he finally admitted—on one of the loneliest stretches of road—that the car in its present state wouldn't get us to Almaty. As I began to worry about missing my plane, he pulled over near a creek and opened the hood. He took a makeshift toolkit out of the trunk and began rooting around, finding at last a tiny can of what appeared to be a light-colored sealer with the consistency of Play-Doh. Removing a cap near the radiator, the driver formed the sealer into a small ball and placed it in a cavity. Noting that it would take thirty minutes for the sealer to set, he sat down on the grass on the roadside, and I pulled out my packed lunch and joined him.

Back in the car after our half-hour pit stop, the driver applied the gas cautiously at first but soon gained confidence in his car's ability to continue the climb toward Kazakhstan. Thankfully, our ascent ended shortly afterward, when we arrived on a high, windswept plain. For a time, nothing interrupted the view toward the high mountains across this vast expanse of grassland located at more than 6,000 feet above sea level. Then two faint objects, alone in the middle of the plain, began to come into view. As we got closer, I could make out two small flags almost next to each other, one Kyrgyzstani and the other Kazakhstani. Pulling up to one of the most isolated border posts in the world, we slowly approached the Kyrgyz passport and customs building and were quickly waved through. Advancing a few yards further to the larger and more modern Kazakhstani facility, officials motioned to us to leave the car and go inside.

It wasn't every day, or perhaps even every month, that an American passed through their border post, and so when I handed the agent my dark blue passport and greeted him in Russian, I knew we'd be there for a while. Carefully leafing through the visa pages and finding the stamp of entry into Kazakhstan two weeks earlier, the Kazakhstani official warned me that my visa for his country was expiring the following day. I responded that, inshallah, I would be departing from Almaty in the early morning hours, a typical arrival or departure time for flights connecting Europe and Central Asia.

With the passport formalities aside, the agent began to inquire about life in the United States. He soon got around to the question that I had come to

Figure 15.1.   The Kazakhstan-Kyrgyzstan border, near Kegen. August 2008

expect from strangers I met in the post-communist world: how much would a person in my job make in your country? When I named an approximate figure, he immediately followed up by asking what that would buy in the United States, and I reminded him and his curious colleagues listening in of the expenditures for various forms of insurance and taxes and other items that would eat into what they imagined would be a generous disposable income in the West. Even these few introductory comments on the complexity of a household economy in the United States were enough to challenge their preconceptions about an easy life abroad.

After stamping my passport, the Kazakhstani official grabbed the documents of my driver and began speaking to him gruffly in Kazakh, a language whose vocabulary, grammar, and pronunciation overlapped considerably with Kyrgyz. Unfortunately, the driver, a Tatar brought up in Russian-speaking surroundings in Karakol, knew only a smattering of Kyrgyz, which provoked the ire of the passport officials. "Even a Tatar growing up in Kyrgyzstan should know how to speak Kyrgyz," they insisted. Had I not been alongside him, the driver, unable to banter with the officials in a local language, would almost certainly have been asked to pay a bribe to cross the border. But no one seemed willing to reveal this unpleasant side of local life to a Westerner, and so we were sent on our way with our documents in order.

Within thirty minutes of leaving the remote border posts on the high plains, I spotted the first settlement in more than three hours of driving. It was Kegen, an agricultural community that had housed a large state farm in the Soviet era. There were few signs of contemporary farm equipment or buildings, but the town of just under 9,000 had a cell tower, and so with a signal for the first time since leaving Tiup, I called my wife from this isolated outpost to advise her that if the old VW did not hold out, I would likely miss my flight from Almaty.

Whether because of the soundness of the repair, or the more favorable terrain—the rest of the trip was either downhill or on flat stretches of road— the car held up bravely the rest of the way. Coming down off the high plains, we wound our way through canyons with occasional switchbacks where the pavement's edge dropped off precipitously to the valley floor below. Just before meeting the main road running west to Almaty, we encountered the magical landscape of the Charyn Canyon, where unusual formations of striped red sandstone towered above riverbeds that snaked their way toward the Ili River to the north.

As we approached the sprawling metropolis of Almaty, a pall of smoke from burning trash hung over the outskirts of the city. With the sun setting around 9:00 p.m., six hours before my flight, we drove down the now famil- iar tree-lined road on the eastern edge of Almaty that led to the airport. With the terminal in sight, I received an unexpected call on my cell phone: it was the public relations department from my university. Not knowing that I was overseas, they asked if I would be prepared to speak to the media about the war that had just begun between Russia and Georgia. It was the first I had heard of the combat between the two sides, though stories broadcast on Russian TV had been preparing Russia's citizens for war for some time.

Entering the terminal, I looked up at the screens to see "cancelled" along- side the flights destined for the Georgian capital, Tbilisi, and other parts of the Caucasus. As my Lufthansa flight took off for Frankfurt early in the morning, it took a northern routing over Moscow, well outside the war zone. Although distant from Kyrgyzstan, the war would change the tenor of rela- tions within the post-Soviet world, and embolden Russia to challenge American interests in Kyrgyzstan. The five-day Russo-Georgian War in Au- gust had consolidated Russia's hold over two breakaway regions in northern Georgia and sent a strong message to the West that Russia was pursuing a more assertive policy toward its "near abroad," including Kyrgyzstan.[1]

Chapter Sixteen

The Netherworld of the Opposition

At a political fundraiser in Orlando in the fall of 2008, a congressional candidate—and former student of mine—Suzanne Kosmas, introduced me to Rahm Emanuel, at the time a prominent member of Congress from Illinois and chair of the House Democratic Caucus. Informed that I was an expert on Kyrgyzstan, Emanuel quipped that if one of his kids ever needed to do a book report on an exotic country, he'd give me a call. Less than three months after this meeting, in his first few days as chief of staff for the newly elected American President, Barack Obama, Emanuel would have received disturbing news out of Moscow. Intent on containing, and if possible rolling back, American influence on the post-Soviet periphery, Russia's President Dmitrii Medvedev met with President Bakiev and offered Kyrgyzstan a $2 billion loan and $150 million in grants. [1]

No sooner had the aid package been announced than Bakiev stated at a press conference in Moscow on February 3, 2009, that "the time has come to close the [Western] military base on our soil," a base that was vital to the support of Western forces fighting in Afghanistan. Once Bakiev was back in Bishkek, however, he reneged on his promise to the Russians and began negotiating with the Americans for an extension to the base lease, which would ultimately increase the West's payment to the Kyrgyzstani government severalfold. [2] Playing two Great Powers off against each other was of course a perilous game for the leader of a small nation.

It was in this window of uncertainty about the future of the American and Western military presence in Kyrgyzstan that I arrived in Bishkek for a short-term teaching assignment and further research on the political opposition. I settled in to a small apartment a few streets removed from the American University of Central Asia, where I would teach a three-week special seminar on Russian politics to fifteen curious and appreciative students. The class was a mixed group in terms of geographical and ethnic background. Although most came from Kyrgyzstan, there were several students from Afghanistan and from Turkmenistan, where quality higher education, never mind quality higher education in English, was inaccessible. In fact, in order to discourage independent thought, Turkmenistan's dictator had recently closed all the country's universities and eliminated the final years of high school, which prevented students from applying for admission to universities abroad. To its credit, the American University of Central Asia lived up to its claim to serve as a resource for the entire region by organizing a special high school completion track for Turkmenistani students who wished to matriculate at AUCA.

My accommodations on this visit were in what might have been the safest quarter of the city, halfway between the headquarters of the regular police at the Ministry of the Interior and the secret police central command in the State Committee for National Security. In earlier years, I would have thought little about personal security in the center of the city, but local colleagues spoke with alarm about rising street crime after dark, usually committed by young Kyrgyz men who were drunk or on drugs.[3] For those active in politics, however, it was the thugs of the state and not the thugs of the street that posed the greater danger.

Less than three weeks before my arrival, the charred body of Bakiev's former chief of staff, Medet Sadyrkulov, had been found in his Lexus on a remote mountain road outside the capital.[4] For reasons that are still unclear, Sadyrkulov had left the service of Bakiev at the beginning of 2009, taking with him an insider's knowledge of the operation of this increasingly authoritarian regime. Seeking to stay in the political game, Sadyrkulov maintained his contacts with representatives of foreign governments in Bishkek as well as opposition figures, one of whom confided to me that they had offered to make Sadyrkulov mayor of Bishkek or foreign minister if he sided with the opposition against Bakiev.[5]

The day before his death, Sadyrkulov drove to Almaty, Kazakhstan, for meetings with persons with whom he apparently did not wish to be seen in Bishkek. On the return trip, he arrived after midnight at the Kazakhstan-Kyrgyzstan frontier, where his car was inexplicably delayed by the Kyrgyzstani border guards, who informed their superiors of his reentry to the country. Instead of going home to Bishkek, a few minutes south, the car traveled to a village east of the capital, where a young man allegedly struck Sadyrkulov's car after a night of revelry and sent it plunging into a ravine. According to police, the car caught fire and the bodies of Sadyrkulov, his driver, and a political consultant who accompanied him to Almaty were burned beyond recognition. In light of the gift of a human ear and finger that Sadyrkulov had received the previous New Year's eve, and the unusual circumstances of this accident, few doubted that his enemies in the regime had carried out an assassination. Mysteriously, the fuel tank of the Lexus had remained intact and the remains of the chauffeur were found in the front passenger's seat. A year later, the young man who took the rap for the "accident" was stabbed to death in prison.

In the aftermath of this event, most of the opposition figures whom I interviewed were unusually sober and cautious. Several in their ranks, including former ministers of foreign affairs and defense, were already in prison or under criminal investigation. One of the opposition politicians I met during this stay, Azimbek Beknazarov, was visibly nervous when I stepped into his parked car on a side street near my apartment. Known as the Bulldozer of the Revolution, Beknazarov had stood up fearlessly to Akaev, but the rules were different now under Bakiev, and when I contacted him about an interview, he insisted on meeting in his car, a run-down GMC Jimmy. With the car radio blasting during the entire fifty-minute interview, Beknazarov unleashed a torrent of criticism against the Bakiev regime in the heavily accented Russian that betrayed his roots in the rural South of the country.[6]

Beknazarov explained that I had arrived in the country at a critical moment: opposition leaders were meeting that week to select a single presidential candidate to stand against Bakiev in the presidential elections to be held in July. With two exceptions, all of the heavyweights in the opposition had come together to back the candidacy of Almazbek Atambaev, the former prime minister and leader of the Social Democratic Party. One of the holdouts was Temir Sariev, a successful young businessman from a small town west of Bishkek whose technocratic demeanor and economic sophistication distinguished him from his older colleagues. To satisfy Sariev's political ambitions, Beknazarov and the other opposition leaders promised Sariev the post of prime minister if Atambaev were elected, but Sariev ultimately decided to break ranks with his colleagues and run as the new face of the anti-Bakiev opposition.

In this period, the opposition operated in a netherworld where normal political activities, like negotiations over the selection of a presidential candidate to challenge Bakiev, occurred alongside political persecution and even assassinations of parliamentary deputies, five of whom had been shot since the Tulip Revolution. It was the shifting, uncertain boundaries of accepted political dissent that many in the opposition found so unnerving, as well as the infiltration of the state by elements from the criminal underworld. This sense of vulnerability was evident as I made my way to an interview with the opposition's consensus choice for the presidency, Almazbek Atambaev.

A successful businessman in his own right, Atambaev maintained an office on the second floor of a highrise that he owned on a major artery just south of the center of Bishkek. As I pulled up to this architectural abomination from the late-Soviet era, whose exterior walls were missing chunks of concrete, I saw what seemed like a group of toughs dressed in black milling about the entrance. Asked what business I had there, I replied that Almazbek Sharshenovich—the polite form of address for Atambaev—was expecting me for an interview. They ushered me into a narrow entranceway where a black-clad guard inspected my passport and, with a jerk of his head, motioned to me to walk up the stairs. Lining the stairwell were more "sportsmen" in black attire, whose eyes followed me closely as I ascended. On the second floor, I entered Atambaev's outer office, where an all-male staff in similar dress seemed to be passing the time rather than working. A soap opera was playing on a television in the corner, the sound muted.

Stripped of my cell phones and umbrella, I stepped into a different world from the grim spaces protected by the security retinue. In an immaculately appointed office befitting a major figure of state, Atambaev greeted me with a graciousness and deference that recalled the quiet style of Akaev. By Russian and Central Asian standards, Atambaev was from old money. Leaving a Soviet government job in 1989 to enter business in the newly liberalized environment of the Gorbachev era, Atambaev made his first millions in publishing in a country where bookstore shelves had been filled for decades with pulp propaganda. On March 8, 1990, International Women's Day, his company published the Soviet equivalent of *The Joy of Cooking*. He then turned to printing Russian versions of popular foreign fiction, including *The Godfather*. As more than one opposition leader told me, Atambaev's ability to finance his own campaign was an important factor in his selection as the presidential candidate of the anti-Bakiev forces.

It was clear from the outset that this would be a different kind of interview. Most of the opposition politicians and NGO leaders with whom I met wanted to describe the underside of political life and the personal weaknesses of other members of the elite. As a seasoned politician, Atambaev spoke in measured, purposeful phrases that never revealed more than he intended. In Atambaev's version of events, he was not anxious to run against Bakiev for the presidency, but other opposition leaders insisted. He recognized that many of them had publicly criticized him for accepting the prime ministership under Bakiev in March 2007, but he claimed that several had agreed at the time to join his Cabinet, and only at the last minute got cold feet. Proof of this fact, he noted, was their willingness now to back him as the opposition candidate for president. He then gave me the small, just-published brochure that he had produced with documents supporting his side of the story.[7]

After refusing to fill out the brief questionnaire that I gave all interviewees to probe their views on why the opposition had found it so difficult to unite against Bakiev, Atambaev raised an issue on his agenda for the meeting. Why, he asked, had the United States government turned its back on him and other members of the country's opposition? After all, he continued,

Figure 16.1. Almazbek Atambaev (with the author). April 2009

> if we don't want a repeat of problems we've had with Bin Laden in Afghani-
> stan, then at least one country in Central Asia should serve as an example. If
> even a single country [in the region] follows a democratic path, then others
> will follow. . . . I recall how on my visits to several neighboring countries
> ministers would confide in me that they were jealous of us.[8]

Obviously seeking to attract support in the West for his own campaign to
unseat the incumbent president, he warned that if the current attempts at
democratization failed in Kyrgyzstan, the alternative to authoritarianism,
poverty, and corruption would be radical Islam.[9]

It was not the first time in Kyrgyzstan that I had heard a politician use the
self-serving threat of radical Islam in a plea for foreign assistance, nor was it
the first time during this stay that I had heard complaints from opposition
leaders and some NGO heads about the new, standoffish approach of the US
Embassy in Bishkek to Bakiev's opponents. According to Atambaev, the
new American ambassador, Tatiana Gfoeller, had been in country for almost
six months yet they had not met, an affront to a former prime minister who
had had ready access to American envoys in the past. Less than a year earlier,
for example, Atambaev had been invited to speak to a high-ranking US
Senate delegation in Bishek, led by Senator Harry Reid.[10] These concerns
about the American government's reticence to maintain key lines of communication with Bakiev's adversaries were at the center of my congressional

testimony in Washington during a crisis the following year that threatened to rupture relations between Kyrgyzstan and the United States. [11]

Like almost all candidates for elective office in Kyrgyzstan, Almazbek Atambaev lacked a carefully crafted political platform. With most voters drawn to candidates because of their personality or their kinship or regional ties—the latter providing assurances to voters that their groups would benefit from having their Big Man in power—there was no attempt to develop a set of specific policies on issues like taxation or employment or foreign affairs. When I asked Atambaev about the message that he would communicate to voters during the campaign, it was that citizens faced a choice in the upcoming presidential election between civilization and barbarism, between accountable government or authoritarianism. In short, much as President Yeltsin sought to frame the 1996 Russian presidential election as a choice between the communist past and a democratic future, Atambaev and other anti-Bakiev forces attempted to cast the July 2009 presidential election in Kyrgyzstan as a contest between family rule and a constitutional order. The difference, of course, was that Yeltsin was the incumbent, so Atambaev was in effect calling for the election to replace not just Bakiev and his loyalists but the mechanisms of rule that had undermined political and economic competition in Kyrgyzstan.

When I asked Atambaev what measures he could take to ensure that the upcoming election was free and fair, he shrugged off suggestions that having his electoral observers at every precinct and counting station would improve electoral administration. In fact, from his comments and those of other opposition leaders, it was evident that they didn't so much expect to win at the polls but during the popular unrest (*volneniia*) that would follow attempts by Bakiev to control the campaign and falsify the results. This perilous strategy rested on the assumption that Bakiev would lose a fair election and that the population wouldn't stand for his accession to a second presidential term through a flawed contest. In essence, the opposition was planning to carry out the second revolution in four years in Kyrgyzstan.

A few days later, on an early Saturday morning, April 25, 2009, I drove with Roza Otunbaeva to Atambaev's home village of Arashan, a few miles southeast of the capital, where hundreds of delegates from opposition parties were gathering to nominate Atambaev as their presidential candidate. Just beyond the village, in a large field at the base of low, treeless hills, a dozen large yurts formed a semicircle around an expansive stage. Stepping out of the car in traditional dress, which included a long black wool coat with wide lapels embroidered with Kyrgyz symbols, Roza encountered a swarm of well-wishers who had come to the convention from every region of the country. As we made our way toward the stage, delegates were streaming onto the field, carrying their party's banners. The blue flags of the Social

Democrats, Atambaev's party, competed for attention with the red banners of Ata-Meken, led by Omurbek Tekebaev.

There were a few trappings of modernity, such as an electric sound system, but in other respects this *Uluttuk Kurultai*, or National Assembly, sought to respect Kyrgyz traditions inherited from its nomadic past. Many in the crowd wore Kyrgyz headgear—with men in distinctive high kalpaks, married women wearing large, pillbox hats tied tightly with a light-colored

Figure 16.2.   Roza Otunbaeva at the Kurultai nominating Almazbek Atambaev for president, near the village of Arashan. April 2009

scarf under their chins, and maidens sporting a conical headpiece topped off by a plume of feathers designed to attract suitors. Just outside the yurts, which served as gathering places for regional delegations, women and children tended large metal pots that boiled water for tea. In the fields beyond, boys rode on horseback against the backdrop of the snow-covered peaks of the Ala-Too.

After several singers in traditional garb warmed up the crowd with well-known Kyrgyz songs, the convention opened with a display of opposition solidarity, as prominent political leaders who were intent on removing Bakiev gathered on the stage. Nominating speeches followed by representatives of each of the country's seven regions and Bishkek. Perhaps because politicians had limited opportunities to speak before crowds—there was no equivalent of the Rotary Club and rubber chicken circuit that honed the oratorical skills of American politicians—most speakers at this convention lacked the ability to inspire the assembled. When the rare impassioned speaker took the microphone, what seemed to fire up the crowd were attacks on the Bakiev regime, not words of praise for the nominee, which were, in any case, relatively few and tepid. After two hours of nominating speeches, Atambaev

Figure 16.3.   Flags of the Social Democratic and Ata-Meken Parties in front of the stage at the Kurultai. April 2009

mounted the stage to give his acceptance address, to which the convention delegates responded with respect but little enthusiasm. In a contest between Atambaev and Bakiev, neither politician would win many votes based on their charisma or rhetorical appeal.

Virtually absent from the convention were representatives of the country's minority groups, who accounted for 30 percent of Kyrgyzstan's population and a significant share of likely voters for parties and candidates opposed to the Bakiev regime. Of the dozens of speakers appearing on the stage that day, only two delegates from Bishkek—ethnic Slavs—spoke in Russian; the rest of the convention was conducted in Kyrgyz, with no interpretation, which meant that the proceedings would have been inaccessible to a fair share of the country's population.[12] Structuring the convention as a distinctly Kyrgyz event allowed the organizers to celebrate the language and traditions of the country's titular people, many of whom considered their small nation to be under threat from the russifying legacies of the Soviet era and the pressures of globalization. As one of the very few non-Kyrgyz at this national nominating convention, I considered it a privilege to witness an event that was both making and reviving history, though I had little doubt that the

Figure 16.4. Kyrgyz boy on horseback at the Kurultai, near the village of Arashan. April 2009

decision to organize a national political nominating convention as an *Uluttuk Kurultai* would deepen the sense among minorities that they were living in a Kyrgyzstan for the Kyrgyz.

When the convention broke up in midafternoon, I traveled a short distance by car with Roza Otunbaeva to Arashan, where a celebratory luncheon had been organized. Walking past an open cafeteria serving convention delegates, Roza and I entered a courtyard and ducked into a small ceremonial yurt with a picnic table and two benches. Much to my surprise, I found myself sitting around a table with eight or nine of the country's leading politicians, most of whom I had interviewed over the years. The last person to arrive was Almazbek Atambaev, who shook everyone's hand and then, revealing his doubts about his performance on stage, asked the assembled how they thought he'd done. He appeared genuinely concerned about the impression he'd made to the convention, perhaps because, like many of his generation who were brought up in and around the capital, he had had limited practice speaking Kyrgyz in public.[13]

After a few minutes of small talk in Russian over a traditional Kyrgyz feast, where, as usual, lamb took pride of place, the politicians switched to Kyrgyz, apparently intent on preventing the foreigner in their midst from following a conversation over the difficult campaign that lay ahead. Catching only a few words and proper names after this point, it was nonetheless evident that the mood had darkened and there were serious disagreements among the politicians. What had initially seemed like a rare opportunity to observe opposition leaders interacting outside the public eye soon left me feeling like an unwelcome guest whose presence threatened to erode Roza's standing in their eyes. More than anything, of course, I regretted not having a command of Kyrgyz that would have allowed me to follow the disagreements that arose among those seeking to remove Bakiev from power.

Following this lunch, I reflected further on what had encouraged such an ambitious and fractious group of opposition leaders to unify at last against the Bakiev regime. It struck me that it was, in no small measure, the perceived "threat level" that they faced in their opposition to the regime. By the end of 2008, the threats to their physical safety and livelihoods were significant enough that they had begun to recognize that they could save themselves only by leaving the country, defecting to the regime, or cooperating among themselves—it was becoming too dangerous for each party and politician to go it alone.[14] And with the regime tightening its grip on the country, it would soon be too late to pursue a strategy of cooperation. In a sense, then, this was a window of opportunity that was rapidly closing. While many politicians I spoke with had argued that Bakiev's regime pursued policies that divided them, they failed to mention the extent to which Kyrgyzstan's increasingly repressive government had brought them together.

Three months after I left the country, on July 23, 2009, the citizens of Kyrgyzstan went to the polls to cast their ballots following a lackluster and one-sided campaign. Despite the opposition's willingness to support Atambaev's candidacy for the presidency, it faced enormous hurdles in mobilizing voters behind Atambaev or Sariev, Bakiev's two strongest opponents. Just as in the latter elections of the Akaev era, the incumbent used government resources, compliant media, and an enormous financial advantage to dominate the campaign: Bakiev outspent Atambaev by thirty-eight million soms to eight. In addition, election day brought widespread reports of ballot stuffing, restricted access to polling places and counting rooms by domestic and foreign observers, and falsification of precinct tally sheets, known as voting protocols. It was unsurprising, then, that the official results showed that Bakiev received 76 percent of the vote, while Atambaev and Sariev garnered just over 8 and 6 percent of the vote, respectively. [15]

In the final days before the election, recognizing that the vote would go against him, Atambaev had urged his supporters to arm themselves with axes and pitchforks to "defend their electoral rights" at the election commissions counting the votes. [16] Then, just after noon on election day, Atambaev and another presidential candidate in the six-person field, Jenishbek Nazaraliev, announced that they were withdrawing from the contest and condemning the as-yet-unannounced results as invalid because of numerous electoral violations. Almost simultaneously, a large crowd of Atambaev supporters assembled in the northern city of Balykchy and attempted to seize control of the mayor's office, but the police intervened to prevent the takeover. [17] When a rally outside Atambaev's headquarters in Bishkek that evening failed to attract a sufficiently large and dedicated crowd, the leading opposition candidate appeared to recognize that the widespread unrest he had predicted in April during our meeting was unlikely to occur. Unable to use a flawed election as a triggering mechanism for the overthrow of Bakiev, as had occurred in earlier color revolutions, Atambaev and other opposition leaders retreated to their corners. They did not, however, abandon the search for an event that could mobilize the population against a president whose official mandate had just been extended for five more years. That event came sooner than almost anyone would have imagined.

Chapter Seventeen

Bakiev Falls, Washington Reacts

On March 23, 2010, I received an unexpected email from the son of one of Kyrgyzstan's most prominent opposition politicians. It contained a simple message, "Here we go again." The URL below this line took me to a Russian website with a broadcast report about Kyrgyzstan: a prominent Moscow TV station had unleashed a harsh attack on the Kyrgyzstani regime, accusing it of corruption and nepotism. It represented a dramatic public break with President Bakiev, whom Russia had faithfully supported until that point, at least in the media.

Over the preceding week, political leaders in Kyrgyzstan had organized two *kurultai*, the popular open-air assemblies, in Bishkek. At the first, thousands of participants heard opposition leaders call for the removal from office of Bakiev's brothers and sons, who had managed to purchase formerly state-owned telecommunications and utility companies at fire-sale prices. The second *kurultai*, labeled an assembly of concord, was organized by the regime in an attempt to defuse the growing social tension. But when opposition supporters sought to deliver a set of demands to the leaders of the event, the authorities intervened and briefly detained thirty persons, including the unsuccessful presidential candidate, Temir Sariev. In its reporting on the pro-regime *kurultai*, Russian media made it clear that Moscow's patience with Bakiev and his family had run out.

The unprecedented Russian criticism came as popular discontent with the Bakiev regime grew in Kyrgyzstan itself. Until the early part of 2010, the expansion of the Bakiev family business empire narrowed opportunities for the country's entrepreneurs, but it was little more than a subject of gossip for the average citizen. That changed on April 1, 2010, when the utility company privatized by Bakiev's son, Maxim, doubled the rates paid by residents. At almost the same time, gasoline and fuel oil became scarcer and more expensive, in large part because the Russian government imposed a hefty export tax on petroleum products after discovering that middlemen tied to the Bakiev family were selling cheaply obtained Russian jet fuel to the Americans operating at the Manas Air Base. Finally, Kyrgyzstan's largest cell phone company, also controlled by the Bakiev family, had just introduced a 60-tyiyn connection charge—a tyiyn is 1/100 of a som—for all phone calls, a wildly unpopular measure in a country where mobile phones were seen as necessities.

While economic conditions worsened for the entire country, demographic and political developments fed northern resentment against the South. As Bakiev drew more southern elites into his inner circle and key government posts, labor migrants from the South were arriving in ever larger numbers in Bishkek. In interviews over the preceding two years, I had heard more and more complaints from northerners about this southern "invasion." In the summer of 2008, Roza Otunbaeva noted that when southerners came in as ministers, they tended to clean house, right down to the cleaning staff.[1] Even Bakiev's former defense minister, himself from the South, admitted that after Bakiev came to power, the first question people began asking was "Where are you from?"[2] When an NGO leader in this period tried to hail a cab in Bishkek, the driver asked her region of origin. Learning she was from the North, he responded: "Get in then. I refuse to take southerners any longer."[3] His relative had lost a government job to a recent arrival from the South. The deepening regional divide was apparent in the results of an opinion poll administered in October 2008. Fifty-eight percent of southerners reported being very satisfied or somewhat satisfied with the way democracy was developing in Kyrgyzstan; only 28 percent of northerners felt that way.[4] If Bakiev was to be toppled, it was northerners who would lead the way.

Lacking the ability to influence politics in the halls of power, the opposition continued to put pressure on the regime from the streets, with new *kurultai* planned for the northern cities of Talas, Naryn, and Bishkek on April 7.[5] Seeking to decapitate the leadership of the opposition before these demonstrations got underway, the authorities began arresting leading members of the opposition on April 6, beginning with Bolot Sherniiazov, who had just arrived that evening in Talas to lead the local *kurultai* the following morning. In response, two thousand opposition supporters gathered in the main square of Talas and burned handheld photos of Bakiev as well as a billboard with the president's image. As sympathizers arrived from neighboring districts that evening, the crowd swelled by several thousand persons, allowing it to overwhelm the 150 policemen on the square and seize the local government headquarters, the *akimiat*, and temporarily free Sherniazov. Back in Bishkek, special forces began arresting opposition leaders, including Omurbek Tekebaev and Almazbek Atambaev, whose heavily guarded home was no match for a large contingent of police.

The following day, April 7, five thousand anti-Bakiev demonstrators entered the *akimiat* in Naryn and "appointed" an opposition-oriented governor, while in Talas crowds estimated to be as large as fifteen thousand persons freed Sherniazov and bloodied and almost killed Bakiev's minister of the interior, who had arrived that morning with special police units to try to reclaim the city and its surrounding region for the regime. Dozens of police, most poorly armed, fought for their lives in Talas as enraged demonstrators broke into the local barracks and attacked those inside with clubs, rocks, and broken bottles. In other northern cities, including Tokmok, Cholpon-Ata, and Karakol, anti-Bakiev forces took control of local government buildings, while in Bishkek, the authorities boarded a plane arriving from Moscow to arrest Temir Sariev, apparently fresh from talks with Russian officials. By midday, ten opposition politicians were in custody.

With the remaining leaders of the opposition in hiding to avoid arrest, crowds gathered on the main square facing the White House to demand the release of those detained. Under gray, threatening skies, thousands of persons, mainly young men, engaged in skirmishes with the police, as clouds of tear gas wafted across Chu Prospect. Demonstrators then seized an armored personnel carrier and tried to ram the gates of the White House. Amid confusion on the streets and fears of demonstrators entering the White House gates, government snipers stationed in the White House began firing into the crowd, killing eighty-six and wounding several hundred. Even as the casualties were being evacuated from the scene, many in the crowd continued to rush the White House, almost like zombies, as my colleague Gulnara Iskakova described them to me after witnessing the events. By early evening, the White House was in the hands of the opposition and President Bakiev had fled with family and close advisors to his home district of Jalal-Abad, hoping to rally supporters in the South against what he described as an unconstitutional seizure of power by his political opponents.

Just as in 2005, anarchy reigned in Bishkek in the aftermath of the president's departure. Looters again took advantage of the collapse of public order to abscond with anything of value in shops in the city center. The headquarters of the national prosecutor's office went up in flames, along with all of the records inside, an act almost certainly ordered by criminal kingpins seeking to destroy evidence against them. For years afterwards the charred skeleton of this building served as a reminder of the lawlessness unleashed by the second popular revolt in five years in Kyrgyzstan.

With Bakiev gone, the leaders of the opposition shut down the parliament and Constitutional Court and claimed power for themselves as an Interim Government, with the promise that a new, more democratic constitution would be presented shortly to the nation for its approval.[6] In the ten weeks separating Bakiev's overthrow from the constitutional referendum, the Interim Government faced an almost unimaginable series of challenges, ranging

from a countercoup attempt by the former president to widespread inter-
ethnic violence. It was a time that called for maximum unity in the new
leadership, but having closed ranks to help depose Bakiev, the former oppo-
sitionists found it difficult to maintain that sense of solidarity and single-
minded purpose once they were in power.

The members of the Interim Government had plenty of executive and
legislative experience among them, but they were unwilling to set aside their
personal resentments and ambitions and govern as a true leadership collective. They created instead little fiefdoms for themselves, with each member
of the Interim Government controlling his or her own area of policy, such as
law, economics, and defense, with minimal oversight from their colleagues.
Roza Otunbaeva assumed the title of Leader of the Interim Government, later
upgraded to President, but the position did not grant her the authority to
impose discipline on the ruling group. While these arrangements may have
limited political infighting in the Interim Government, they did little to promote sound and effective governance at a critical time in the nation's history.

Bakiev's removal caught numerous foreign governments off-guard. Angered by the removal of Bakiev, neighboring Kazakhstan closed the border
with Kyrgyzstan for months, which cut off much-needed trade. Kazakhstan
would later build a razor-wire fence along the more populated sections of
Kyrgyzstan's northern border, an unfriendly act that reminded Kyrgyzstanis
of their dependence on their better-off neighbor to the north. For its part,
Washington had bet heavily on Bakiev as a guarantor of Western access to
the Manas Air Base in Bishkek, and now the Northern Supply Route into
Afghanistan appeared endangered by the accession to power of a group of
opposition politicians who felt they had been ostracized by the US Embassy
in Bishkek.

With the two former Superpowers—each with its own base in the country—vying for Kyrgyzstan's favor, the overthrow of Bakiev generated enormous interest and angst in policy and media circles in the United States.
Regimes in small, developing countries regularly collapse in fits of violence,
but only rarely are the potential consequences for the regional and international order as far-reaching as they were in Kyrgyzstan in April 2010. There
was great demand, therefore, for detailed information about a country that
few in the United States had ever heard of, let alone read about. Suddenly,
years of academic research in Kyrgyzstan had immediate practical applica-
tion and I spent the next few weeks trying to explain developments in a small
Central Asian country to American government officials and the broader
public.

The day after the revolution in Bishkek, I pulled from my drawer a five-
thousand-word draft of a popular article on Kyrgyzstan that I had written a
few months earlier, anticipating Bakiev's day of reckoning. Quickly bringing
the piece up to date, I emailed it out early the next morning to Salon, an

online publication on cultural and political affairs. Within an hour, I had received a note from an editor, Steve Kornacki, a writer and political junkie who would later work as an on-air journalist for MSNBC. He had good news and bad news: "The writing is very strong and the information superb," he noted, but they were not in a position to pay me for the piece. With a day job as a professor, getting the story out quickly was payment enough, and after some minor editing and a dramatic change of title, the piece went live at eight o'clock that evening. Kornacki had wisely passed on my proposed title, something only an academic would have loved, and labeled the piece, "If You Want to Understand Kyrgyzstan, Read This." All it lacked was an exclamation point.

Where professors normally wait weeks, if not months or years, to receive responses to their work, the reaction to the Salon article was disorientingly immediate and intense. Within minutes, readers began adding comments to the piece; some managed to find my email and send me messages of appreciation for the work. Within an hour, the article joined the list of the most-read Salon publications of the day, and it was soon at the top of the chart. Fame is fleeting, however, and by the next morning an article providing recipes for mashed potatoes had replaced my article at the summit. It was a reminder that in a battle for the attention of the American public, food will trump Kyrgyzstan every time.

Early the following week, I was speaking to a very different audience: government officials in Washington. I had been scheduled for some weeks to travel to DC to take part in a small conference on Eurasian affairs with analysts from the intelligence community and a couple of other academic specialists on post-communist politics. My topic was "Trajectories for Russia's Power-Sharing Arrangements," a fitting theme given the arrival of President Medvedev in Washington on the day after the conference. As a graduate student I had worried that such encounters between professors and government officials could pose risks for the independence of academic inquiry, but having participated in several of these sessions over the preceding quarter-century, I recognized that each side benefitted from vigorous debates over how to interpret political developments in a part of the world where the exercise of state power was often opaque.

My first exposure to the world of intelligence analysts had come in 1986, when I was invited by the CIA to explain to young analysts-in-training how to read Soviet newspapers. In those days the meetings were held at CIA headquarters in Langley, Virginia, where security measures were in full view, with entering cars checked carefully for explosives and offices inside the building secured by combination locks. The protocol later changed and sessions took place instead in the Washington suburbs in commercial office buildings whose markings gave no indication of the nature of the business conducted there. On entering the building, one relinquished cell phones and cameras and, after 9/11, the ID badges of intelligence officials no longer revealed their last names, which immediately distinguished them from the academics present, whose full names and institutions were prominently displayed.

Learning that I would be in town for a conference on Russian politics organized by the intelligence community, State Department officials asked me to come by the following morning, Wednesday, April 14, to discuss developments in Kyrgyzstan with foreign service officers specializing in Central Asia. In a seminar attended by about twenty State Department personnel, I laid out the causes and likely consequences of the previous week's change of regime, and then spent much of the discussion period providing background on the former opposition politicians, now the young country's leaders. Not all of my assessments of American policy toward the Bakiev regime went down well with the participants. An official who had served in the US Embassy in Bishkek challenged my criticisms of the ambassador for turning her back on the opposition. It is usually State Department officials who receive criticism for "going native," that is accepting uncritically the outlook of those they live among overseas, but in this case it was a foreign service officer who implied that I had taken on the opposition cause.

It was not the first time that week that observers had called into question the Kyrgyzstani opposition's motives and methods in overthrowing Bakiev. A fellow academic, Eric McGlinchey, had just published an op-ed in the *New York Times* arguing that the only thing differentiating Kyrgyzstani politicians was whether they were in or out of power.[7] While admitting that the means the opposition used to topple the former president were suspect, there was little doubt in my mind that if the Bakiev family had remained in power, Kyrgyzstan would soon have resembled the harsh authoritarian regimes in several surrounding states. In short, the rebellion of April 2010 ensured that the country remained a Stan like no other.

After a brief lunch in the State Department cafeteria with a former student, who was one of State's leading specialists on the former Soviet republics, I hurried onto the streets of Foggy Bottom to see if a tentatively planned meeting with a White House official had been confirmed. The previous evening Michael McFaul, special assistant to President Obama for Russian and Eurasian affairs, had written to ask if I could stop by his office to brief him on the new leadership in Kyrgyzstan, noting that his secretary would email me with a time around midday. Unlike everyone else in Washington at the time, I did not yet have a smartphone, and so with no way of checking my emails on the street, I did what any good Luddite would have done: I called my daughter in Tulsa and asked her to access my emails to see if a message had arrived from Mike McFaul, who had been a professor of Russian politics at Stanford before taking a leave to join Obama's National Security Council staff. Finding a note from his secretary in my inbox, my daughter wrote back to her with my cell phone number, and within minutes I was climbing the steps of the Executive Office Building (EOB) for a 1:00 p.m. meeting with McFaul. As the host of the Western air base at Manas and the sole country in the region where competitive politics seemed to have a chance, Kyrgyzstan clearly had the attention of the Obama administration—perhaps even Rahm Emanuel.[8]

Located on the grounds of the White House, the EOB is a grand, if slightly tatty, structure whose long hallways and high ceilings have the familiar feel of an aging academic building. Arriving at McFaul's office on an upper floor, I knocked several times before the secretary opened the massive door, secured by a special lock. Within minutes, McFaul came out to the small reception room to greet me and usher me into his office, which had the air of a large professorial carrel, with books everywhere, including a number by McFaul. It was quickly apparent, however, that the comparisons with a university setting had their limits. Gazing out the window behind McFaul, I saw marksmen dressed in dark clothing patrolling the White House roof next door.

Structures of power are the stock and trade of political scientists, but in Kyrgyzstan at this moment it was personalities and not institutions that mattered. Having tossed out the Constitution's provisions on governing arrangements, the Interim Government was making up the rules as it went along, and so for officials like McFaul, who had responsibility for helping to shape American policy toward Kyrgyzstan, it was vital to know who was leading a nation in transition. For half an hour, I provided detail on the backgrounds, values, and temperaments of Kyrgyzstan's new leaders to McFaul, who would travel to Bishkek later that week to meet with Roza Otunbaeva and several other members of the Interim Government. Just after 1:30 p.m., a gracious and attentive McFaul apologized to say that he was late for a National Security Council meeting, and as we hurried out of the office he grabbed two of his own books from the shelf to give me, including a just-published volume entitled—appropriately for the time—*Advancing Democracy Abroad*.

On arriving in Florida that evening, I received an invitation from the House Subcommittee on National Security and Foreign Affairs to return to Washington the following week to testify before Congress on developments in Kyrgyzstan. Like most of Washington, the subcommittee's primary focus was on the Transit Center at Manas, but Chairman John Tierney and the subcommittee staff were less interested in whether the Interim Government would extend the base lease than in whether the US government had violated legal or ethical standards in their dealings with the Bakiev regime. Put simply, the question was whether the United States cozied up to a repressive and corrupt ruler—and helped to enrich his family—in order to maintain access to the base. At the center of the controversy were shadowy contractors, the

Gibraltar-based Mina Corporation, and its affiliate, Red Star Enterprises, which had served as middlemen for $2 billion in jet fuel purchases by the US government from a Kyrgyzstani group with suspected ties to the Bakiev family.

Just before the testimony began on the morning of April 22, I joined three other specialists in a lounge off the congressional hearing room to await the arrival of Chairman Tierney, who would give us a brief orientation on the proceedings. The other experts were Scott Horton, a New York–based human rights lawyer who had helped to found the American University of Central Asia; Alexander Cooley, a Columbia University international relations specialist whose book, *Base Politics*, detailed the local political entanglements that often accompanied US basing rights overseas; and Baktybek Abdrisaev, former ambassador of Kyrgyzstan to the United States.

As congressional hearings go, this one was relatively low key. There was little media presence and only a smattering of observers in the gallery, among them a few representatives from the embassies of neighboring Central Asian countries. Nonetheless, the formal swearing in and the room arrangements gave the proceedings a solemn and almost menacing air. Those of us testifying sat at tables that faced members of Congress and their staff, who were seated on raised rows above us. Although Chairman Tierney and members of the subcommittee expressed their appreciation for our willingness to share our expertise with Congress, the questions were at times pointed, as appropriate for a serious matter affecting the country's national security and its adherence to its own legal standards, most notably the Foreign Corrupt Practices Act.

"We are here today because the United States tried to please a dictator." With these words I opened my testimony, which contained blunt criticism of what I considered to have been an unnecessarily deferential American policy toward the Bakiev regime. I went on to argue that "the Manas airbase had granted President Bakiev a kind of get-out-of-jail-free card with the US." This approach, I noted, had played into Russia's hands. With the US Embassy in Bishkek turning a cold shoulder to the opposition, the Russian Embassy had begun to seriously engage civil society in Kyrgyzstan for the first time since the collapse of the USSR. While the United States hesitated in its response to the overthrow of Bakiev, Vladimir Putin, then Russia's prime minister, was the first foreign leader to congratulate Kyrgyzstan on its successful revolution. Given my critical comments, I shouldn't have been surprised that the next day several international publications, including Paris' *Le Monde* and Moscow's *Izvestia*, cited my testimony in articles about the hearing.

Where I spoke primarily to the American government's inappropriate treatment of the opposition under Bakiev, Scott Horton and Alexander Cooley discussed the more sensitive issue of American government contracts for jet fuel supplied to the Transit Center at Manas. As Horton noted in his testimony, and the subcommittee later confirmed after months of investigation, there was, at a minimum, the widespread perception in Kyrgyzstan that the Bakiev family had benefitted financially from American military procurement practices at Manas. In essence, Horton argued, the presidential family's control over the airport, which had begun under Akaev, continued in the Bakiev era. The US government's use of obscure companies like Red Star and Mina to purchase millions of gallons of jet fuel only made sense, Horton continued, if it was seeking to remain at arm's length from the Kyrgyzstani supplier in order to avoid a direct relationship with members of the Bakiev family. In this case, therefore, Red Star and Mina, whose principals had previously worked for the US government, appear to have been created expressly to serve as shell companies that could act as a go-between in dealings between the American military and Kyrgyzstani firms with ties to the Bakiev family. Neither company had business interests outside of those at Manas. For their part, members of the Interim Government, with whom the United States was now dealing on matters relating to the airbase, had no doubt that the United States had tried to cover up a corrupt practices scheme at Manas that implicated the Bakiev family. In a meeting with Robert Blake, the Assistant Secretary of State for South and Central Asian Affairs, Roza Otunbaeva reportedly sent a clear warning to the US government, "Clean up your act at Manas."[9]

After the hearing, those of us testifying joined colleagues at a restaurant on Independence Avenue, a short walk from the Cannon House Office Building, the site of the hearing. On my way out of the restaurant after lunch, I saw my congressman, John Mica, strolling back to his office with his chief of staff. Stopping him on the street, I couldn't resist mentioning that I missed seeing him at the hearing—he was a member of the Subcommittee on National Security and Foreign Affairs but had not attended the hearing, at which an expert from his district had testified. Mica took it in good stride, and I understood well that members of Congress had to be highly selective about their commitments. For a congressman whose special concern was domestic transportation, an inquiry into a scandal in a small nation a half a world away was no doubt of limited interest.

Congressman Mica's indifference to events in Kyrgyzstan aside, Washington's foreign policy establishment had responded to the crisis in Bishkek with a speed and intensity that was remarkable for "a city of southern efficiency and northern charm," as President Kennedy described it. The following day I participated in yet another event in Washington devoted to the crisis in Kyrgyzstan, a half-day workshop organized by the National Endowment for Democracy (NED) that brought together a handful of Central Asian specialists from the US government, academic institutions, and the NGO community. Created under President Reagan and funded almost exclusively by the federal budget, the NED was a classic instrument of American "soft power," offering support and guidance for political forces overseas seeking to build democratic institutions. In the case of Kyrgyzstan under the Interim Government, this meant providing unsolicited "technical assistance" on a recently released draft constitution that promised to replace Kyrgyzstan's presidency-dominant model of government with a parliamentary republic.

Crafted by the former opposition leader and now member of the Interim Government, Omurbek Tekebaev, Kyrgyzstan's draft constitution sought to inoculate the country against a repeat of repressive rule by offering provisions that reduced the power of the presidency and granted special protections to the political opposition. It imagined a political system like no other in Central Asia: open and competitive with numerous institutional checks and balances. In the view of many of us attending the workshop, however, there were several deficiencies in the proposed constitution as well as in the procedures for constitutional adoption, deficiencies that we outlined in a memo to the Kyrgyzstani ambassador to the United States and Tekebaev's constitutional working group in Bishkek. First, Tekebaev's working group allowed only a two-week period of public debate for the draft, to be followed by a single week for review of the comments received. By world standards, this timeline suggested a rush job. Although we understood the dangers of delaying the adoption of a new constitution in a country where the current political leadership had limited legitimacy, we also recognized that without adequate time for drafting and review, a new constitution could create unexpected political consequences and an indifference to the document by a citizenry that should be given time to understand, and buy into, the country's basic law.

The draft constitution proclaimed that Kyrgyzstan was to be a parliamentary republic, but traditionally such models of governments have presidents or monarchs who perform a largely ceremonial function. They usually assume their position either by dynastic succession, as in Great Britain, or by indirect election, with parliament traditionally choosing a president. In such systems, it is the prime minister who exercises real executive power and the parliamentary majority that has the authority to confirm and remove the prime minister as well as to approve legislation. However, the provisions of the new constitution in Kyrgyzstan ensured that the president would be far more than a figurehead. As a politician directly elected for a six-year term, the president would enjoy a popular mandate, making him or her the only national executive figure who could claim to have been chosen by the people. Moreover, the president would retain control over what was called the "power bloc" in the post-communist world, that is the ministries that are responsible for law enforcement, national security, and foreign affairs. In developing societies like Kyrgyzstan, where governments often target their political enemies for criminal prosecution, granting a president the power of appointment and oversight of the "power bloc" ensured that the interests of the head of state—the president—would in some cases clash with those of the head of government—the prime minister, which is a frequent feature of semi-presidential, not parliamentary, political systems. Balancing the considerable authority invested in the president by the new constitution were provisions eliminating the president's right to call referendums and limiting his or her tenure to a single term. With no possibility of reelection, future presidents would, in theory, have less incentive to abuse their office or manipulate presidential elections.

Several provisions of Kyrgyzstan's draft constitution were oddities by international standards. Having spent many years out of power, Omurbek Tekebaev and his working group in Bishkek sought to protect opposition forces in the future by requiring that members of a minority party chair two important parliamentary committees, those on legal affairs and the economy. This novelty in constitutional engineering seems at first glance like a reasonable way to introduce checks and balances into the parliament itself, but good government requires efficiency as well as accountability and restraint. By leading two key committees, the opposition would be in a position to impede the majority's legislative agenda, which violates basic principles of parliamentary government.

Because Presidents Akaev and Bakiev dramatically expanded their formal powers through constitutional amendments, the framers of the new constitution introduced two provisions designed to make it more difficult to change the country's basic law. The draft retained a two-thirds parliamentary vote as the threshold for constitutional amendments, but it introduced a rule that prohibited any single party from winning more than 65 seats in the 120-seat single-chamber parliament, thereby ensuring that no single "party of power," such as that operating under Bakiev and other post-communist rulers, would have enough seats on its own to alter the constitution. While the logic of this rule was understandable, it undermined a basic principle of democracy by limiting the will of the people; in effect, it had the potential to award parliamentary seats to parties that did not merit them, given that some of the votes cast for a highly popular party would in effect be transferred to its opponents. The draft also provided that no amendments to the constitution made by the parliament would be permitted until 2020, though the constitutional language did not forbid the use of a referendum to alter the constitution. Although the intent of Tekebaev and his working group was to allow the new political system to put down roots before a leader could tamper with the country's institutional arrangements, the failure to prohibit constitutional amendments through referendums provided an opening that would later be used by those impatient to alter the values and the institutional arrangements championed by the 2010 Constitution.

Finally, the draft constitution envisioned a new voting system that would elect parliamentary deputies using a closed-list form of proportional representation, where all voters across the country cast their ballot for parties and not individuals. In this system, the parties are awarded the percentage of the parliamentary seats that correspond to the percentage of the votes received. Designed to encourage strong parties, which had not been a feature of Kyrgyzstani politics to this point, the voting system had the disadvantage of ignoring the strong local loyalties of the electorate. Because deputies were elected on the same ballot across the whole country, citizens would no longer have a local representative, which in the view of many of us in the workgroup was inappropriate for a country where identities often aligned closely with geographical areas and where remote and less-developed areas could be more easily ignored if they did not have their own representatives in the capital.

Participating in this Washington workshop on Kyrgyzstani constitution-making reminded me that "democracy-promotion" was in some respects a presumptuous exercise. The technologies and values in place at the end of the eighteenth century ensured that the framers of the American constitution were not subject to the advice of foreigners who felt that they possessed special expertise on the drafting of constitutions. One could well have argued that the citizens of Kyrgyzstan should have been left alone as they put in place their own constitution. And yet the world was a more integrated place at the beginning of the twenty-first century, and Kyrgyzstan was a small country with only a handful of persons who understood the subtleties of constitutional drafting. One of those was my colleague, Gulnara Iskakova, a member of Tekebaev's staff who threw up her hands at times in reaction to the limited expertise among members of Kyrgyzstan's constitutional working group. In any event, the Interim Government had already sought the assistance of constitutional experts on the Council of Europe's Venice Commission which, as one of its leaders noted, "had a moral duty to answer the call" of new democracies seeking assistance.[10] Kyrgyzstan's ambassador to the United States welcomed the National Endowment of Democracy's carefully prepared memo on the draft constitution, though our advice, and that of the Venice Commission, did not prevent Kyrgyzstan from adopting several constitutional provisions that would complicate political life in the country in the years ahead.

Chapter Eighteen

Revolutionary Legality versus Transitional Justice

While politicians and experts debated the fine points of constitution-making in Bishkek, Washington, and Strasbourg, ordinary citizens in Kyrgyzstan were focused on the Interim Government's inability to provide order and justice on the ground in the wake of the April rebellion. Thanks in part to patrols of volunteers, calm returned to the capital within days of Bakiev's departure, but some citizens in outlying areas took advantage of the collapse of public order to lash out against wealthier minority communities. Intoxicated by the potent elixir of popular revenge and more mundane stimulants, impoverished ethnic Kyrgyz attacked and robbed their Meskhetian Turkish neighbors in the northern village of Maevka in the days after the April rebellion. A dispute pitting recently arrived and landless Kyrgyz against relatively prosperous Meskhetian Turks led to attacks on a third of the eighty Meskhetian Turkish families in the village. Five Meskhetian Turks were killed in the violence and several of their homes were completely destroyed. Similar scenes played out in other towns and villages in the Chu and Talas regions of the North, where better-off minority families, including Uighurs and Dungans, found themselves targeted by poor Kyrgyz seeking to use the revolutionary moment to redistribute the country's wealth.

Where minorities were most susceptible to vigilante justice, a far wider circle of citizens suffered from the abuse of authority by the country's police and prosecutors. The April Revolution only heightened the sense of impunity long felt by Kyrgyzstan's law enforcement officials, who took advantage of the regime transition to settle political scores with those who had prospered under Bakiev and to extort bribes from the vulnerable, whatever their ethnic or regional background. As poorly paid civil servants, police and prosecutors in Kyrgyzstan, as in other developing societies, often supplemented their incomes by accepting money to release those who violated the law. What distinguished the aftermath of the April Revolution was the scale of the cases that were manufactured by police and prosecutors in order to pursue their own form of wealth distribution.

Although the Interim Government had granted one of its members, Azimbek Beknazarov, broad powers to manage the country's legal institutions, the actions of law enforcement officials had become so controversial in the first weeks after Bakiev's removal that the new government intervened and issued a special decree on April 30 designed to bring a halt to the wave of state-sanctioned intimidation and extortion. Introduced as a means of "unifying the population, eliminating social tension, and stabilizing the political situation in the country," the decree freed from criminal responsibility any government official or businessperson who had committed a wide range of illegal actions on the orders of superiors in the period from January 1, 1994, to April 7, 2010, as long as they cooperated with the authorities.[1] In addition, citizens surrendering weapons to the authorities by May 25—weapons that in many cases had been seized from government armories during the revolution— would also avoid prosecution. Among those let off the hook by the decree were law enforcement officials themselves. There would be no penalties for police or prosecutors who, under the encouragement of superiors, abused office for commercial gain or engaged in torture. Perhaps unknown to its members, in offering de facto pardons for torturers, the Interim Government was violating a fundamental principle of international law, and specifically Article 12 of the United Nations Convention Against Torture, to which Kyrgyzstan is a signatory.

A few days after the issuance of this decree, I received an invitation from the International Center for Transitional Justice in New York to join a small investigative team heading to Kyrgyzstan at the end of May. As I would soon learn, transitional justice was an umbrella term that covered a range of legal, political, and social mechanisms employed in societies where violent conflict and state repression produced widespread violations of human rights. The traditional components of transitional justice are truth seeking about the causes and consequences of social violence, often through truth and reconciliation commissions; reparations, which recognize the debt that society owes to the victims of persecution and violence; the criminal prosecution of senior officials responsible for repressive policies; and finally the reform of political and legal institutions in order to discourage a repeat of the violence. The task of the week-long mission was to assess the nature of the violence and social divisions in Kyrgyzstan as well as the receptiveness of the Interim Government to applying transitional justice approaches. As the country specialist on the mission, with a knowledge of Russian and the local legal and political environment, I worked with two experts in transitional justice who had extensive experience in conflict zones in Latin America and the former Yugoslavia.

As we were making preparations for the trip, the Bakiev family launched a countercoup in mid-May against the Interim Government by provoking a rebellion in their native region of Jalal-Abad. Taking a page from the opposition's playbook, the pro-Bakiev forces organized popular demonstrations and seized several government buildings in the South. The scene was chaotic and especially troubling for an Interim Government that lacked loyal local officials in Jalal-Abad or crack crowd-control units that could be deployed from Bishkek. Desperate to suppress the uprising, the Interim Government reportedly authorized Omurbek Tekebaev and his brother, who hailed from the region, to mobilize the local Uzbek population against the pro-Bakiev forces. At one point while helping to put down the revolt, an Uzbek posse seized the Bakiev family home and burned the Kyrgyzstani flag and a ceremonial yurt on the property. The Interim Government ultimately won the battle against the pro-Bakiev rebels, but the images of ethnic Uzbeks serving as a sword of the state and desecrating Kyrgyz cultural symbols enraged many Kyrgyz nationalists, especially those in the South. Within weeks the resentment unleashed by the events in Jalal-Abad would explode in inter-ethnic violence on a scale that Kyrgyzstan had not witnessed since June of 1990.

Exactly twenty years earlier, as the Soviet Union was collapsing, a land dispute between ethnic Kyrgyz and Uzbeks near the southern town of Uzgen had reached an impasse. Intervening on behalf of landless Kyrgyz who demanded parcels belonging to a collective farm populated by Uzbeks, the local authorities—themselves Kyrgyz—granted a portion of the *kolkhoz* to their co-ethnics. This decision ignited two days of inter-ethnic violence that was only halted by the intervention of the Soviet Army. Memories from the fighting haunted Kyrgyzstan as it emerged from Soviet rule, with images of Kyrgyz men on horseback arriving from the mountains to reinforce their local kin, combatants from both sides using knives, machetes, and other traditional weapons, and dead bodies floating in irrigation canals at the edge of the *kolkhoz*.[2]

It was hoped that the memory of this mass slaughter, where more than two hundred persons were killed, would serve to inoculate the country against a descent into another inferno. And yet little was done to bring about a genuine reconciliation between the Kyrgyz and Uzbek communities. With distinct positions in the national economy—the traditionally nomadic Kyrgyz were generally less successful in adapting to a more market-based economy than the traditionally sedentary Uzbeks—each side had deeply held grievances about their fate in an independent Kyrgyzstan. Ethnic Uzbeks resented the official and unofficial affirmative action policies that privileged ethnic Kyrgyz in government hiring, in education and language policy, and in political representation. With the country in turmoil in the wake of Bakiev's departure, some Uzbek leaders took advantage of the fluid political environment to demand expanded cultural rights for the Uzbeks. At the forefront of this effort was the prominent Uzbek businessman, Kadyrjon Batyrov, who had founded an Uzbek university in Jalal-Abad and now pushed for the expansion of Uzbek-language instruction in schools in areas of the South with large Uzbek populations.

For their part, many ethnic Kyrgyz found Uzbek demands for greater cultural and political expression both presumptuous and potentially dangerous for Kyrgyzstani sovereignty. There was already an Uzbekistan for the Uzbeks, they argued, and given the high concentration of Uzbeks living along Kyrgyzstan's border with its larger and more powerful neighbor, an increase in the rights afforded Kyrgyzstani Uzbeks could threaten the centrality of Kyrgyz language and culture in that part of the country. In neighboring Uzbekistan, they pointed out, the much smaller Kyrgyz minority found it far more difficult to advance economically and politically, or to retain their sense of identity, than Uzbeks did in Kyrgyzstan. Kyrgyz sensitivities on this issue derived in considerable measure from their perception that their small country had further to go to revive their language and culture than other post-Soviet states. As a result, what was needed, in their view, was not more minority rights but an even more prominent place for the majority people, many of whom languished at the margins of the national economy while minority groups like the Uzbeks appeared to enjoy a higher living standard.[3]

It was background of this kind on Kyrgyzstan's ethnic and regional divisions that I provided to my transitional justice colleagues as we settled into the Park Hotel in Bishkek on May 31 to begin an intensive week of interviewing. The Park is like no other hotel in Kyrgyzstan—modern, well-run, tastefully decorated, and reasonably priced—and for us it had the added advantage of being located across the street from what was then the headquarters of the Interim Government. Its competitor—and the standard option for government delegations or foreigners in Kyrgyzstan on business—was the Bishkek Hyatt, pronounced Hi-Yacht by the locals, unaware of the irony. The Hyatt occupied generous grounds at the edge of downtown, and its prominent security fence and guardhouse served as a point of contention at times with local authorities.[4] As the only Western hotel in the city, the Hyatt charged $300 and up for a room and surroundings that made you forget you were in Kyrgyzstan, which may have been attractive to some, but not to anyone curious about life in Central Asia.

Interviewing on a fact-finding mission for an international nongovernmental organization (INGO) was a departure from my normal research routine as a scholar. For one, I had a dual role as interpreter as well as questioner. Thankfully, a translator assigned to us handled most of the interpreting duties, though I often began the interviews with a Russian-language overview of the nature of transitional justice, a little-known concept in the West, never mind in Kyrgyzstan. My primary responsibility, however, was cultural interpretation, that is, adding the political and social context needed to understand the answers provided by our interviewees. Interviewing as a member of a foreign delegation also meant that the meetings were more formal and longer than I was used to. Waiting for—and at times correcting—the translations of responses from our interlocutors more than doubled the time required to conduct an interview. In addition, the mere presence of five persons in a room probing the openness of the country to transitional justice mechanisms prevented the development of a camaraderie between interviewer and interviewee that had marked many of my meetings with politicians and citizen activists in earlier visits.

We arrived on our mission in Kyrgyzstan with the acquiescence but not the blessing of the Interim Government, whose energies were focused on holding the country together and organizing a constitutional referendum that was less than a month away. Using its close connections to Acting President Roza Otunbaeva and members of her new staff, the local office of Soros' Open Society Institute arranged the invitation and helped to choreograph an intense meeting schedule that had us rushing from appointment to appointment, a total of twenty-six over the course of five days. Keeping to this demanding schedule was complicated by the city's arcane system of addresses, another legacy of the Soviet era. Especially for meetings with leaders of NGOs, whose offices were often located in residential apartment units, it was not enough to drive to the right street address. A single building number could contain a dozen or more separate entrances, usually accessible only from an inner courtyard rather than from the street. And finding the right entrance did not mean that the access keypad would work or that the name of the individual or institution would be present or decipherable on the keypad.

Changes in street names presented their own challenges for navigating around the capital. Most streets in Bishkek had two designations, a russified name from the Soviet era and a Kyrgyz name from the post-communist period. In a few cases, the street name had undergone more than one revision in the independence period; in other instances, local residents of whatever ethnic background continued to use the old Soviet reference. Merely stepping into a cab, therefore, was an exercise in language and cultural politics. If the driver appeared to be Russian, I used the Soviet-era name to identify my destination; if Kyrgyz, especially a Kyrgyz who seemed to be a recent arrival from the countryside, I provided instead the indigenized street name. My transitional justice colleagues were no doubt unaware of the code switching that went on as we took taxis to meetings across the city.

One of our first meetings was with the presidential chief of staff, Edil' Baisalov, who worked in a corner office of the parliament building, to which executive officials had been relocated from a White House badly damaged by the April violence. Walking past the broken windows and damaged gates of the White House on this visit was a stark reminder of the limited capacity of a young, poor state, which had not been able to repair the damage done almost two months earlier. Edil' Baisalov was an unlikely candidate for presidential chief of staff. Rather than a retiring behind-the-scenes organizer, Baisalov was a young political activist who loved the limelight. Exceptionally bright and a superb English speaker, Baisalov had the intensity of a 60s radical, and his critiques of the Bakiev regime became so pointed that he was among the numerous opposition figures who fled the country, in his case to Sweden, where he pursued graduate studies in post-communist affairs at Uppsala University. Returning to Kyrgyzstan in the days after the April rebellion, he clearly relished the role of vizier to a revolutionary government that was writing its own playbook.

Baisalov listened intently to my colleagues' explanations of how transitional justice mechanisms might be employed in Kyrgyzstan, but he exhibited some impatience when answering their questions about abuses in the legal system and the recent inter-ethnic violence. It was evident that he felt the Interim Government already had enough on its plate without embracing institutions like a truth commission, which could dredge up animosities that the Interim Government was trying to put behind it. Besides, a month earlier an independent commission consisting of leading civil society activists had presented its own findings about the April Revolution and its aftermath, and an official parliamentary inquiry into the events was already underway, with representatives from the government and civil society. In this environment, the prospects of employing internationally facilitated transitional justice mechanisms in Kyrgyzstan excited a few NGO leaders but government officials approached the idea with curiosity but little, if any, enthusiasm. Further complicating our talks with government officials was our institutional affiliation—emissaries from intergovernmental organizations like the UN or OSCE had an official status that we lacked as the representatives of an international NGO.

Among the several human rights activists we interviewed was Dmitrii Kabak, the head of an NGO called Open Viewpoint. With a mandate to collect information on violations of legality as well as inter-ethnic violence, my transitional justice colleagues were drawn to the descriptions and materials provided by Kabak on the arrest of a large group of observant Muslims in the southern town of Nookat in October 2008.[5] In the wake of the Tulip Revolution of 2005, Muslims in Kyrgyzstan were allowed for the first time to organize public celebrations to mark Eid al-Fitr, the end of the holy month of Ramadan. In the fall of 2008, however, as the Bakiev regime tightened its grip on the country, local officials in Nookat cancelled at the last minute a planned celebration at a local sports stadium. When celebrants gathered in the vicinity, they were attacked by the police, with dozens taken to local jails, many on suspicion of belonging to the banned Muslim organization, Hizb ut-

Tahrir. Numerous witnesses reported that while detained, the State Committee for National Security, Kyrgyzstan's secret police, subjected the suspects to physical and psychological torture ranging from beatings and sleep deprivation to ethnically based humiliation. Jailed Uzbeks, who accounted for the vast majority of those detained, were forced to learn the Kyrgyz-language version of the national anthem and sing it five times a day. If any episode should be the focus of a truth commission, Kabak argued, it was the repression of observant Muslims in Nookat. Interviews with Kabak and other civil society activists provided evidence of widespread human rights violations that were all too familiar to my two transitional justice colleagues, who had experience in some of the world's most violence-prone states.

Given the nature of the questions we posed about past and present interethnic conflict and abuse of power by state legal institutions, it was unsurprising that our interviews provoked two different reactions. Local NGO organizations that monitored state behavior welcomed us with open arms, seeing us as partners in their efforts to unearth past wrongdoing and hold the Interim Government to account. On the other hand, representatives of state institutions, who included Kyrgyzstan's chief prosecutor and its minister of justice, tended to give us a chilly reception, offering responses that were for the most part laconic and defensive. They clearly had other priorities. The prosecutor's office, for example, gave me a list of thirty-six leading members of the Bakiev administration that had recently been indicted in absentia or placed under house arrest. The first six names on the list were members of the Bakiev family.[6]

One law enforcement official, however, greeted us warmly: Bolot Sherniiazov, the head of the Ministry of Internal Affairs (MVD) which oversaw the regular police force. A native of Talas, Sherniiazov was the opposition leader whose arrest in his hometown ignited the April uprising. In the wake of this event he shortened his name to Sher, meaning mountain lion in Kyrgyz, as a way of promoting his image as a popular hero. Imprisoned by the police on April 6, he became the leader of the police the following day.

Sher was not well when we visited him at MVD headquarters on Saturday morning, June 5, our last day in Bishkek. He had recently suffered a heart attack and two strokes, and as a result had submitted his resignation to Roza Otunbaeva, but she refused to accept it. Speaking with Sher for just a few minutes, we understood why. In an institution known for its corruption and lack of professionalism, he was a breath of fresh air. His diagnosis of the ills of the MVD and the police force under it was frank and disturbing. He estimated that only about 70 percent of the staff were loyal to the Interim Government and insisted that it would take at least five years to reform the institution. Undermining the professionalism of the force, in his view, were clan and tribal loyalties; miserly salaries in the ministry, which averaged only about $250 per month; the penetration of some segments of the MVD by criminal elements; and the low educational level of ministerial personnel. He believed that 70 percent of his staff would have failed their entrance exams if they had been properly scored, an indication of the widespread bribery that allowed many state employees to buy their way into their positions.[7]

As part of his ambitious reform agenda for the ministry, Sher had already closed down the MVD's Ninth Department, which the Bakiev regime had used to persecute the political opposition. He was also moving the ministry away from a heavy reliance on statistical indicators to assess the performance of MVD personnel, which had distorted policing practice for decades. Inspired by the Republic of Georgia's experiment in law enforcement, which he learned about on a US government–sponsored junket to Washington, Sher also proposed sending one hundred promising young police supervisors to the United States for training in an English-language environment. If we continue to rely on Russian as our international language, he argued, we will remain exposed to the worst policing practices emanating from the Russian Federation.

Sher recognized that there were political limits to rapid reform. He revealed to us that he had already removed all of his deputy ministers carried over from the Bakiev era and many of the heads of regional and district MVD offices, but he needed to fire additional high-ranking personnel in the ministry. He didn't dare carry out these personnel changes, however, until the constitutional referendum had passed, lest jilted officials mobilize their kinship and regional networks to vote against the new constitution. In response to our questions about holding police accountable for torturing suspects, he recognized the need for justice to be done, but he said that they were having a hard time prosecuting officials for fabricating cases against innocent citizens, so "how can we talk about bringing charges in cases as sensitive as torture?" The interview with Sher was a sobering reminder that even with the best of intentions, Kyrgyzstani officials pushing reform met resistance at every turn.

Despite the language barriers and the cultural specificities of Kyrgyzstan, my transitional justice colleagues had little trouble connecting with the interviewees, with one exception. He was Duishon Abdyldaev, a Muslim activist who was a member of the Constituent Assembly, which had issued less than two weeks earlier the final constitutional draft to be put before the nation in late June. Wearing a skull cap and an impenetrable gaze, Abdyldaev seemed intent on expressing as little emotion as possible as he answered our questions in slowly delivered, carefully formed sentences. His major concern was that, over his fierce objections, the new constitution would reaffirm Kyrgyzstan's status as a secular state. Insisting that a Muslim-majority society like Kyrgyzstan was obliged to accept Islamic law as its foundation, he was uninterested in ameliorative measures advanced by foreigners or Western-oriented Kyrgyz to fight injustice when the embrace of Islamic principles would itself assure a just society.

Engaging in a conversation focused on mechanisms that introduced incremental change made little sense to Abdyldaev, and so for the first and only time in our week of interviews, there was no meeting of the minds on even minor matters. It was as if we had entered a parallel universe where virtually all of our assumptions about political, economic, and cultural institutions were contested by our interviewee. As non-Muslims, we avoided, however, the standards to which he subjected his co-religionists during interviews. On entering a room to interview Abdyldaev, a Kyrgyz journalist had greeted him with "How are you doing?" Abdyldaev asked him to exit the room and reenter, this time with the appropriate Muslim greeting: "Assalamu alaikum."[8]

In a week full of troubling revelations from government officials, NGO activists, and local representatives of international organizations, such as the UN and OSCE, among the most disturbing were accusations of corruption and retribution by certain members of the Interim Government. It was the rare interview where the word *mest'*—or revenge—did not figure prominently in the descriptions of the actions of the new government, whether related to the removal or prosecution of officials who had worked under Bakiev. Even some public figures who were seen as insufficiently critical of Bakiev were targeted for retribution. In mid-May, the authorities arrested Iskhak Masaliev, the leader of Kyrgyzstan's small Communist Party and the son of the last Communist Party first secretary of Soviet Kirgizia. A southerner who had not joined the opposition to Bakiev, Masaliev was suspected of collaborating with the Bakiev family in plotting the abortive countercoup launched in May in Jalal-Abad, though the evidence of his involvement was circumstantial at best. One interviewee claimed that the Interim Government finance tsar, Temir Sariev, had remarked to her that "Masaliev had to suffer like we did."[9]

Prominent civil society activists, including Nazgul Turdubekova and Cholpon Jakupova, accused some Interim Government members of taking bribes, in one case to arrange free passage out of the country for Bakiev's prime minister, Daniiar Usenov, in others to release suspects arrested on trumped-up charges. We also heard claims that some leaders of the Interim Government shook down businesses, in one instance forcing the concession of an ownership share in a successful company. Protests by these businesses that they had had no choice but to work with the Bakiev regime fell on deaf ears. In the two months that separated the April uprising from the adoption of a new constitution, what the Soviets had called "revolutionary legality" seemed to rule, with some individuals in power using this interregnum to settle scores and fill their own bank accounts.

Unable to fit a trip to the South into our schedule, we arranged a teleconference with representatives of four human rights groups based in Jalal-Abad on the day before our departure. Working at the geographical epicenter of resistance to the policies introduced by the Interim Government, the southern activists perceived an acute need for more careful monitoring of the justice system and for educational measures to build trust between the local Kyrgyz and Uzbek communities in the South. They expressed no concerns, however, that relations between southern Kyrgyz and Uzbeks were on the verge of descending into the kind of inter-ethnic violence that plagued the North in recent months and prompted our mission to Kyrgyzstan.

After drafting a preliminary report in the waning hours of our mission, we left a country still on edge in the early morning of June 6.[10] Although the population had settled back into its daily routines after the April Revolution, there was growing uncertainty about the upcoming referendum and rumors persisted about an impending attempt by the Bakiev family to reclaim power through another popular uprising. Some reports even provided a precise date, June 22, just five days before the scheduled referendum.[11] Those rumors—like many others circulating at the time—proved false, but another event, unforeseen by us or any of those with whom we spoke, soon presented the young nation with its greatest test since independence. A mere four days after our departure, Kyrgyzstan descended into a bacchanalia of violence between Kyrgyz and Uzbeks in Osh.

Chapter Nineteen

June 2010

The Month That Remade a Country

The long-neglected capital of Kyrgyzstan's South, the city of Osh, lies at the eastern end of the Ferghana Valley, a densely settled agricultural region divided among Kyrgyzstan, Tajikistan, and Uzbekistan. A predominantly Uzbek settlement for centuries, Osh absorbed increasing numbers of ethnic Kyrgyz after Soviet authorities placed the city just inside the borders of the newly established Kirgiz Socialist Republic in the 1930s. While the Kyrgyz moved into newly built highrise apartments on Osh's periphery in the second half of the twentieth century, ethnic Uzbeks continued to live in their own quarters, the *mahallas*, in the historic city center. Running off the wide Soviet-era streets were narrow passages, some still unpaved, that wound through the *mahallas*, whose residents lived as multigenerational families in one-story walled compounds that would have been familiar to any visitor from a traditional Muslim country.[1]

Frustrated by the prominence of ethnic Uzbeks in Osh, whose western edge abutted the Uzbekistani border, local Kyrgyz leaders had searched for ways to assert the city's Kyrgyz identity. Through demographic gerrymandering—redrawing the city's borders to absorb adjoining Kyrgyz villages while detaching Uzbek-dominated neighborhoods along the periphery—ethnic Kyrgyz finally outnumbered Uzbeks in Osh in the 2009 census. Proposals for urban renewal projects called for the replacement of the largely monoethnic *mahallas* with modern residential neighborhoods inhabited by a mix of ethnic groups. Kyrgyz nationalists also sought to diminish the status of the Uzbeks living in Osh by referring to them as a diaspora, that is, a people living outside its original homeland. Local Uzbeks took offense at this label, noting that it was not they who had moved but the borders. Moreover, the

Bakiev regime had placed new barriers in the way of Uzbek-language education and cultural expression in the South, and so when the April Revolution emboldened Uzbeks to push back against their cultural and political marginalization, many Kyrgyz resented the newfound confidence of local Uzbeks.

In the early days of June 2010, altercations between groups of young Kyrgyz and Uzbek men in the South of Kyrgyzstan began to increase in frequency and intensity. With both communities on edge, the police struggled to quell fights between ethnic gangs, some driven by criminal turf wars unleashed by the collapse of the Bakiev power structure and, on June 7, the murder of an Uzbek criminal kingpin known to all as Black Aibek.[2] On Thursday evening, June 10, a disagreement between groups of Kyrgyz and Uzbek youth in a casino in the center of Osh quickly escalated into a confrontation along ethnic lines between hundreds of young men. With each side prepared to believe the worst about the actions and motives of the other, rumors began to circulate that local Uzbek men were raping young Kyrgyz women living in a nearby university dormitory. Through text messages that were the lifeblood of modern communications in Kyrgyzstan, word of this alleged sexual violence spread rapidly to local Kyrgyz and to the families of female students living in districts throughout southern Kyrgyzstan. As Kyrgyz men from mountain settlements set off for Osh, Uzbeks began to erect barricades at the entrances to their *mahallas*.

Reports of the impromptu mobilization of the two ethnic communities in Osh and surrounding territories reached the Interim Government in Bishkek around midnight, prompting an emergency cabinet meeting at 2:00 a.m. on Friday, July 11. Shortly after dawn that morning, a small delegation dispatched by the Interim Government flew into Osh to assess the conditions on the ground and to restore order. Headed by the Interim Government's defense chief, the southerner Ismail Isakov, the group arrived amid renewed confrontations between Kyrgyz and Uzbeks that only grew in intensity as the day progressed. Whatever steps were taken by Isakov and the uniformed personnel under his command—and those remain in dispute—they were inadequate to prevent a mass slaughter of innocent civilians in Osh and the spread of the violence to adjoining districts as well as the city of Jalal-Abad, sixty-five miles away.

Deeply distrustful of the Kyrgyz-dominated army and police, local Uzbeks set up roadblocks at strategic intersections, strengthened the barricades leading to their neighborhoods, and armed themselves with hunting rifles and other weapons. Many young Kyrgyz and Uzbek men died in confrontations on the streets, but the most savage violence against innocent civilians resulted from ethnic Kyrgyz groups marauding through the *mahallas*, some taunting Uzbek residents with cries of "Sarts," a term of derision reserved for urban residents of Central Asia.[3] Whether out of fear, poor training, or sympathy with their Kyrgyz peers, some personnel in the police and armed forces abandoned their positions and their weapons to the crowd, including several armored personnel carriers (APCs). Some reports insisted that Kyrgyz uniformed personnel became active participants in the violence.

On Friday, shortly after *Asr*, the afternoon prayer, Kyrgyz manning APCs broke through the barricades to the Cheremushki *mahalla* near the city center. A few Kyrgyz and Russians living in the *mahalla* were able to shelter Uzbek families from the onslaught, but most Uzbek residents either fled for their lives or were terrorized in their own homes. Rampaging groups of Kyrgyz youth often torched the Uzbek homes they entered, and in one case an entire family died in a fire while hiding in their basement. Of the six family members killed, three were children and one was a woman over seventy years of age.[4]

Just as in the northern village of Maevka two months earlier, members of the majority ethnic group used a collapse in public order to expropriate the wealth of minority families, with women as well as men among the perpetrators. Although much of the violence erupted spontaneously, and many Kyrgyz died as a result of brutal attacks on the streets by young Uzbeks, because of their superior numbers Kyrgyz were able to conduct systematic assaults on Uzbek homes in the *mahallas*, targeting the lives and property of innocent civilians of all ages. Once the APCs had cleared a path into Uzbek neighborhoods, angry Kyrgyz youth broke down the large gates securing Uzbek residences, attacked the individuals inside, and then looted the property. In many cases, middle-aged Kyrgyz women arrived in the wake of the initial assaults to coordinate the theft of household valuables, which were removed to waiting vans or KAMAZ trucks.

The sheer exhaustion of the combatants and occasional rumors of intervention by outside powers provided some breaks in the hostilities, with young Kyrgyz men temporarily retreating from the *mahallas* when they heard reports of the impending arrival of Uzbekistani troops. As Felix Kulov reminded me a few weeks after the violence, if Uzbekistani President Islam Karimov had not restrained his countrymen from crossing the border to assist their co-ethnics under assault, there would have been a total bloodbath and a full-scale war between the countries of Kyrgyzstan and Uzbekistan. For that, Kulov observed, "we have to give Karimov his due."[5]

Unlike in 1990, when the Soviet military intervened, no outside forces arrived to quell the violence, and the Kyrgyzstani uniformed services only appeared to regain control of the streets once the passions of the crowds had been exhausted. Whether because of the incompetence or complicity of law enforcement organs, or the indecisiveness of the country's leaders in Bishkek, who initially refused to allow soldiers and police to fire on civilians, half of the deaths from the inter-ethnic conflict occurred in Osh on Saturday and Sunday, June 12 and 13, that is, more than twenty-four hours after the hostilities began. The absence of foreign troops was not for lack of an official invitation. On Saturday, desperate to halt the violence, President Otunbaeva wrote to Russia's President Dmitrii Medvedev:

> From yesterday evening the situation [in Osh] has gotten out of control and we need the intervention of foreign forces to gain the upper hand. As a result, we are turning to Russia for help.[6]

Reluctant to be drawn into what Medvedev's spokeswoman called an "internal conflict," Russia deployed a battalion of several hundred paratroopers on Sunday to its base in Kant, just outside Bishkek, but the move was only designed, according to the Russians, to beef up base security at a time of crisis. Russia did promise to raise the issue of peacekeeping troops on Monday with the other members of the Collective Security Treaty Organization, a regional security body that included both Russia and Kyrgyzstan. By then, however, the violence was all but over, and the Interim Government was less keen to sacrifice its sovereignty by having Russian troops patrolling the streets of southern Kyrgyzstan.[7]

As the smoke cleared and bodies were being buried, the residents of Osh and surrounding communities confronted the staggering costs of four days of inter-ethnic violence: 470 persons killed, more than 2,000 wounded, and 2,700 homes and businesses destroyed. The toll was highest in the Uzbek community, which accounted for three-quarters of the dead and the lion's share of the property damage, though significantly more Kyrgyz than Uzbeks were wounded. Thanks to modern satellite technology, it was in many ways easier to assess the damage to property than the loss of life. In the immediate aftermath of the conflict, UNOSAT, the United Nations satellite imagery division, published photographs of the city of Osh that illustrated the precise scale and location of the destruction, with whole swaths of Uzbek *mahallas* lying within the "damage clusters" on the satellite images.

For days, haunting photographs from Osh filled the internet and the pages of the world's press. Some portrayed the damaged houses that occasionally bore the spray-painted label of the ethnic background of the family living there. "KG" appeared on houses whose occupants hoped to be spared by Kyrgyz youth who were targeting Uzbeks; "SOS" was visible on the outside walls and roofs of some Uzbek houses, whose occupants hoped to be saved by foreign troops. Other images captured the difficulty that local authorities had in dealing with the dead. Makeshift morgues cropped up on the streets, with bodies wrapped in bedding and placed on prayer rugs. Photographs from the Kyrgyzstan-Uzbekistan border revealed long lines of Uzbek women in wildly colored satin robes and head scarves trying to escape the violence with their children and aged parents. In order to minimize civilian deaths during the violence, President Otunbaeva had opened the border with Uzbekistan, and over 100,000 Kyrgyzstani Uzbeks found temporary refuge there.

The violence displaced another 300,000 persons inside Kyrgyzstan itself, so that in the wake of the Osh events, almost 10 percent of Kyrgyzstan's population were refugees.

An information war with competing narratives of the Osh events accompanied the physical battles on the ground. In what became the dominant interpretation of the conflict, advanced initially in Uzbek-controlled news outlets and then embraced by most international observers, the blame for the massive violence lay disproportionately on the Kyrgyz side. Some commentators even likened the assaults on the Uzbek community to genocide.

The Kyrgyz would have none of it. In their view, Uzbeks were the primary instigators of the violence, and so there was no need to accept responsibility for acts of commission by local Kyrgyz or acts of omission by the Interim Government. The co-leader of a prominent political party with its base in the South told me shortly after the violence that Uzbeks had been stockpiling weapons for some time. "For the last two years," he insisted, "for every 200 high-caliber hunting rifles sold in gun shops in the South, 199 had been purchased by Uzbeks and only one by a Kyrgyz."[8] He claimed to have seen with his own eyes the naked, mutilated, and violated bodies of young Kyrgyz women that had been thrown three floors to the street below their dormitory, an assertion for which international investigators subsequently found no corroborating evidence.[9] Even the most highly educated and politically moderate Kyrgyz were often prepared to accept uncritically outlandish explanations of Uzbek conspiracies that led to the violence. With each side wedded to its own narrative, which absolved it of responsibility for the violence, there was no opening for a truth commission or other forms of reconciliation that would bring the two communities together.

In the wake of the June events, the growing international criticism of the Kyrgyz only heightened an already strong sense of victimization in the Kyrgyz community. When an international commission headed by a Finnish diplomat published its conclusions on the violence a year later, the government attacked what it regarded as the report's tendency to portray Uzbeks as defenseless victims. The parliament then voted by a large majority to declare the Finnish commission chair persona non grata.

In the informational fog that surrounds such events, commenting from afar on the course of hostilities, never mind opining on the causes of the violence, is a hazardous undertaking. Yet scholars have an obligation to use their expertise to provide the backstory behind outbreaks of mass violence. Two days after hostilities began I received a call from Al Jazeera English Service in Qatar, a network that provides sophisticated and detailed coverage of developments in Central Asia and the Middle East. Appearing by Skype at the top of that evening's TV newscast, I sought to explain the confluence of factors that contributed to the inter-ethnic conflict in Osh, among them a weak state, a more assertive Uzbek community, and frustrated southern Kyrgyz, whose native son had been deposed and whose views of the proper place of Uzbeks were being challenged by the actions of the Interim Government. In subsequent interviews with the Canadian and Australian broadcasting companies, I emphasized that countries having a combination of strong ethnic identities and the virtual absence of an overarching loyalty to the state were often incubators for political conflict. Such a mixture creates a favorable environment for "ethnic entrepreneurs" who seek to stoke inter-ethnic tensions as a means of advancing their own careers.

The Osh events generated not only competing journalistic narratives about who was responsible for the violence but also diverse academic assessments of the causes of the conflict. By highlighting ethnicity as a lens through which Kyrgyzstani citizens viewed the world around them, I was employing an interpretive framework that has become less popular in academic circles in recent decades. In discussing the causes of the violence in Osh, Alexander Cooley noted that he "didn't believe in a narrative of long-simmering ethnic tension." Cooley and other scholars interviewed for an article in the *New York Times* on June 15 argued that "ethnic distinctions between Uzbeks and Kyrgyz are so slight as to be hardly distinguishable. . . . [b]oth are predominantly Muslim and they speak a mutually comprehensible Turkic language."[10] In fact, differences in language, housing, dress, and other cultural markers did serve as identifiers of the two ethnic groups.

In the view of Cooley and many others, the violence grew out of a class conflict between the rich and poor, a conflict that had its origins in the earlier nomadic versus sedentary lifestyles of the Kyrgyz and Uzbeks and the ways in which those traditions positioned the two groups in the modern economy. Although it is certainly true that economic resentment played a role in the hostilities, it did not trigger the violence nor determine its targets. The enemies for poor Kyrgyz youth rampaging through the *mahallas* were not rich Kyrgyz but Uzbeks of any economic class. Russians in Osh were not targets of either side. In short, ethnic loyalty mattered more than class loyalty, or perhaps more accurately, ethnic enmity trumped class enmity, a lesson that I learned from my own childhood in the segregated South. Living in a society deeply divided along racial or ethnic lines illustrates the limitations of economic analysis.

Having been the primary targets of rioters during the inter-ethnic violence, Uzbeks in southern Kyrgyzstan now emerged as the main subjects of criminal prosecutions filed in the wake of the June events. International human rights groups warned that the Uzbek population was being victimized again, this time at the hands of Kyrgyz state officials, many of whom seemed intent on extorting money from the accused, protecting their kith and kin from prosecution, and supporting the narrative of Uzbeks as the primary perpetrators of the violence. Law enforcement statistics revealed that 79 percent of those facing criminal charges were Uzbeks while only 18 percent were Kyrgyz; of the twenty-seven murder cases opened, twenty-four had Uzbek defendants. The ethnic breakdown of those arrested illustrated a similar ethnic imbalance: 230 Uzbeks, 39 Kyrgyz, and 2 persons of other ethnic backgrounds.[11] Put generously, state authorities did not pursue the transparent and evenhanded criminal investigations that specialists in transitional justice would have ordered for a conflict zone.

As police completed controversial mopping-up operations in small Uzbek-dominated settlements around Osh,[12] the Interim Government turned its attention to the constitutional referendum that was less than two weeks away. Numerous local NGOs and international organizations urged the Interim Government to postpone the voting, arguing that the country needed time to recover from the national trauma and to resettle the large number of internal refugees. However, postponement of the referendum was a luxury that the fragile Interim Government felt it could not afford. It desperately needed a popular mandate to shore up its waning authority at a time of crisis, and so it insisted on adhering to its original timetable for the reestablishment of democratic rule, the first step of which was the June 27th referendum.

Assuring a successful referendum required a few unusual measures. Because the existing electoral law did not permit voting to occur during a state of emergency, which had been declared during the inter-ethnic violence, President Otunbaeva lifted the state of emergency before the polls opened and reinstated it at ten o'clock the same evening, shortly after the polls closed. To accommodate citizens displaced by the violence, the authorities allowed voters to cast their ballots in any electoral precinct in the country. In order to discourage repeat voting, they revived the practice of inking fingers for this election. Finally, the Central Election Commission composed a ballot that contained three distinct questions bound into a single option, for which voters had to give a "yes" or "no" response: do you accept the new constitution, confirm Roza Otunbaeva as Kyrgyzstan's president, and approve the firing of the justices of the Constitutional Court? By denying citizens the right to split their vote, this all-or-nothing ballot enhanced the chances that the Interim Government would achieve all of its goals in the referendum.

Despite some voting irregularities and doubts about the accuracy of the voter rolls, election day seemed to surprise all observers, foreign and domestic. Conditions were peaceful, voters showed up in large numbers, and, if the official electoral statistics can be believed, there was broad support for the Interim Government's proposals. Voter turnout was over 72 percent and more than 90 percent of those casting ballots approved the referendum.[13] Having won their high-stakes gamble, members of the Interim Government now began to turn their attention from governing to politicking. The most important parliamentary elections in the country's history were only four months away.

Chapter Twenty

"We Either Have Fair Elections, or We Have Violence"

While Osh and its environs descended into chaos in mid-June, I was making final preparations for a long-planned trip to Kyrgyzstan to introduce the country to my wife and younger daughter and to wrap up research on the opposition to Bakiev's rule. As a scholar, following the dramatic events in Kyrgyzstan from afar prompted concerns for the country's future as well as a host of research questions about the transition to a new regime. As a husband and father, tracking developments in Kyrgyzstan aroused a different senti-ment altogether: apprehension about the wisdom of taking my family into the political whirlwind. To hedge our bets, we planned alternative itineraries through Istanbul, and it was only after two days in Turkey that we decided that conditions had improved sufficiently in Kyrgyzstan to allow us to ven-ture on to Bishkek together.

With its immense, modern airport in Istanbul and its self-declared role as the leader of the far-flung Turkic-speaking world, Turkey had emerged in the post-communist era as a competitor to Moscow as the gateway to Central Asia. Both Moscow and Istanbul exude the grandeur of imperial capitals, but as we rode the ferry up the Bosporus, and climbed to a promontory on the Asian side, with its dramatic views of the Black Sea to the north, it was difficult not to conclude that Turkey's largest city had an even richer trove of sights and sounds than its Russian counterpart. While plying the Bosporus that day, I tried to imagine what was running through the minds of Soviet sailors in earlier decades as they passed through the narrow straits separating Europe from Asia, eyeing the miles of elegant residences overlooking the water. Even without entering the palaces, mosques, and markets that are the pride of Istanbul, they would have found it hard to square what they saw with what they had heard in their country about the lower level of development of their southern neighbor.

Flying Turkish Airlines for five-and-a-half hours to Bishkek exposed Turkey's position as a country between East and West, traditionalism and modernity. Boasting impeccable food and service in the cabin, and pilots whose English was honed in NATO training exercises, Turkish Airlines offered a far more pleasant flying experience than American carriers. Yet at times the differences were not in the airline's favor. One such moment occurred as we were landing in Bishkek in the early morning hours of Friday, July 16. The flight attendants circulated through the cabin reminding passengers to fasten their seat belts for landing. A young Turkish father toward the front of the plane refused to strap in his young daughter, despite a mildly worded objection from a flight attendant, who was in a position to see an accident waiting to happen. Seconds after landing, as the pilot applied the brakes more firmly than usual, the girl hurtled forward, head first, into the seat in front of her, mercifully without suffering serious injury. Instead of expressing concern for the welfare of the child, the father berated her for not staying in her seat.

Even though the airport at Bishkek had undergone recent renovations, and it was now possible to deplane using a jetway rather than descending to the tarmac, once inside the terminal passengers still had to carry luggage down two flights of stairs. As we passed the first landing, my daughter looked up to see a sign in English bearing my name, held by a stranger. With the other passengers continuing down the stairs, he shepherded us into a VIP lounge where he took our passports for processing and asked for our beverage order. It was a welcome—and a visit—like no other in my two-decade experience in Kyrgyzstan, made possible by members of the Interim Government who were intent on extending the red carpet to a scholar and his family willing to visit a country at one of its darkest hours.

Entering the Park Hotel with my wife and daughter just before 3:00 a.m., I saw the familiar face of the desk clerk, who said with a broad smile, "Welcome Back to the Park." After a few hours of sleep, we walked past the White House to find broken windows dotting the upper floors and the iron fence surrounding the grounds still mangled in places. Near the gates facing Chu Prospect, makeshift memorials with photos of those killed during the April Revolution had been replaced since my visit the previous month by a permanent plaque with the names of the dead. As I headed off to conduct interviews, my wife and daughter visited the Historical Museum next door, where a hastily curated exhibit on the overthrow of Bakiev had just opened.

Besides the occasional physical reminders of the recent violence in Kyrgyzstan's capital, the city gave little indication of having been through dramatic political upheavals in recent months. The only residual discontent evident in Bishkek came from the families of the dead and wounded in the April Revolution, who sought to claim for themselves generous financial support from the government as well as a special voice in policy-making. Returning to the hotel one afternoon, my wife and daughter encountered an angry group of demonstrators demanding justice for the victims of the April Revolution, whose families would ultimately receive from the government a free apartment and one million soms each (about $20,000).

Although I was not overly concerned about our physical safety during the stay, Kubatbek Baibolov, the recently appointed head of the MVD, took no chances. Generously offering to serve as our patron for the trip, he had arranged the special airport reception and then provided transportation around the city and to Lake Issyk-Kul', usually with his official car and driver. Coming out of the hotel on the second day of our stay, we found a black, oversized Mercedes waiting for us. The license plate read MVD 100. As we rode in style across northern Kyrgyzstan, our college-aged daughter reveled in the surprised looks of passersby when they spied the license. Even more striking was the reaction of the traffic police, who man guard posts at entrances to the city and at strategic locations along the highways. The much-reviled traffic cops stand alongside the roadways pulling over cars with a demonstrative wave of their black-and-white striped batons, sometimes for infractions, sometimes for no particular reason except to collect a small bribe, and then send drivers on their way. On several occasions while we were driving at speed past the guard posts, police would angrily motion us over with their batons, only to spot the license, which caused them to snap sharply to attention and to raise their batons stiffly in the air as a sign of deference to their superiors.

In many other ways, this stay exposed my wife and daughter to a side of Kyrgyz life that I had rarely, if ever, experienced on earlier research or consulting visits. On one of our first nights in Bishkek, we decided to go to the outskirts of the city to eat dinner at one of the grand, gaudy restaurants that lined Tokombaev Street, the closest thing in Kyrgyzstan to the Las Vegas strip. Accompanied by Gulnara Iskakova and her husband, Timur, we shunned the glaringly bright banquet hall, adorned with garish statues evoking ancient Babylon, for a large table in a dimly lit corner of the patio. We had just begun to order when Gulnara received a text from Roza Otunbaeva, now president of the country. Within minutes a small fleet of official-looking cars pulled up and Roza hurried over to join us at the table, which was soon surrounded by expressionless men in bulging jackets. Ever the diplomat and politician, Roza greeted my wife and daughter effusively, recalling her visit to our house many years earlier in Florida and noting how much our daughter had matured since then. It was a far cry from my previous meeting with Roza when, as an opposition leader uncertain of her political and personal future, she had prepared a simple dinner for me in her apartment in a Stalinist-era building on Erkindik.

It may not have seemed the time or place for a serious discussion of politics, but in Kyrgyzstan in the wake of the April Revolution, the subject was on everyone's lips. Roza's lighthearted demeanor changed rapidly as she began to raise concerns about the rise of armed militias attached to increasingly popular southern Kyrgyz politicians, such as Kamchibek Tashiev. A general and former head of the Ministry of Extraordinary Situations, Tashiev had assembled a group of one thousand highly trained men who were personally loyal to him. Roza worried that the current forces available to her were no match for such militias, and she believed that the only solution was for the United States to help Kyrgyzstan train a small, effective domestic strike force, as she understood we had done in the Republic of Georgia. She also revealed her plans to dismiss peremptorily a large number of corrupt and politically compromised judges, a measure that Gulnara and I immediately questioned on the grounds of its legality and political wisdom. I promised to send her a copy of the report I had cowritten for the International Center for Transitional Justice, which laid out in detail international best practices for vetting and dismissing judges during regime transitions.

Curious about the reaction Roza received from Russia when she requested assistance during the inter-ethnic violence the previous month, I asked her how President Medvedev had justified his refusal to intervene. Medvedev insisted, she said, that Russia already had its hands full in South Ossetia, the breakaway Georgian territory occupied by Russia during the 2008 war, and it did not wish to assume other open-ended commitments. It seemed an unlikely response by the Russian president, and I wondered if Roza was being forthcoming with me. There were many other plausible explanations, such as resistance from other members of the Collective Security Treaty Organization, most notably from neighboring Uzbekistan, which would not have been keen to see Russian troops patrolling in Uzbek neighborhoods only a few miles from its border.

As it turned out, Russia's rejection of Roza's request greatly simplified her leadership in the transition toward a more competitive political system. In the wake of the April Revolution, President Medvedev and other Russian leaders had repeatedly condemned Kyrgyzstan's plans to introduce a parliamentary republic, fearing that the development of a genuinely democratic country in Central Asia would complicate Russian foreign policy in the region and serve as an inspiration for reform-minded forces in Russia itself. Had Russia intervened with peacekeeping forces, Moscow's heightened political influence in the country would almost certainly have altered significantly Kyrgyzstan's developmental path.

Later that week, we had dinner with another politician in a very different setting. Bolot Sher, Baibolov's predecessor as MVD chief and the hero of opposition forces in Talas in April, invited us to his house to share a meal with his family. Arriving at dusk to find a plainclothes security guard standing outside Sher's residence, we were ushered through an expansive and tasteful house to a dining pavilion in the back garden, a common feature of Kyrgyz homes. Under the pavilion was a large table surrounded by a raised platform covered in carpets, designed to replicate traditional dining on the floor. Joined by his wife and children, who were not much younger than our daughter, Sher presided at the head of a table that was filled with cherries, apricots, and other fresh fruits, cut-up pieces of naan, and bowls of *lagman*, a popular dish in Kyrgyzstan that combines meat, vegetables, and noodles in a hearty broth.

Still weakened by a heart ailment that had forced him to retire temporarily from politics and government service, Sher was nonetheless a formidable presence. On this occasion, he steered the conversation away from current events and toward the challenges facing young people throughout the world. As we moved back and forth between Russian and English—his son and daughter were already quite proficient in English—he pushed his own children and my daughter to speak about how they imagined the future and their place in it, not an easy subject for a person of any age. As we were finishing dinner, the distinctive crackle of gunfire could be heard nearby, but Sher dismissed it as harmless after the security guard came inside to whisper something in his ear. It was the only dissonant note in the kind of encounter that makes work in foreign lands so enticing: two families from different traditions sharing food and conversation outside on a pleasant summer evening. As an American, I always left such meals with a sense of indebtedness that could not be repaid, knowing that despite our best efforts, we could never match in our own homes the generous hospitality accorded to us in Central Asia.

Several days later, Kubatbek Baibolov arranged yet another dinner for us, this time in the presidential compound south of the city, a sprawling collection of buildings where the president lived with several other members of the country's political elite. Because the rapid descent to Bishkek by car from Lake Issyk-Kul' earlier that day had left our daughter feeling unwell, I headed out alone to the dinner. I had driven by the high walls of the presidential complex on numerous occasions on my way to Ala-Archa National Park, but this was my first time inside the gently rolling grounds, whose thick stands of pine trees and haphazardly arranged low buildings gave the place the air of a summer camp. Shortly after passing through the guardhouse, whose personnel waved Baibolov's car through routinely, I spotted a middle-aged man walking toward us on the opposite side of the narrow asphalt roadway. As we passed, I recognized him as the head of the country's secret police, Keneshbek Duishebaev. He was taking his evening constitutional, followed at a close distance by a young bodyguard in uniform with an automatic weapon at the ready.

Entering an empty restaurant and banquet hall in the presidential compound, the contrast between the simple exterior of the building and the elegant furnishings inside could not have been more dramatic. After I sat down with Baibolov and several of his colleagues at an oversized round table, handsomely dressed waiters presented us with a custom-made menu for the evening, which in the still current usage from the Soviet era promised European rather than national—meaning in this case Kyrgyz—cuisine. With waiters hovering nearby during the dinner, and simultaneously lifting the domed metal dish covers from our entrees, it was hard to square the formal meal service with the rough and tumble political world in which those partaking of such dinners operated. Just a few weeks earlier, Baibolov had been called back from self-imposed exile in the United States to serve as commandant of Jalal-Abad, a city under siege by warring Kyrgyz and Uzbek groups. Now as head of the MVD, he oversaw an agency long-tainted by corruption and by personnel who, to put it mildly, often refused to respect the procedural rights of suspects and defendants in their custody.

My concern that evening was not the challenges facing Baibolov as the new head of the MVD but the initial maneuvers in a just-launched electoral campaign that was supposed to usher in a more stable and democratic era in Kyrgyzstan. With only a little more than three months remaining before the October parliamentary elections, political elites were busy positioning themselves for the upcoming contest. Forbidden from contesting the election while holding executive office, members of the Interim Government were beginning to resign their positions in order to devote themselves fully to forming new parties or strengthening existing ones. As Edil' Baisalov commented to me that week, these departures represented an opportunity to replace a group of highly politicized leaders with a team of technocrats who could work with President Otunbaeva to restore confidence in Kyrgyzstan's government.

For many years, Baibolov had been a prominent member—and one of the most generous financial backers—of Tekebaev's Ata-Meken Party. I had expected that he would continue to play a supporting role to Tekebaev, but over dinner in the presidential compound he revealed that if Ata-Meken obtained the most seats in the new parliament, he would likely emerge as prime minister, while Tekebaev would assume the position of parliamentary speaker. If the Social Democrats gained the most seats, he noted, their leader, Almazbek Atambaev, would become the prime minister. I had no way of knowing whether he had the ability to deprive Tekebaev of what was designed to be the most important executive position in the country under the new constitution. Certainly, Baibolov possessed a greater will to power than Tekebaev, who had exhibited indecisiveness at various points in his career, including in an interview with me two days earlier, but on one issue Baibolov was clearly mistaken: given the likelihood of a highly fractured parliament, where no party would win a majority of the seats, there was little prospect that leaders from a single party would be able to claim both the roles of prime minister and parliamentary speaker.

As a leading member of Kyrgyzstan's northern political establishment, Baibolov was dismissive of the electoral chances of prominent southern Kyrgyz politicians who were harsh critics of the Interim Government and erstwhile political allies of President Bakiev. He also downplayed Roza's concerns about the large militias attached to some of these politicians, noting with bravado that "we would take care of them if they started anything." In any case, he added, criminal charges would soon be filed against Kamchibek Tashiev, one of the most outspoken southern Kyrgyz politicians.

When I met with Tashiev several days later, he offered a very different perspective on Kyrgyzstani politics and the upcoming elections. Gaining access to southern politicians like Tashiev was not easy—they were often suspicious of Western scholars and journalists. Having heard a great deal about Tashiev from former members of the opposition, very little of it flattering, I didn't know quite what to expect when I arrived at the recently opened headquarters of his party, Ata-Jurt (Fatherland), for the interview. Occupying two vacant floors in a modern highrise building in Bishkek's commercial district, the operation did not even have desks and partitions in place yet. After sitting alone for a few minutes at a makeshift table, the only piece of furniture in a vast open room, I spotted a familiar face approaching. It was Talant Sultanov, a bright young Kyrgyz man who, like Tashiev, was a southerner. I had met Talant a few years earlier in Florida when he was an exchange student in San Francisco and happened to visit a friend who lived near my university. This thoughtful, introspective fellow seemed an unlikely aide to a brusque politician of martial bearing like Tashiev, but then in Kyrgyzstan, as in many parts of the world, it was not an affinity based on ideas or temperament that shaped political networks but geographical and kinship connections.

For all his reticence to meet, once Tashiev sat down for the interview, he talked openly, almost eagerly about his own background and the prospects for the newly revived party, Ata-Jurt, for which he served as co-leader. A caricature of a gruff military man, Tashiev spoke in a basso profundo, using short, clipped sentences that seemed designed to intimidate his interlocutor. Launching immediately into a defense of his career, Tashiev expressed pride in his promotion to the rank of general at an earlier age than anyone in the country's history. He also touted his role in preventing greater bloodshed in May in his home district of Suzak in the Jalal-Abad region.

Alarmed by the crowd of twenty thousand Kyrgyz teenagers and young men—some of them armed—who had gathered in the center of Jalal-Abad in May to exact revenge on the Uzbeks for the burning of Bakiev's home, Tashiev met with Azimbek Beknazarov and local elders, the *aksakals*, in order to defuse the tension. That meeting produced a list of three demands that he proposed to submit to local Uzbek leaders: that the Uzbeks issue an apology to the Kyrgyz people for what they did; that they renounce the local Uzbek leader, Kadyrjon Batyrov; and that they hand over their weapons. Even these harsh demands were not enough for the angry mob of young Kyrgyz, who began to surge toward the Uzbek settlement of Suzak a short distance away. At this point, Tashiev claimed, he jumped on an armored personnel carrier and addressed the crowd, in his words, "with no bulletproof vest, no pistol, nothing."

> Dear fellow Kyrgyz, my brothers, if you want to go to Suzak to kill Uzbeks, you'll first have to kill me. . . . I am prepared to give my life for you and for the Uzbeks. . . . Only at this point did people recognize the seriousness of the situation . . . and then they dispersed.[1]

A recurring theme in his accounts of the recent inter-ethnic violence in the South was that only he and other tough-minded southern Kyrgyz politicians were capable of protecting local Uzbeks against angry Kyrgyz. There were echoes here of George Wallace's claims decades earlier in the American South that he was the best friend of the colored people.

Like Baibolov, Tashiev spoke about the likely results of the upcoming election with supreme confidence only, in his telling, it was the southern-based parties, and Ata-Jurt in particular, that would emerge as the victors. Whether that meant achieving an absolute majority of the seats in the parliament he wasn't sure, but he insisted that Ata-Jurt would win 80–90 percent of the votes in the South, an extraordinary claim given that it faced competition from another up-and-coming southern party, Butun Kyrgyzstan (United Kyrgyzstan), as well as a host of longstanding, well-financed northern-based parties. When I added that Uzbeks represented a quarter of voters in the South, and Ata-Jurt might find it difficult to win their support, he asserted again that he had a special bond with Uzbeks in Kyrgyzstan.

> Uzbeks in every mosque now say their prayers and bless me. In every mosque. Who saved the Uzbeks? Did Atambaev save them? Sariev? Tekebaev? . . I consider the Uzbek portion of the population our voters.

Tashiev was surprisingly optimistic about the prospects for a free and fair election as well as the electoral strength of his party. "We now have a chance, a historic chance, for elections to be conducted fairly," he said. To realize that goal, his party was planning to station electoral observers at the more than two thousand voting precincts around the country and to encourage foreign observers to monitor the election. He was all too aware, of course, of Kyrgyzstan's checkered electoral history, and so he recognized that there would be efforts to derail his party. The criminal case being built against him, mentioned to me earlier by Baibolov, was one such effort, in Tashiev's view. He claimed that law enforcement officials had held several people for questioning for two or three days in order to extract evidence against him. The regular and secret police, he noted, had also summoned members of Ata-Jurt and issued threats like the following: "Quit the party or things will get worse for you. Your business will fail or your brother will lose his job."

Where a criminal prosecution would have disqualified Tashiev from running for parliament on the Ata-Jurt Party slate, electoral manipulation could have denied representation in parliament to the entire party. Ata-Jurt appeared especially vulnerable to the provision in the electoral law designed to discourage the election of parties with a purely regional orientation. Just as in the 2007 parliamentary elections, in order to receive seats in the new parliament, which would be filled by granting each party the percentage of seats that accorded with its share of the vote, a party had to receive at least 5 percent of the total national vote as well as at least .5 percent of the votes in each of the country's seven regions, plus Bishkek and Osh.[2] For southern parties that were just beginning to make inroads in rural northern regions like Naryn and Talas, this last provision was a potential hurdle to representation. Tashiev scoffed, though, at the thought that Ata-Jurt would not clear this barrier. The only way they could lose, he insisted, was if those linked to the Interim Government falsified the election results.

What would happen if the elections weren't conducted fairly, I asked Tashiev. "We either have fair elections, or we have violence [*konflikty*]," he answered, making clear that he saw the threat of violence as a kind of guarantor of competitive elections. The co-leader of Tashiev's party, Akhmatbek Kel'dibekov, provided an equally sobering response to this question. In the wake of an unfair election, he asserted, "We would block the highways between North and South."[3] When I noted that such action would be tantamount to the beginning of a civil war, he did not disagree. In effect, then, the potential for both northern and southern political blocs to obstruct the other side from campaigning on the visitors' turf produced an unusual political truce during the campaign that minimized, without eliminating altogether, harassment of parties operating outside their home territory. Tashiev conceded that if his party lost fairly, they would not encourage people in the South to rebel, but in the next breath he added that if the elections were free, there was no way that Ata-Jurt would not gain seats in the parliament.

He then informed me that he had just returned from a visit to the South, where he had held twenty meetings across the Osh, Jalal-Abad, and Batken regions. He found a population that was still on edge. In Tashiev's words:

> People have a very negative view of the interim authorities. We won't have to work to mobilize them, it will be enough to say that the authorities aren't

acting properly on some issue, and the people will be out on the streets. They
are prepared to act now; all they need is an excuse.

One such excuse would have been a decision by the Interim Government to
introduce peacekeeping forces in the South from the OSCE, the political
organization that grew out of the Helsinki Accords. Some in the Interim
Government were willing to consider the introduction of a small contingent
of OSCE peacekeepers in Osh, but Tashiev asserted that "our people" in the
South would not allow it. In fact, he was dead set against the presence of any
foreign "consultants," as he called them, who would only come here "to spy
on us."

Earlier in the week, I had heard opposition of a different sort to foreign
peacekeepers from Felix Kulov, the head of the Ar-Namys Party. "When I
ask people what these peacekeepers will do," Kulov said, "they tell me
they'll walk around unarmed."

What kind of policemen are these, not knowing our language, our customs,
and patrolling without weapons with our policemen? Someone will kill them
just to compromise the new regime.

In the end, the objections of Tashiev, Kulov, and others kept foreign peacekeepers out of Kyrgyzstan.

As my interview with Tashiev drew to a close, and I thanked him for his
willingness to speak to me, Tashiev began to soften his tone for the first time.
"I think I should thank you for the interest you've taken in our country," he
said, "and I hope very much that your visit and your work in our country will
be beneficial to our people." He then noted that one of these days, once
everything was peaceful, he'd pack his bags and come to see America. As we
shook hands, he left me with these unexpected words: "You are a very, very
fine conversation partner" (*Vy ochen', ochen' prekrasnyi sobesednik*). Having gotten in only a few questions and comments during our hour-long interview, I could only take that to mean that he appreciated my curiosity and
attentiveness.

In our final days in Bishkek, campaign billboards began to appear in the
city. Although the formal start to the campaign was still several weeks away,
Ata-Jurt was already making its presence known in the capital. Almost overnight, a party that several northern-based politicians dismissed as a haven for
bandits was dominating the physical landscape of the capital. It was a moment like no other in the short life of Kyrgyzstan or the long history of
Central Asia. A popular election was in the offing whose outcome no one
could predict.

Chapter Twenty-One

First Steps on the Parliamentary Road

Early Sunday morning, October 10, 2010, voting precincts began opening their doors across Kyrgyzstan. After a two-month campaign waged by twenty-nine different parties seeking places in the new 120-seat parliament, the country's fate was in the hands of its citizens. At the polling stations, voters placed a mark against their preferred party, under which appeared the names of the top five politicians on the party's list. They then dropped their ballots into a transparent voter's box and exited the precinct to await the results. In the absence of reliable polling, even the most seasoned political observers were unsure of the outcome.

Most of the parties and politicians on the ballot were obscure newcomers to Kyrgyzstani politics. They refused to defer to more established figures, in spite of the impossible odds facing smaller, poorly funded parties. In a crowded contest where a party needed 5 percent of the national vote to obtain any parliamentary seats, the vast majority of candidates and parties in the October election were tilting at windmills, but that was a venerable Kyrgyz tradition. Better to live a few weeks as a potential leader of a parliamentary party than years as a mere back-bencher.

Early in the electoral campaign, seven parties had separated themselves from the pack as viable contestants for parliamentary seats, in no small part because of the generous funds they received from wealthy party leaders or other candidates on the party's list. Each of these parties sought to establish a distinctive brand for itself based less on specific policy proposals than on the persona of its top leader or leaders, its geographic and kinship connections, and its general political orientation. In this sense, voters arriving at the polls had a clear choice. They could select an incumbent party that had supplied leaders to the Interim Government or a party whose leaders were out of power following the April Revolution; a party with its primary roots in the

North or the South—or a new party, Respublika, that drew its leaders in almost equal numbers from both regions of the country; a party that championed a vigorous Kyrgyz nationalism or a party that sought to retain some of the internationalism of the Soviet era; a party whose foreign policy had Russia as the touchstone or one that advocated a multivectored approach to international relations. Although the leaders of numerous parties traveled to Moscow to seek the backing of Russia, only Felix Kulov, the head of the northern-based Ar-Namys Party, was able to arrange a photo opportunity with President Medvedev and therefore the implicit backing of the Russian president. Seeking to attract ethnic Russians and other minority voters as well as those who favored closer ties to Russia, Ar-Namys made the photo of Kulov and Medvedev the symbolic centerpiece of the party's electoral campaign.

As suspense built throughout election day about which parties would cross the five-percent threshold, poll workers were busy registering and distributing ballots to almost 200,000 citizens voting outside of their home precinct. These same-day registrants, primarily labor migrants or persons who had fled the violence in the South, represented almost 12 percent of the total electorate that day, an extraordinarily high share by Kyrgyzstani or international standards. Kyrgyzstan was also unusual in its method of determining which parties met the minimum threshold to receive seats in parliament. Parties had to receive 5 percent of the registered voters, not the actual voters, a standard that reduced the number of parties represented in parliament.[1]

The results announced the following day by the Central Election Commission fundamentally altered the correlation of political forces in the country. Of the five parties that passed the five-percent threshold, and thereby qualified for parliamentary seats, only two—the Social Democrats and Ata-Meken—had been affiliated with the Interim Government. The other three—Ata-Jurt, Respublika, and Ar-Namys—ran as outsiders that, in different ways, criticized the leadership of the incumbents. Perhaps the sharpest shock to the northern political establishment was the exceptionally strong showing of Ata-Jurt. Although it may not have achieved the ambitious goals set for it by its co-leader, Kamchibek Tashiev, it won the most votes and therefore the most seats in the new parliament—28 out of 120 seats. Another major party dominated by southern elites, Butun Kyrgyzstan, fell just shy of the five-percent threshold, which prompted vigorous protests by its leader, Adakhan Madumarov. Had there not been so many same-day registrants, Butun Kyrgyzstan would have gained seats in the parliament and further undercut northern dominance of the country's political system.

Serving as a window on society as well as a means of distributing political power, elections allow us to piece together a portrait of key political divisions in a country's population. In the immediate aftermath of the election, my colleague David Hill and I collected results from each of Kyrgyz-stan's 2,333 voting precincts and compared those results with district-level demographic data on the age, economic, education, ethnic, and linguistic backgrounds of voters.[2] Unlike in the United States and most Western countries, where parties are associated with certain age, occupational, or income groups, in Kyrgyzstan voters aligned with parties primarily along regional, local, kinship, and ethnic lines. Ethnic Kyrgyz tended to cast their ballots for parties associated with their region of origin—North or South, or for parties whose top leader or leaders hailed from their particular district. Geography did not explain everything, however. Butun Kyrgyzstan, the southern party that fell just shy of qualifying for parliamentary seats, did especially well in districts where ethnic Kyrgyz voters shared the same tribal identity as the party's leader.

Not surprisingly, the election results did not bear out Tashiev's prediction to me that his party, Ata-Jurt, would sweep the Uzbek vote. In fact, Uzbek voters shunned the aggressive Kyrgyz nationalism of parties like Ata-Jurt and Butun Kyrgyzstan, choosing instead northern-based parties, like Ar-Namys, that openly appealed to minority voters by stressing their internationalist outlook and by including Uzbek and Russian candidates near the top of their party lists. Although Kyrgyzstan's electoral rules mandated that minority candidates occupy 15 percent of the places on each party's list, most parties positioned those candidates so far down the party list that they had no chance of claiming a parliamentary seat. As a result, only five Russians and three Uzbeks gained seats in the new parliament. This token concession to minority groups contrasted with more robust provisions designed to achieve greater parity between male and female deputies. When composing their list of candidates, parties were required to place a woman in every fourth slot, which resulted in a parliament whose membership was 31 percent female.[3]

Because no single party received more than a quarter of the parliamentary seats, a minimum of three parties was needed to form a majority coalition that would select—and provide political support for—a prime minister and his or her government. In circumstances like this, when an election fails to produce a majority party, the president asks the leader of one party to try to form a ruling coalition of parties. Not surprisingly, President Otunbaeva selected as the *formateur* Almazbek Atambaev, the leader of her own party, the Social Democrats, which received 26 seats, only two less than Ata-Jurt. After several weeks of negotiations with other parties over how political offices would be allocated, Atambaev announced that three parties were willing to serve in a governing coalition—the Social Democrats, Ata-Meken, and Respublika. This attempt at coalition formation collapsed, however, when Omurbek Tekebaev, the head of Ata-Meken, failed to receive enough votes to become parliamentary speaker, a post that the interparty negotiations had designated for him. It turned out that several rank-and-file members of

Respublika refused to support his candidacy, thereby undermining the arrangement entered into by the party leader, Omurbek Babanov.

After the failure of Atambaev to form a new government, President Otunbaeva asked Babanov to serve as *formateur*. Babanov was a Moscow-educated businessman whose wealth and extensive connections across the North-South divide assured the success of his recently created party, Respublika. A relatively fresh face on the political scene, Babanov succeeded in convincing the dominant parties of the North and South—the Social Democrats and Ata-Jurt—to join Respublika in a ruling coalition that could claim support in all geographical areas of the country. In this first coalition to govern under Kyrgyzstan's new constitution, which held 77 of the 120 seats in the parliament, Almazbek Atambaev served as the prime minister, Babanov as deputy prime minister, and Akhmatbek Kel'dibekov (Ata-Jurt) as parliamentary speaker.

The lengthy and difficult process of forming a government in Kyrgyzstan at the end of 2010 illustrated that the popular vote is only the first stage in selecting leaders when parliamentary elections produce a highly fragmented parliament. After the voters had their say in late October, the country's political elites took six weeks to form a viable ruling coalition, and so it was only in the middle of December, 2010, that the new deputies gathered in Bishkek for the first session of Kyrgyzstan's unicameral legislature. It did not take long for cracks to appear in the new system. Much like the Interim Government earlier that year, the new government under Prime Minister Atambaev found it difficult to rule as a single, coordinated team. In the absence of the usual cooperation found in Western parliamentary coalitions, Kyrgyzstani leaders tended to assign responsibility for decision-making in specific arenas to different parties. On personnel matters, for example, each of the three parties in the ruling coalition assumed responsibility for making appointments of high-ranking officials in certain ministries or of *akims* in certain districts of the country. These quota arrangements may have satisfied the ruling parties' natural desire for patronage power but they did little to advance a common governing agenda or to assure the efficient operation of executive institutions at the national or local levels. When combined with the widespread corruption that still plagued state institutions, the fissures in Atambaev's government prevented Kyrgyzstan from effectively addressing its many challenges in social and economic development.

The lack of discipline and coordination within the ruling coalition was also evident in the parties themselves. No sooner had the new parliament begun its work than serious intraparty disputes arose over matters of policy and patronage. Given the absence of unifying party ideologies, and the tendency for parliamentary candidates to be placed on the party lists because of their wealth or visibility rather than their loyalty to the party, it was not surprising that rank-and-file deputies had little incentive to follow the party leadership. Further weakening party discipline was the absence of the standard patronage rewards that party leaders can dole out to back-benchers in most parliamentary systems. Because Kyrgyzstani deputies in this period had to relinquish their parliamentary mandate if they accepted an appointment in the executive, there was little reason to defer to party leaders when there was no prospect of moving onto a front bench.

The most colorful intraparty disputes involved members of Ata-Jurt, and in the first rank, its quick-tempered co-leader, Kamchibek Tashiev. At the end of March, 2011, Tashiev got into an argument in the speaker's chambers with a fellow party member and began pummeling his colleague, which sent the latter to the hospital and prompted the opening of a criminal investigation against Tashiev for assault. The following day, amid heated parliamentary discussions about Deputy Prime Minister Babanov's business ties to a leading telecommunications company, Tashiev again set upon a fellow member of parliament, this time a deputy from Babanov's Respublika party. In an attempt to overcome the controversy surrounding these embarrassing episodes in the halls of parliament, the country's political leaders invited a group of Kyrgyz elders, the *aksakals*, to intervene. In a series of rituals designed to "purge the parliament of evil spirits," Tashiev and his pugilistic partner from Respublika traded traditional Kyrgyz hats and robes and participated in the slaughtering of seven sheep outside the parliament building.[4]

Where Tashiev's forceful personality led several Ata-Jurt deputies to form an alternative parliamentary faction called "For Reforms" at the end of 2011, Felix Kulov's domineering style produced a schism inside the parliamentary faction of Ar-Namys. Against the wishes of many of his members, in December 2010 Kulov had refused to accept the terms of an offer to include Ar-Namys in the ruling coalition. By April 2011, frustrated with their position in the opposition, ten of the party's twenty-five parliamentary deputies sought to enter the majority coalition on their own.

Contributing to these intraparty tensions were the murky relations between Kyrgyzstani political parties and their parliamentary factions. Unlike in most established democracies, those running on the party list often had tenuous ties to the party organization, and so while leaders like Kulov may have enjoyed an unchallenged position as head of the party outside parliament, they had limited control over the deputies in their party faction inside parliament. In the case of Ar-Namys, this awkward coexistence of two parts of the party was on full display in July 2011, when a majority of the members of the Ar-Namys parliamentary faction met without Kulov and tried to remove him as leader. Kulov contended that such an action was illegal because the full party membership, and not just the party's parliamentary deputies, was responsible for selecting and removing the party leader. Although Kulov won this battle, the war inside the Ar-Namys parliamentary faction continued, which prevented Kulov from playing a role commensurate with the twenty-five seats his party received in the parliament.

Despite the ill-discipline in the ruling coalition, and within the parties themselves, the new system worked in its own messy and unpredictable fashion. In its first session, from December 2010 to June 2011, the parliament passed more legislation than at any other six-month period in the country's history. Perhaps more importantly, the new parliament successfully carried out the primary function of a legislature in any democratic country: it kept most political conflicts in the halls of parliament and off the streets. It did so in part by limiting the amount of power concentrated in the executive and establishing protections for the political opposition. Put another way, the country's revised institutional framework reduced the stakes of elections and forced northern and southern elites to work together in parliament. Instead of concentrating authority in the hands of a first secretary—as under communism—or a president—as in the first two decades after communism—the 2010 Constitution distributed power more evenly across the political landscape. Like no other country in the region, Kyrgyzstan was willing to sacrifice some governing efficiency for popular accountability.

The increased prominence of parliament and prime minister following the October 2010 elections reflected not just the design of the new constitution but the lame duck status of President Otunbaeva and her own leadership style, which sought to minimize conflicts with the new prime minister, Almazbek Atambaev. Even on those issues where Otunbaeva tried to act decisively, her limited authority and the weakness of the central Kyrgyzstani state often prevented the implementation of her initiatives. In the late summer of 2010, for example, she made an abortive attempt to remove the mayor of Osh, Melis Myrzakmatov, a flamboyant Kyrgyz nationalist whose provocative speeches and actions deepened the divide between Kyrgyz and Uzbeks in the South in the wake of the inter-ethnic violence. Myrzakmatov was among a number of Kyrgyz nationalists who advocated the closing of Uzbek-language schools in the South. He also spoke at a rally attended by seven hundred persons in the main square of Osh where the crowd burned a book that accused the Kyrgyz of genocide against local Uzbeks in the June events.[5]

Further limiting Otunbaeva's authority was her path to the presidency, and therefore the nature of her mandate. Instead of choosing her from among a list of candidates, voters in June 2010 had only been able to vote "yes" or "no" on whether the Interim Government's nomination of her as president should be confirmed, and even that question was packaged with another, unrelated issue. In contrast, her successor—the first to be elected to a full six-year term under the new constitution—would enjoy a popular mandate acquired in the contested presidential election of October 30, 2011.

Chapter Twenty-Two

Without Abuse, Power Loses Its Charm

To the surprise of those who regarded the post of prime minister as the most authoritative executive office under the new constitution, virtually all of the heavyweights in Kyrgyzstani politics tossed their hats in the ring for the presidency in 2011, including the incumbent prime minister, Almazbek Atambaev. For Atambaev and others, the presidency had one great advantage over the office of prime minister: the presidential mandate was for a fixed six-year term, whereas the prime minister could be removed at any time by a majority in the parliament. In addition to job security, there was a residual allure to an office that had dominated the political landscape for more than two decades. And the presidency still carried practical as well as symbolic weight. The heads of all the uniformed services, such as the police and armed forces, continued to answer directly to the president on operational matters, and the president remained the leading figure in international affairs.

When I arrived in Bishkek with my wife in the middle of October 2011, the presidential election campaign was at its zenith. The eighty-three candidates initially registered for the race had dwindled to sixteen contenders, still an unwieldy number of participants and additional evidence, if any was needed, that most Kyrgyz politicians harbored wholly unrealistic expectations about their prospects. The unseen face of power in this and other presidential races was the horse trading that went on before the election among the gaggle of potential presidential candidates. Although voters may choose among the candidates on the ballot, it is the leaders who supply the choices available to the voters. In earlier presidential races in Kyrgyzstan, incumbents used various techniques to disqualify prominent opponents from the race, but in the 2011 contest many candidates removed themselves from the contest. They did so because they received a promise of favors from a likely victor or because they feared that their continued presence in the race would siphon votes from a candidate with whom they shared common interests.

The greatest beneficiary of early retirements from the campaign was Prime Minister Atambaev, who became the de facto standard bearer of the northern political class when several other well-known politicians with northern roots abandoned the race. With the built-in advantages of personal wealth and incumbency as prime minister, Atambaev towered above other northern candidates. The situation in the South was quite different. There the two leading candidates for president, Kamchibek Tashiev and Adakhan Madumarov, were evenly matched in terms of their outsized personal ambitions and their popular support across the region. As a result, both remained in the race, which ensured that they would split the southern vote while Atambaev carried the North convincingly.

While neighboring "Stans" held elections distinguished by their lack of competitiveness—and often their lack of frequency—Kyrgyzstan was embracing modern techniques of electoral campaigning and administration. With funding from the United States Agency for International Development (USAID), Kyrgyzstan's election commission launched an initiative that encouraged voters to familiarize themselves with, and defend, their electoral rights. Plastered around the country were stickers with the message "Don't Remain Silent: Report Violations of Your Rights." To facilitate this campaign of "see something, say something," the stickers urged citizens to send a text to a common national number—4414—with details of electoral violations and the number of the voting precinct involved. Voters could then follow reports of alleged violations on a map accessible at a heavily publicized website. Although it's unclear to what extent this initiative deterred electoral fraud, this presidential election earned generally positive assessments from domestic and international observers.

One of the most impressive elements of the campaign was a series of formal televised debates among the candidates. Instead of holding a debate or debates with the full sixteen-man field—there were no female candidates in this contest—the election authorities organized four separate three-person debates and one four-person debate, all of which were broadcast over national television during the last three weeks of the campaign. Led by one male and one female moderator whose political knowledge and media professionalism put many of their American counterparts to shame, the forums allowed the moderators, members of the studio audience, and the other candidates present to pose hard-hitting questions to the presidential contenders. Although some questions encouraged candidates to speak on policy issues, many forced those seeking the presidency to defend their records during controversial moments of the rule of Bakiev or the Interim Government. Adopting the aggressive questioning style of British television news figures, one moderator asked Madumarov about his actions as a member of Bakiev's

Security Council. Dissatisfied with the response, the moderator pressed on, "How many times can you possibly repeat the same [unconvincing] answer?" Madumarov's answer: "And how many times do I need to?" (*A skol'ko nado*).[1]

Less than two weeks before the election, I attended a forum in the Park Hotel ostensibly devoted to the role of the media in the presidential campaign. It was in fact an opportunity for representatives from campaign staffs and NGOs to air their grievances about the conduct of the election, with officials from the country's chief legal agency, the Procuracy, in attendance. The primary target of most of those present was the front-runner, Almazbek Atambaev, whose campaign was accused of using the administrative resources available to the sitting prime minister to gain an unfair advantage in the race. A spokesman for the campaign of former MVD and Procuracy head, Kubatbek Baibolov, complained that the senior administration of the Kyrgyz National University instructed all members of staff and their families to vote for Atambaev. In the city of Naryn, Baibolov's campaign alleged, officials on the state payroll—the so-called *biudzhetniki*, such as teachers, doctors, and local government employees—were encouraged to take six persons each to the polls to vote for Atambaev. For his part, the Tashiev representative reported that the head of the Bishkek city bus company had refused their ad for posters on the buses. He also complained that groups of provocateurs—women, students, and drunks—had been hired to disrupt campaign meetings for Tashiev in smaller northern cities such as Tokmok and Karakol.

In her usual dramatic fashion, Cholpon Jakupova, the head of a prominent legal aid organization in Bishkek, raised the specter of a civil war between North and South if such episodes prevented this winner-take-all election from being perceived as free and fair in all regions of the country. Although the general consensus was that electoral abuse was less blatant and widespread than in the past, there were still efforts afoot to gain unfair advantage in the voting. Quoting the French writer Paul Valéry, Jakupova reminded participants in the closing minutes of the forum that "power [exercised] without abuse loses its charm," a not-so-veiled reference to the administrative resources employed by Atambaev and his allies in the campaign.

Unlike in the United States, with its long and shameful history of suppressing electoral participation by minority groups, voter registration in Kyrgyzstan had generated little controversy in earlier electoral cycles. The authorities traditionally constructed voter rolls using data on eligible citizens drawn from residency records compiled by the local police. In this election, however, the authorities shifted responsibility for voter registration to the country's election commissions, which relied on different datasets to draw up the voter rolls. Although voters were encouraged to check the accuracy of their registration in the ten days before the election, either online or in person at their local election office, many did not avail themselves of this opportunity, and a significant number of voters arrived at the polls on October 30 to find their names missing from the registration lists. Whether by accident or design, a disproportionate share of those absent from the rolls in Bishkek were recent arrivals in the capital from the South, which prompted complaints of unequal treatment of voters by region of origin.

A more serious issue for southern voters—and the politicians that drew most of their votes—was the unusually large number of citizens from the South who were working outside the country, primarily in Russia, on election day. A study of the election that I conducted with David Hill illustrated that voter turnout in the South was a stunning 22 percent lower than in the North, due in large measure to the absence of so many southern labor migrants.[2] In the parliamentary election the previous year, the election commission had tried to operate voting precincts in major Russian cities, but the turnout was relatively low and there were so many irregularities that they threw out all of the ballots cast outside the country. In this election, the authorities did not even attempt to mobilize voters abroad, either through absentee balloting or on-site voting in foreign embassies. The effective result was the suppression of the franchise in the South.

While many fewer southerners voted in this election, northern voters turned out in record numbers—15 points higher than in the 2010 parliamentary elections. Part of the explanation for the high turnout in the North lay in the effectiveness of the Atambaev campaign's "ground game," that is its ability to use networks of prominent local loyalists to get voters to the polls. In the West, one thinks of voting as a quintessentially individual act, but in many rural areas of Kyrgyzstan and other developing societies, going to the polls is almost a community obligation—if we don't vote as expected, our village could be denied much-needed government support. And where Western political scientists like to think that voting involves "costs"—you have to devote time to collecting information and traveling to the polls—in many parts of Kyrgyzstan there are arguably higher costs in staying home and having your friends and neighbors recognize that you failed to support the community and its leaders.[3]

Southern presidential candidates, of course, had their own networks of local mobilizers, many of whom were very effective at the "ground game," but what they did not have was supporters who were voting to keep their leaders in power. In a memorable passage from his novel, *A Man of the People*, the Nigerian writer, Chinua Achebe, wrote the following about the indigenous leaders who had replaced British rulers in the early 1960s:

> A man who has just come in from the rain and dried his body and put on dry clothes is more reluctant to go out again than another who has been indoors all the time.

In the case of Kyrgyzstan, it was the northern-dominated elite who had suffered most under Bakiev, and now that they were in power they were desperate to stay out of the rain. What social psychologists call "loss aversion"—the fear of loss is a stronger incentive than a desire for gain—ensured that voters and leaders in the North, with their recent memories of Bakiev's rule, had good reason to rally around the candidacy of Atambaev.

A further incentive for northern voters to cast their ballots was the unsavory reputation in the North of the two leading southern candidates for the presidency. The behavior of both Tashiev and Madumarov fed into northern stereotypes about the backwardness and brutality of southern leaders, and of course segments of the press and some local and national politicians only reinforced those stereotypes with their observations about the race. In the case of Madumarov, his alleged comments on the status of the country's minority groups also repelled Russian and Uzbek voters throughout the country. In the infamous phrase attributed to him on the relative standing of the country's ethnic groups, Madumarov stated that "the Kyrgyz are the owners of the house, the rest are just renters."[4]

With more than 90 percent of voters turning out in heavily Kyrgyz districts in the North of Kyrgyzstan, Almazbek Atambaev emerged as the victor in the presidential election, with over 62 percent of the vote. He had put together a winning coalition that drew on some southern Kyrgyz as well as the overwhelming majority of northern Kyrgyz and ethnic minorities living in all parts of the country. Just over a month later, on December 1, 2011, Atambaev took the oath of office, succeeding Roza Otunbaeva as the country's fourth president, this at a time when Uzbekistan and Kazakhstan were still on their first presidents. And unlike in the other four Central Asian countries, the constitution of Kyrgyzstan limited President Atambaev to a single term.

As the election campaign was winding down, I took off one afternoon from participation in a local conference to board a bus in front of the campus of the American University of Central Asia. Filled with students, members of the faculty and administration, conference participants, and university well-wishers, it was part of a convoy of buses heading out of Bishkek's city center for a rock-strewn field twenty minutes south of town. On arrival we found a makeshift stage and banners announcing the groundbreaking for the new campus of AUCA. Having fought for years against powerful political forces that sought to evict the university from its historic buildings in the heart of Bishkek, AUCA's board finally agreed to abandon the charming but decrepit structures in the city center for a more modern, spacious, and secure facility on the outskirts of the capital.

Instead of government buildings and lush parks, the new site had as its neighbor the city's twelfth micro-district, a sprawling assortment of unremarkable Soviet-era highrises fronted by the occasional phone card or tobacco booth and small produce stands. The setting may have appeared inauspicious on this gray October day, but there was the promise of a self-contained campus with resources equal to those anywhere in the post-communist world. In her remarks at the groundbreaking, the American ambassador noted that the project represented an investment of the US government and other donors in the transformative power of high-quality education for future AUCA students and for the country. With so much American money having been spent on short-term projects in the military and political fields, this commitment to English-language higher education seemed a small price to pay for an opportunity to expose generations of Kyrgyzstani youth to the rigors and values of an American liberal arts education. In fact, the rewards of earlier investments were already apparent in the early days of the Atambaev presidency, when a recent AUCA graduate, Kadyr Toktogulov, was appointed presidential press secretary.

A few days later, while leaving Kyrgyzstan by road for the airport in Almaty, my wife and I joined a long line of people waiting to cross the border into Kazakhstan, just north of Bishkek. Waiting patiently in a slow-moving queue that was ten persons wide and well over 100 yards long, my diminutive wife—whose Mexican American features were hardly distinguishable from those of an Uzbek—was jostled continually by the crowds of female shuttle traders who were dragging their overstuffed plastic and cloth sacks toward the border. As we got within shouting distance of the border post, a uniformed Kyrgyz official spotted me, standing a head above the rest of the crowd. He called out an order to those in front of me: "Let the academician through!" Having come directly from a lecture at the American University of Central Asia, I was dressed in a coat and tie and a deer stalker cap from Scotland, the very picture of a British fop. As the long-suffering Kyrgyz and Kazakhs in the line hurled epithets in my direction, I struggled to help my wife take advantage of the privilege that I had been accorded by a generous Kyrgyzstani official who was intent on protecting a foreigner from the everyday indignities experienced by his own people.

Amid the discussions of white privilege in the United States in recent years, the Soviet Union and many of its successor states are the places where I have been most conscious of the advantages of being an American of European descent. In Moscow and Leningrad in the 1970s and 1980s, I was astonished at times by the contrast between the favorable treatment I received from the same Soviet citizens who dealt with their compatriots as if they were part of an inferior race. On this occasion, as we fought our way through the large crowds on the Kazakhstani-Kyrgyzstani border, this deference to a well-dressed person of European background was at once welcome and disturbing.

Chapter Twenty-Three

Goodbye to Manas

No sooner had Almazbek Atambaev declared victory as president than he announced that Kyrgyzstan would not renew the lease with Western countries for the Manas Transit Center at Bishkek's airport. Pro-Russian politicians and Kyrgyz nationalists alike had been using the occasional incident at the base, such as an American serviceman's killing of a local truck driver entering the facility, to stir up popular resentment against the continued presence in the country of a large contingent of foreign troops and aircraft.[1] Expressing a concern that had been growing for some time in Kyrgyzstan, President Atambaev justified the termination of lease arrangements by referring to his country's fear that if the United States launched an attack against Iranian nuclear installations—a much-discussed possibility in this period—Iran would retaliate by bombing the Manas Transit Center in Kyrgyzstan.

Over lunch at an outside cafe in Bishkek's Oak Park during Atambaev's second year in office, I spoke with a Kyrgyzstani official who had sought to allay popular fears about the base.[2] As chair of the Transparency Commission, which brought American military representatives together with local residents, the official explained that much of their work was devoted to dispelling unfounded rumors about environmental and other hazards posed by the base. Although he pointed to numerous instances when this joint working group had intervened to calm the nerves of citizens in the area, he recognized that the consensus in the country was against retaining the base, which was one of the few cash cows for the local economy. It did not help that, just a month earlier, an American KC-135 refueling aircraft had crashed in the mountains near the transit center, killing all five crew members on board. A year later, in June 2014, the last Western forces departed from the base, a move that coincided with the end of large-scale American military operations in Afghanistan.

The closing of the Manas Transit Center was one of a series of initiatives that brought Kyrgyzstan more firmly within Russia's security, diplomatic, and economic orbit. As Western governments and NGOs scaled back their commitments to Kyrgyzstan, Russia increased its footprint in the country. Russian companies expanded their ownership in the telecommunications and energy sectors and, under considerable pressure from Moscow, the government of Kyrgyzstan agreed to join the Russian-dominated Eurasian Economic Union, Putin's answer to the European Union. Kyrgyzstan's integration into the union, whose members also included the post-communist countries of Russia, Kazakhstan, Belarus, and Armenia, was not without economic costs, especially with regard to the vibrant trade in cheap imported goods from China, which were then resold in markets across Central Asia. However, Kyrgyzstan's neighbors had already begun placing barriers in the way of such reselling, and so the decision to join an economic market of some 200 million persons in 2015 was seemingly one of the few viable options for a small, resource-poor country in an isolated region of the world.

In many ways, Russia was a natural partner for Kyrgyzstan. Many members of the political establishment, including President Atambaev, had close personal and/or business ties to Russia, and the steady stream of labor migrants to Russia from impoverished regions of Kyrgyzstan increased linkages at the grassroots level between the two countries. As economic ties with China deepened, Kyrgyzstan worried about excessive dependence on its eastern neighbor, which had been the bête noire of the Kyrgyz for a millennium; with ties to the United States fraying, only Russia could serve as an effective counterbalance to Beijing's influence. Finally, most citizens of Kyrgyzstan, of whatever ethnic or linguistic background, continued to view the world largely through the lens of Russian-language media from Moscow, whose steady stream of half-truths and anti-American conspiracies undermined attempts by Western countries to improve their fading image in Kyrgyzstan.

Russia's position as the favored nation in the consciousness of Kyrgyzstanis was apparent in a survey conducted in February 2012 by the International Republican Institute, an American-funded NGO. When asked to assess current relations with a host of countries in the region and abroad, 98 percent of respondents reported that relations with Russia were good; the corresponding figure for the United States was 42 percent. When asked which countries were the most important partners and biggest threats to Kyrgyzstan, 96 percent considered Russia to be among the closest partners, with the United States garnering only 8 percent of the responses on this question. Whereas less than 1 percent of those questioned viewed Russia as one of the biggest threats, the figure for the United States was 42 percent. Only Afghanistan, at 48 percent, was perceived to be a more serious threat to Kyrgyzstan.[3]

A few years earlier I had met several Kyrgyz for drinks at a new biergarten near the city's sports stadium. After several pints, the conversation turned to Vladimir Putin's leadership in Russia. A minor government official in the group started singing his praises, noting that Putin was a real *muzhik*—a man's man. With all of its factional politics, Kyrgyzstan should be so lucky, he noted, to have such a "strong hand" in charge. Taken together with a growing nostalgia for the stability and order of the Soviet era, when politics were controlled from Moscow, this admiration for the leadership of Putin was yet another reason for Russia's popularity among citizens of Kyrgyzstan.

In the early summer of 2013, I returned to Kyrgyzstan for a month as a US Embassy Specialist, a grand-sounding title that belied my status as an independent scholar conducting research on a subject that was of interest to the local office of the US Agency for International Development (USAID). A previously stand-alone government agency that the State Department had recently absorbed, USAID had extended financial support through its Bishkek office to a good governance initiative launched under the presidency of Roza Otunbaeva. The idea was to create citizen advisory boards to monitor the operations of the country's executive agencies.

Arriving in Bishkek to assess the first two years of this ambitious experiment in citizen involvement in the oversight of government, I had barely stepped off the plane when I was summoned by the coordinator of these volunteer advisory boards to attend a small workshop in a mountain retreat near Bishkek. Leading the workshop was ex-President Otunbaeva, who considered the advisory boards to be an important part of her legacy. As I quickly learned, the backing of the former president was essential to maintaining the visibility and integrity of this reform and to fending off its many ministerial critics who were understandably unenthusiastic about subjecting their work to the scrutiny of outsiders.

When the workshop broke up, Roza asked me to stroll with her up a path where couples and young families had come to take in the mountain air. As she explained her vision for the public advisory boards, and the impediments she saw to its implementation, plainclothes security personnel walked along at a discreet distance. From time to time, well-wishers shouted out their greetings, and one family insisted on taking a photograph surrounding the former president. Although some visitors to the park seemed surprised to see President Otunbaeva walking among them, most greeted Roza matter-of-factly, speaking to her as they would to an acquaintance. Kyrgyzstan was, after all, a small country, and the Kyrgyz, never ones to respect social hierarchy, preferred familiarity to deference. The very existence of a surviving former president was, of course, another measure of Kyrgyzstan's distinctiveness—Kyrgyzstan now had three, compared to none in the other four Central Asian states.

Over the succeeding weeks, my interviews with advisory board members revealed that, against all odds, many of the boards were achieving the initia-

tive's goals of enhancing transparency, reducing corruption, increasing effi-
ciencies, and eliminating favoritism in hiring practices in Kyrgyzstan's governing institutions. Success was not universal, of course, and some of the
boards had become moribund, either due to disinterest on the part of their
members, irreconcilable differences within the board, or bureaucratic resistance from ministers and their staff. In many cases, however, the public
advisory boards were impressive instruments of reform in government ministries, whose bureaucratic culture and practices had changed little since the
Soviet era. The advisory board monitoring the Finance Ministry, for example, helped to introduce an e-government reform that granted citizens online
access to detailed information on the national budget, foreign assistance, and
procurement matters. For its part, the board of the Ministry of Energy published an exhaustive study of inefficiencies in procurement in the country's
electricity grid.[4] It was as if a local branch of McKinsey had volunteered its
consulting services to state entities.

In the ministries where state officials were unwilling to partner with these
citizen overseers, some activist boards chose to go public with their criticism
of bureaucratic wrongdoing. In November 2012, the public advisory board of
the State Property Committee exposed a massive corruption ring in the agency responsible for agricultural procurement. When I asked a prominent member of the advisory board of the Ministry of Energy, Rita Karasartova, to
summarize her view of the work of the public advisory boards, this supreme-
ly confident and forceful citizen activist responded: "What have we been able
to achieve in two years? I don't want to say that they [the ministries] began to
fear us, but they had to reckon with our point of view."

Members of the public advisory boards were not the only supporters of
the reform. Even some government officials whose agencies were subjects of
citizen oversight spoke of a productive partnership with their public advisory
boards. Many boards were filled with talented and civic-oriented young professionals who brought a knowledge of international standards in their fields
that was often lacking among long-serving and poorly paid government officials. Astute and enlightened public managers recognized the advantages of
tapping into this free labor, among them Baktybek Ashirov, the head of the
State Service on Fighting Economic Crimes. While he was in charge of
Kyrgyzstan's State Tax Service, Ashirov had drafted a modern tax code with
the assistance of that agency's public advisory board, and so when he assumed his new position, he insisted on creating a board in the recently
formed State Service on Fighting Economic Crimes. Speaking with Ashirov
in his unassuming but well-protected headquarters on a dead-end street well
outside the city center of Bishkek, I asked him about the appropriate relationship between citizen boards and the agencies they monitored. A good public
advisory board, he noted, "will know when to praise and when to curse the
minister."[5] In Kyrgyzstan, as elsewhere, it was not every leader who was

willing to be cursed, and the fact that some in Kyrgyzstan exposed themselves willingly to such scrutiny and criticism was another indication of the
country's distinctiveness.

Amid the continuing drama and conflict of high politics, where parliament, prime minister, and president were center stage, the public advisory
board initiative received little attention in Kyrgyzstan. Few ordinary citizens
I spoke with had ever heard of it, and yet such quiet reforms of public
administration were key to improving governance and living conditions in
the country. Under pressure from some members of the MVD's public advisory board, most notably Aziza Abdirasulova, one of Kyrgyzstan's most
tireless advocates for criminal justice reform, the MVD granted the board
unlimited twenty-four-hour access to places of detention across the country.
As Abdirasulova explained to me in her dimly lit office overlooking one of
Bishkek's industrial zones, this concession discouraged mistreatment of the
detained by allowing her to follow up immediately on any reports of abuse.[6]
Although the board itself had stopped meeting regularly—they convened a
session one evening in MVD headquarters just for me, where four persons
turned up with no agenda and nothing of substance to discuss—the heroic
work of a single activist member was helping to hold the government to
account.

Because many members of the public advisory boards that I met were
drawn from the business community—from the head of the local stock exchange to successful company executives—I gained access for the first time
to the world of vibrant young entrepreneurs that gave Bishkek an energy that
is lacking in some neighboring countries. One such entrepreneur was a female real estate agent who sat on the public advisory board attached to the
State Registration Committee, the agency that registers all forms of property.
After a meeting with the leading members of the board, this smartly dressed
woman, a Uighur by nationality, drove me in her Lexus SUV to lunch at her
family's restaurant just east of Bishkek's main department store, TsUM.
Over traditional Uighur dishes, our conversation moved quickly from her
role on the advisory board to her work as a realtor and the challenges facing
ethnic minorities in the business world.

Related culturally and linguistically to Uzbeks, her ethnic group, the Uighurs live predominantly in western China's Xinjiang province, where their
way of life as agrarian Muslims has been threatened by the influx of tens of
millions of Han Chinese sent to the region by Beijing. Violent Uighur reaction to this Sinicization policy, fed initially by ethnolinguistic resentment,
has in recent years drawn succor from radical interpretations of Islam. Although the relatively small numbers of Uighurs living in Kazakhstan and
Kyrgyzstan have shown few signs of radicalization, they have been the subject of intense scrutiny by governments on both sides of the old Sino-Soviet
border. A suicide bombing at the gates of the Chinese Embassy in Bishkek at

the end of August 2016 only heightened fears that the widespread violence unleashed by Uighurs in Xinjiang could be spreading to Central Asia.

The prejudice faced by my Uighur lunch partner on this early June day in 2013 had nothing to do, however, with regional politics and everything to do with the virulent nationalism unleashed against Uzbeks and their Uighur cousins by the events of 2010. The real estate agent lamented that she was regularly forced to forgo some of her sales commissions because of her ethnic background—some Kyrgyz simply refused to pay her what she was owed, and in most cases pursuing the matter would have been unprofitable or even dangerous. In one instance, she insisted, a Kyrgyz woman, the wife of a high-ranking government official, threw a $100 bill in her face following a closing in which she was to have received $1000. Such was the impunity enjoyed by those in power.

As I learned during dozens of interviews with members of the public advisory boards, the fate of this experiment in citizen oversight of government depended on the support of the current political leadership as well as the everyday interactions between the boards and the executive agencies they monitored. President Otunbaeva had created a three-year mandate for the institution at the end of 2010, and I had arrived in the country at a time when the friends and foes of the public advisory boards were fighting over whether to extend or end this mandate. Like many policy questions that do not excite the public, the battle over the future of the public advisory boards mobilized only a small circle of interested parties. On one side was Roza Otunbaeva and the coordinating council of the public advisory boards, led by another of Kyrgyzstan's tireless female activists, Nuripa Mukanova; on the other was a smattering of ministerial officials, all male, who saw the boards as an unwelcome monitor of their activities, and a handful of parliamentary deputies who believed that the parliament alone should exercise oversight of executive institutions. Positioned between these two sides were two female staffers in the presidential apparatus who had responsibility for reviewing the activities of the public advisory boards.

When I arrived midafternoon on June 12, 2013, at the suite of presidential offices on the sixth floor of the White House, one of these staffers, Mira Karybaeva, was holding a phone to each ear while barking out orders to subordinates. The head of the presidency's Department of Ethnic and Religious Policies and Civil Society Relations, Karybaeva along with her assistant, Janna Saralieva, were the go-betweens in relations between the public advisory boards and the country's political leadership. Because President Atambaev was reluctant to be drawn into this fight over the extension of the mandate, Karybaeva and Saralieva played an outsized role in steering the debate in favor of public advisory boards.[7] It was a common feature of governance throughout the world—the lower the visibility of the issue, the greater the influence of staff.

Traveling to an advisory board retreat the following week with Janna Saralieva, I came to understand the extent to which she and Mira Karybaeva had served as quiet champions for citizen oversight of government. Once at the retreat, where twenty members of public advisory boards had just finished two days of training on government monitoring, I had the unenviable task of offering my assessment of the first generation of public advisory boards in Kyrgyzstan to persons who knew the institution from the inside. Rather than dwell on the achievements and shortcomings of the boards, which they understood better than anyone, I sought to place Kyrgyzstan's experiment in direct public participation in government in a comparative framework, starting with the novel approaches to participatory budgeting adopted in Brazil two decades earlier. I concluded with a paradox about experiments with citizen participation in government: they can be successful, but not too successful. State institutions that should be performing these functions may cede some space to citizen competitors but they are unlikely to tolerate the work of amateurs when it begins to seriously undermine their own prerogatives or image.

At the end of my month in Bishkek, I headed to the American Embassy for an "outbrief" on my research with the US ambassador, Pamela Spratlen. In search of more space and security, the embassy had recently moved from its modest digs on Erkindik in the very center of Bishkek to facilities in a large, open field twenty minutes south of town. While a permanent structure was gradually rising on the site, American diplomats worked out of a series of modular buildings surrounded by a high iron fence. Turning off the main road into the embassy compound, my taxi halted at a series of concrete barriers that stood some 40 yards from a large guardhouse. After walking to the guardhouse and presenting my identification, I proceeded across an open courtyard into the main complex, where an ethnic Russian employee of the embassy performed a second document check and then asked me to be seated. Within minutes, my escort, Larry Held, approached. I had known Larry since the early 1990s, when he'd contacted me for advice about living in Kyrgyzstan after receiving his Peace Corps placement in the country. As deputy head of the USAID mission in Bishkek during my time as an Embassy Specialist, he was generous in organizing meetings relating to my research as well as social gatherings that introduced me to members of the expatriate community in Bishkek.

As I was about to learn, Pamela Spratlen was not the typical American ambassador. A middle-aged African American woman with a warm persona and keen mind, she had experience in practical politics in the United States, having worked for the better part of a decade as a staffer in the California State Assembly. No doubt because of this background in the rough and tumble of American politics, she had a greater appreciation for the interpersonal and institutional dynamics of Kyrgyzstani politics than most diplomats who entered the foreign service directly from college or graduate school. As I explained my research findings on the public advisory boards and my broader views on contemporary Kyrgyzstani politics, she interjected questions and comments that indicated a sophisticated appreciation of the challenges of reform efforts in Kyrgyzstan.

Departing Ambassador Spratlen's office after a half-hour debrief, Larry turned to me furtively in the hallway and revealed that the meeting almost didn't happen. Hearing that I was in the country, several members of the Political Section who had served under the previous ambassador, Tatiana Gfoeller, had vowed to block any attempt to arrange a meeting with the current ambassador. Given my congressional testimony three years earlier, in which I had roundly criticized Ambassador Gfoeller, Larry had risked his own reputation by circumventing several political officers in the embassy to organize the meeting.

Chapter Twenty-Four

In Osh the Past Is Never Dead

The imposing, cupola-topped building that houses the International University of Kyrgyzstan sits across Bishkek's Chu Prospect from the Metro Pub, where expatriates disappointed by the lackluster food of the Obama Bar and Grill come for a meal or drinks in a setting that is a strangely appealing fusion of coffeehouse and sports bar. This high-priced hangout for Westerners attracts few students or staff, however, from the International University, whose name belies a student body and curriculum that have little international flavor. The exception is the University's controversial medical school, which enrolls approximately one thousand students from India and Pakistan. Unable to gain admission to a medical school at home, a surprising number of students from the Indian subcontinent train to become physicians in postcommunist countries like Kyrgyzstan, where tuition is very modest by Western standards and admission standards are low. Students spend approximately $20,000 for a five-year medical degree at the International University, with a third of that payable in the first year, a financial boon for the University in light of the high attrition rate.[1]

On an early summer afternoon in 2014, small groups of Indian and Pakistani medical students were conversing outside the University entrance as I made my way to visit Daniyar Tokobaev, a thirty-something Kyrgyz scholar on the social science faculty of the International University. A Soros-funded program that matched young Kyrgyz researchers with more experienced American and West European scholars sponsored my collaboration with Daniyar, who was working on grassroots efforts to improve educational opportunities for special needs students in his country. Daniyar had been in residence at my university during the fall semester of 2013, and now it was my turn to visit his institution.

To walk the narrow, unlit stairs and hallways of the International University was to return to an earlier time, when buildings lacked elevators and other accoutrements of the modern era. One feature of the university that was altogether up-to-date was the end-of-year faculty discussion of "learning outcomes," which Daniyar and his colleagues were concluding when I entered the department office. Once that painful task was over, faculty members began to pepper me with questions about opportunities for cooperation with my university in Florida—overtures that I had come to expect from scholars in Kyrgyzstan, many of whom were desperate to travel overseas or establish new revenue lines for their poorly funded programs. Unfortunately, opportunities like the one enjoyed by Daniyar were rare, and getting rarer— Soros halted the program that funded our collaboration the following year.

The following day, anxious to receive an update on developments in the public advisory boards I'd studied the previous summer, I arranged to meet a member of one of the boards for dinner later that week. Waiting for her one evening outside my hotel, the imaginatively named Touristan, I saw a stranger pull up in his car and approach me. It was her cousin, who would serve as our driver and chaperone. Although my dinner companion was a savvy young scholar, she was understandably sensitive about being seen alone with an older American man at the sprawling Sapura entertainment complex on the outskirts of Bishkek, whose restaurant was known for intimate meals served in small yurts and stone huts.

Entering the grounds of this Kyrgyz-themed restaurant, we made our way through vendors offering goods or experiences tied to local traditions. My Kyrgyz hosts prevailed on me to shell out a few soms to hold a famed golden eagle, which was sitting proudly on the arm of its wizened handler. Still used as hunters of wild animals by some rural Kyrgyz, the favorite prey of the eagles these days was tourists, and as I cautiously approached the massive raptor, I was hoping that it had been well and truly tamed. After I'd slipped on the thick leather gauntlet that extended above my elbow, the golden eagle perched on my arm, which I struggled to keep elevated because of the weight of the bird. I was equally unprepared for the sharpness of the talons, which dug into my arm through the leather. Staring directly into the eyes of this menacing creature was hardly the prelude I had expected to a meal where the primary topic of conversation was the selection of the next generation of public advisory board members.

Before departing from Florida on this visit, I had booked a flight from Bishkek to Osh, where I would spend the last days of this stay in Kyrgyzstan working with Daniyar on his research project. Not enamored of the safety record or reliability of the domestic Kyrgyz airline companies that operated between the country's two largest cities, I decided to try a new Turkish-Kyrgyz joint venture, Pegasus Asia, a companion airline to a reputable Turkish discount carrier, Pegasus. Finding a convenient early morning flight on the webpage of Pegasus Asia, I clicked through to find the price—$12.99, an amount that seemed more fitting for a bus pass than an airline ticket. Thinking that the usual add-ons required by deep discount carriers might inflate the price to a more reasonable level, I signed up for an exit row seat and priority boarding, after which the fare increased to the slightly more reassuring figure of $27.99. Not knowing whether to be grateful for my good fortune or fearful for my life, I printed out the e-ticket and filed it with my other travel documents.

On arrival in Bishkek, I received a computer-generated email from Pegasus Asia with the subject line: "Your flight has been cancelled." Remarkably, the airline's call center—a new concept for Kyrgyzstan—picked up on the second ring. The competent-sounding agent informed me that they couldn't find an airplane for that flight and I should call back closer to the date of departure. A breakthrough came on the eve of our trip to Osh, when Pegasus Asia asked us to come to their headquarters that afternoon to update our tickets: they had managed to borrow a plane from another airline. To ensure our places on the forty-minute flight to Osh, we spent an hour searching for the fledgling airline's office, which was located on a dusty road in a remote district of Bishkek. Finally arriving at a two-story house, whose only marking was a small brass plate on the gate, we entered to find a thoroughly modern facility with the latest technology and a bevy of young, well-trained personnel.

Reassured by the quality of the back-office operation, Daniyar and I arrived early the next morning at the Bishkek airport to begin check-in. Approaching security, we encountered a lengthy queue of young European passengers with backpacks. They were adventure tourists who were returning home via the Persian Gulf on a new Middle East discount carrier, Fly Dubai. Kyrgyzstan's natural beauty and its relative openness were finally beginning to attract the visitors that the deputy minister of tourism had dreamed about during our trip to Issyk-Kul' two decades earlier.

Squeezing past the Fly Dubai crowd, we joined a short line filled with Osh-bound citizens of Kyrgyzstan. After registration and a few minutes in a waiting room, we walked onto the tarmac to find an airplane with a distinctive red Kyrgyz emblem and the words "Air Kyrgyzstan" on the fuselage. At least it was a Boeing 737 and not a Yak-40 or other remnant from the Soviet fleet. Gathering at the base of the airstairs, we melded into the usual impatient and disorderly crowd of passengers, whose democratic instincts resisted rituals like boarding by zones. The most insistent passengers were young women with children, whom the flight attendants motioned through first. As I looked up past the line of passengers mounting the stairs, I saw the face of a Russian pilot through the cockpit window, which for some reason offered a modicum of comfort as my turn came to enter the plane. Never mind that he was puffing away on a cigarette, whose smell permeated the cabin.

Arriving at my seat on the exit row, I found it occupied by a young Kyrgyz woman with a babe-in-arms. After gently reminding her about infants not sitting in exit rows, and getting no response, I quietly took the open seat next to her and was grateful for that. As I looked around the plane at the exit signs and the instructions on seat backs, I noticed that they were all in English and Greek. Not only was the aircraft on loan, it was a well-used cast-off from a Greek carrier. Once airborne, though, the flight was like any other, except for the stunning views over the wing toward the Ala-Too Mountains, which we cleared within twenty minutes of take-off. Beyond those peaks were high mountain valleys and the majestic Naryn River, which the Toktogul Dam tamed for electricity before the water continued its westward journey toward the farmlands of Uzbekistan and the arid steppe beyond. As we descended into Osh, the southern foothills of the Ala-Too Range gave way to the fertile Ferghana Valley, where we briefly overflew the troubled Kyrgyzstani-Uzbekistani borderlands before touching down a mile inside Kyrgyzstani territory.

Osh's airport served almost a million passengers a year and the entire southern region of Kyrgyzstan, but it had the look and feel of a large bus depot. The luggage arrived at an open-air wing of the terminal on baggage trucks with uncovered dollies, from which passengers removed their own bags. Marveling at the easy, unsecured access to the tarmac, Daniyar and I grabbed our luggage and negotiated a fare into Osh in one of the unmarked taxis in front of the terminal. Before we got in the cab, the driver shook our hands, a ritual repeated before other taxi rides in Osh, and a point of contrast with the growing standoffishness in relations between strangers in the capital.

The short ride into Osh offered physical reminders of the weight of history in the region, which celebrated its three thousandth anniversary in 2000. A monument to Manas on horseback towered over a roundabout near the airport. A few blocks further along we merged onto the main north-south thoroughfare into Osh, which bore the name of Iskhak Razzakov, a former Communist Party first secretary from Kirgizia who had ties to the South. As we got closer to town, Razzakov Street became Masaliev Street, in honor of yet another favorite son of the South who had served as Communist Party leader of Kirgizia. Once in the center city, we passed an imposing statue of Lenin on the city's main square, occupying the same perch over the Ak-Buura River that it had commanded in the Soviet era. In some respects, as Faulkner observed with regard to the American South, it seemed that in southern Kyrgyzstan "The past is never dead. It's not even past."

Yet with the exception of the statue of Lenin, most of the grand monuments in Osh were not relics of a bygone era. Local authorities had erected a spate of monuments in recent years to celebrate national heroes of the pre-communist era. Acting as the prototypical "ethnic entrepreneur," Osh's defiant mayor, Melisbek Myrzakmatov, viewed the nationalizing of public spaces as a means of enhancing his own authority and reshaping the national narrative in ways that emphasized the central role of the ethnic Kyrgyz in a region of the country that had been home to various peoples over the centuries, including Uzbeks. Unveiling the Manas monument just two years earlier near the airport entrance, Myrzakmatov boasted that only the statue of Genghis Khan in Ulan Bator, the Mongolian capital, was a larger memorial to a national hero. In the words of the mayor, Osh's monument to Manas "was designed to instill in the rising generation a sense of the greatness and courage [of the Kyrgyz people]." A few months before this, the mayor had christened a new statue in the city center to the nineteenth-century Kyrgyz heroine, Kurmanjan Datka, who succeeded her husband, Alimbek, as the military and political leader of Kyrgyz in the nearby Alai district, long known for its defiant nationalism. Commanding ten thousand local horsemen, Kurmanjan had served as a protector of her people by resisting further integration into the Kokand Kingdom, based in territory that is now Uzbekistan. She bore the same title, Datka (General), as her husband, who was honored with his own monument in Osh shortly after my departure from the city.[2]

On the first anniversary of the Osh events, in June 2011, President Otunbaeva had visited the city to unveil a poignant monument designed to facilitate the reconciliation of the Kyrgyz and Uzbek communities in the South. Entitled "Mothers' Tears," this tribute to the victims of the inter-ethnic violence depicted two weeping mothers embracing, one Kyrgyz, the other Uzbek. Yet reconciliation had not yet come to Osh and the communities surrounding it. Instead, there was a growing Kyrgyz dominance of the city's educational, cultural, political, and economic life. Fewer Uzbeks now sat on the city council, there was less access to Uzbek-language education or media, and retail establishments, once the preserve of Uzbek businessmen and women, fell increasingly into the hands of Kyrgyz owners.

With a population of 250,000, Osh was less than one-third the size of Bishkek and it lacked the tony shops and cafes and the "elite" apartments that graced the Kyrgyzstani capital. Although there were vibrant pockets in Osh, many restaurants on the city's historic commercial avenue remained virtually empty over lunch. The city's famed central market, a maze of small shops giving on to winding alleys, was still teeming with locals, but like other bazaars in Kyrgyzstan, it had become a venue for reselling cheap Chinese goods rather than a source of artisanal wares. For handmade Kyrgyz fabrics one had to cross the Ak-Buura River to a small set of boutiques, whose prices and selection were no match for those in shops in Istanbul offering Central Asian artifacts.

What Osh lacked in economic vibrancy it made up for in its physical and cultural landscape. Perched directly above the heart of the city was Solomon-

Too, or Solomon's Mountain, a massive stone outcropping that rose improbably out of the Ferghana Valley. I arrived at the base of the mountain early one morning to find an old woman ready to make a pilgrimage to the top with several young girls in tow. On the summit was a miniature mosque that had been destroyed in the Soviet era and then reopened in the immediate aftermath of communism's collapse. For Muslims in Central Asia, Solomon-Too was one of the holiest shrines in the region and a popular pilgrimage site. According to legend, both the Prophet and Solomon had prayed at the summit, which affords pilgrims a panoramic view of the expanse of the Ferghana Valley to the west and the mountains that separate Kyrgyzstan from China and Tajikistan to the east and south. Hard against the southern face of Solomon-Too was a gleaming new mosque, which could hold 5,000 faithful inside its grand prayer hall and 20,000 on the surrounding square. Funded in part by donors from small Persian Gulf states, the mosque was the largest in Kyrgyzstan, an appropriate honor for a city where Islam had deep roots.

Crossing the street from the new mosque on a sweltering summer afternoon, I stopped into a small lunchroom and grabbed a bottle of water from the refrigerated display case. When I approached the hijab-wearing young assistant behind the counter to pay, she scolded me in Kyrgyz and broken Russian, noting that nothing would be sold during the early afternoon prayers being held across the street. Slinking out of the establishment, I headed down dirt roads that snaked through the heart of the Uzbek *mahalla*. It was a maze of narrow alleys and dead-ends, with houses hidden behind high walls and decorative metal gates, and little physical evidence of the destruction wreaked on the neighborhood four years earlier. Rounding a corner, I fell into a stream of men and boys pouring out of a small mosque, one of more than fifty that dotted the city. Osh had contained three times that number of mosques in the tsarist era, before the Soviet authorities virtually eliminated houses of worship of all kinds. At the end of the communist era, the entire country of Kyrgyzstan had less than forty mosques; less than a quarter-century later, it boasted more than two thousand.[3]

That evening I met a prominent ethnic Uzbek journalist for dinner at an outdoor restaurant along the banks of the Ak-Buura River. Like other residents of the city that I encountered, he was not eager to speak about the violent events of June 2010 and their aftermath. In his view, each of Osh's two major communities—Kyrgyz and Uzbek—had turned inward, and in his own case he had found solace and meaning in Islam, a religion that he had largely ignored before the inter-ethnic violence. Deeply suspicious of American and Russian influence in the region, he sought to probe me during dinner about my own motivations for conducting research in his country, apparently convinced that I was on a mission relating to something other than academic research. When I happened upon him the following day in front of the new mosque, he was walking from prayers at the head of a group of young Uzbek men. He all but ignored my greeting, seemingly embarrassed to acknowledge to his minions that he was acquainted with an American.

Scheduled to leave Osh for Istanbul on an early flight the next morning, I booked a taxi to pick me up at my hotel at 3:00 a.m. The hotel was one of a small number of self-styled "boutique" establishments that offered an attractive alternative to the sprawling, Soviet-era lodgings in the center of the city. For a reasonable price, the hotel offered a serviceable breakfast, well-appointed rooms with comfortable beds, a modern bathroom with its own Ariston water heater—the true mark of luxury in Central Asia—and a view of a factory in ruins less than a hundred meters away. Located in a former industrial zone on the road to the airport, the hotel sat on an outparcel of an abandoned plant that was a relic of the once-dominant cotton industry in the region. Absent the usual planning and zoning rules adopted in urban communities in the West, the peripheries of cities in Kyrgyzstan presented unlimited opportunities for novel uses of land.

Descending the stairs with my suitcase just before 3:00 a.m., I walked toward the glass entrance doors of the hotel and found them locked. With no one at the reception desk or in the small suite of offices behind it, I continued along the darkened corridor in search of another exit. There was none. As I walked back down the hallway, past a series of guest rooms, I tried to roust whoever was "on duty" from his sleep by asking if anyone was there, in ever louder cries. As something approaching panic began to set in, I noticed what seemed to be a door partly ajar and opened it. Inside, a young man, the night clerk, was asleep, fully dressed, on the bed. Unable to wake him with verbal encouragement, I resorted to shaking him, and at last he came to, apologized profusely, and freed me from the hotel and the locked gates beyond.

Not finding a taxi waiting, I called the cab company, but no answer. Undeterred, I set out on foot with my suitcase along an unlit stretch of rough-tarred road that separated the hotel from the main thoroughfare to the airport. Reassured by the glow of lights and the sound of traffic emanating from Masaliev Street in the distance, I arrived at the intersection just before 3:30 a.m. and did what had become customary over three decades of visits to Russia and surrounding regions: I stuck out my arm in the hopes of flagging down a *chastnik*, the Russian word for a driver willing to pick up strangers for a fare. Within seconds, a young male driver veered to the curb from a center lane to see where I was going. After agreeing on a fare, I hopped in the seat alongside him, shook his hand, and spent the ten-minute ride to the airport discussing, in Russian, the NBA and his cousin's new life as an emigrant in Kansas City.

Chapter Twenty-Five

Preparing for a Presidential Afterlife

On board a Turkish Airlines flight to Istanbul two hours later, I began to marvel at how far Kyrgyzstan had come in opening itself to the world over the previous quarter-century. Besides a growing diaspora that now stretched from Eurasia to Europe and the United States, Kyrgyzstan's transport and communication links—previously routed through Moscow—had diversified into an ever-growing web of direct connections with the outside world, with my nonstop flight from Osh to Istanbul on a major international carrier only the latest example. Although citizens of Kyrgyzstan still got much of their news and entertainment from Moscow-based TV and radio channels, rapidly expanding access to the internet—available initially in ubiquitous internet cafes and later through a growing network of Wi-Fi hotspots—was removing the last vestiges of the country's isolation. With over a third of the population connected to the internet at home in 2016—three times the figure of a decade earlier—Kyrgyzstanis had become eager users of social media, which were available without the government-imposed restrictions in place in many neighboring countries. [1]

The five-hour flight to Turkey also allowed me to reflect on Daniyar's unexpected parting words the previous evening. Not usually a person to reveal his feelings, Daniyar had confided in me that our visit to the country's South—the first he had made since a brief school-led excursion in his youth—had opened his eyes to the shared culture of the Kyrgyz, which transcended regional boundaries. He was clearly troubled by the thought that many ambitious politicians from North and South had played the regional card as a means of advancing their own careers. Living just a few days among southerners had helped to dispel for him myths about the region embraced by many of his fellow northerners. It was an encouraging sign—especially amid the construction of a second, and more modern, highway connecting Osh with the capital—that increased contact between North and South could serve as an antidote to regional tensions that had brought the country to the brink of civil war in 2010.

Besides improving transportation and communication links between North and South, the emergence of a virulent brand of ethnic Kyrgyz nationalism after the 2010 violence in Osh served to rally many Kyrgyz from all parts of the country behind a common identity. Yet an ethnic nationalism with the potential to bring North and South together threatened to drive a deeper wedge between the Kyrgyz and the country's minorities, especially the Uzbeks. It also undermined efforts by moderate politicians to advance a national identity that transcended individual ethnic groups by encouraging loyalty to a state of Kyrgyzstanis instead of separate Kyrgyz, Uzbek, or Russian communities. The idea of a civic nation, Roza Otunbaeva admitted, had yet to be created.[2]

There were also plenty of political and economic challenges ahead for what seemed at times to be an "interim country," to use Thomas Lahusen's phrase.[3] A quarter-century into its development as an independent state, Kyrgyzstan had yet to settle on a model of government. To its credit, the 2010 Constitution had tried to give the new institutions of state time to take root by prohibiting the parliament from amending it for ten years. However, President Atambaev and his allies could not resist fiddling with the rules of the political game, just as his predecessors had done repeatedly in the 1990s and 2000s.

Claiming a need to "idiot-proof" the constitution, with just over a year left in his single term Atambaev supported the adoption of constitutional changes that would shift more power from the presidency to the prime minister's office. Ostensibly designed to prevent the abuse of presidential office by a would-be strongman, the measure aroused suspicion that Atambaev, as the de facto leader of the country's dominant party, the Social Democrats, was simply trying to ensure his continued relevance in politics after his term ended in 2017. If Atambaev's successor as president exercised less influence, the prime minister stood to dominate the political landscape. In that case, even if Atambaev himself did not occupy the prime minister's office, he would be a powerful force behind the scenes if, as expected, the prime minister was drawn from the largest parliamentary party, the Social Democrats.

The proposed constitutional changes ignited a firestorm in Kyrgyzstani politics in the second half of 2016. In an unprecedented move, Atambaev's former colleagues in the Interim Government of 2010—among them Roza Otunbaeva and Omurbek Tekebaev, the de facto father of the constitution—signed a collective letter condemning any attempt to revise the constitution before 2020. President Atambaev responded almost immediately to the letter with an intemperate speech, the harshest of his presidency, which accused his former colleagues of spreading "malicious lies." Delivered in the presence of these colleagues on Bishkek's main square on the occasion of Kyrgyzstan's Independence Day, Atambaev's speech reminded them that they could be held to account legally for their misdeeds in office six years earlier, a threat that prompted former President Otunbaeva to rise from her seat and walk demonstratively off the stage. It was no doubt of little comfort to Otunbaeva that Atambaev concluded his speech by assuring the nation that he had no intention of seeking any formal political post after his departure from the presidency in 2017.[4]

The issue for Atambaev's critics was not just allowing political institutions to mature before making constitutional revisions; opponents of the amendments also objected to several of the proposed changes to the constitution, which they believed would weaken the independence of the judiciary and strengthen the hand of Kyrgyz nationalists and those seeking to silence opponents of the regime. As both sides understood, constitutional language mattered. Article 1 of the 2010 Constitution contained a simple, one-sentence statement of the country's basic principles, which included the state's secular, law-based, and democratic character. The proposed alternative had nine separate points, several of which appeared to be inspired by growing currents of nativism and social conservatism in Russia. Among the country's "highest values" in the new draft were "love of country," "the development of the national [Kyrgyz] language and culture," and, perhaps most worrying for the opposition, "a respectful attitude toward the country's history." It was a phrase that the Russian authorities had used to condemn domestic and foreign critics and that the Kyrgyzstani authorities could employ to silence unpopular interpretations of events such as the inter-ethnic violence in Osh in 2010.

Because the existing constitution imposed a decade-long moratorium on constitutional amendments made by parliament, Atambaev and his allies were forced to place the revisions before the country in a referendum, which took place on December 11, 2016. After a heated campaign, the referendum passed, but in desultory fashion. Despite dominating media coverage during the campaign and mobilizing government employees, most notably teachers, to get out the vote on election day, President Atambaev and his political allies were only able to convince 42 percent of the voters to cast their ballots—the previous low turnout for a constitutional referendum was 71 percent. A seemingly respectable 79 percent of those voting approved the referendum, though this too was significantly lower than in the previous six constitutional referendums. The lack of popular enthusiasm for changes to the constitution testified to the waning authority of President Atambaev as well as the depth of divisions in the country.[5]

The constitutional changes turned out to be the opening gambit in a series of moves designed to guarantee the continuing political influence of Almazbek Atambaev after his presidency ended in December 2017. Just as Boris Yeltsin and his team had engineered the handoff of power to Vladimir Putin, President Atambaev launched his own succession plan. He first identified his preferred successor, a longtime political ally and fellow Social Democrat, Sooronbai Jeenbekov, and then employed the still formidable powers of his office to disqualify or denigrate other contenders in the presidential race. Among those targeted for prosecution in the run-up to the October 2017 presidential election was the long-time leader of the Ata-Meken Party, Omurbek Tekebaev, whose eight-year sentence for fraud, handed down in August, kept him out of the race.

During the campaign itself, Atambaev subjected Jeenbekov's main opponent, the wealthy Respublika Party leader, Omurbek Babanov, to a steady stream of smears and innuendo. These included accusations that Babanov was subservient to the Kazakhstani government and to Kyrgyzstani Uzbeks. At a campaign rally in the South, Babanov had told an assembly of ethnic Uzbeks that under his presidency, "if a policeman messes with (*tronet*) Uzbeks, he will be fired." This seemingly innocuous statement prompted the prosecutor's office to investigate Babanov for sowing inter-ethnic enmity. More importantly, its wide dissemination in the media served as a "dog whistle" directed at Kyrgyz nationalist voters, who had no interest in the state assuring equal treatment for ethnic Uzbeks.[6]

At a moment when deeply divisive nationalist rhetoric was proving useful to politicians in the United States and Europe, Atambaev was riding out of the Kyrgyzstani presidency on his own populist wave. Buoyed by the populist attacks on his opponent and the mobilization of administrative resources on his behalf by President Atambaev and his lieutenants, Sooronbai Jeenbekov won in the first round of the presidential election, with 53 percent of the vote. The result made it unlikely that the sixty-one-year-old Atambaev would spend his presidential afterlife learning to play the piano, as he had promised a year earlier.

Unfortunately, the campaign against the political opponents of Atambaev did not end with the election. In the wake of the voting, the authorities brought lawsuits against Omurbek Babanov and his businesses, which led the defeated presidential candidate to flee the country. To save himself and his companies, Babanov announced several weeks later on his Facebook page that he was resigning from parliament and quitting politics. It was an inauspicious beginning to the presidency of Sooronbai Jeenbekov and yet more evidence of how difficult it is for new states, even those with relatively open societies like Kyrgyzstan, to accept the idea of a vibrant political opposition.

Chapter Twenty-Six

A Stan Like No Other

One of the most intriguing puzzles of Central Asian studies is why Kyrgyzstan has been a Stan like no other in the region. Over the years, scholars, journalists, and politicians have offered competing explanations for Kyrgyzstan's exceptionalism. Some emphasize the importance of cultural traditions of the Kyrgyz that predate Russian and Soviet rule. As vertical nomads with a long history of decentralized governance, the Kyrgyz developed attitudes toward political authority that distinguished them from sedentary peoples, who pursued religious and political practices that encouraged greater deference toward centralized rule. It is easy to overstate the importance of this cultural legacy, but it would be wrong to ignore the sinews of history that shape the mental map of people who share a common experience.[1]

Other observers point to the decisive role played by an accident of history as Kyrgyzstan took its leave from the Soviet Union. Unlike in other Central Asian states, Kyrgyzstan's first president, Askar Akaev, was a reform-minded scholar rather than the local leader of the Communist Party. His will to power did not match that of neighboring presidents, and so he was willing to tolerate a level of dissent that was unusual for the region. Although his extended family would later seek to mimic the behavior of ruling dynasties in neighboring states, where the presidents' kin brought leading businesses under their control, Akaev initially granted generous space for enterprising men and women to amass independent wealth. The result was a wide circle of private businessmen who used their considerable means to support opposition parties as well as informal networks of clients and citizen-followers who checked presidential power and, on two occasions, overthrew the country's leader.[2]

Some would also argue that Kyrgyzstan benefitted from an accident of physical geography. Unlike most states in Central Asia, Kyrgyzstan was resource poor. The paucity of easily marketable resources like oil and gas, which exist in plentiful supply in Kazakhstan and Turkmenistan, denied Kyrgyzstan much-needed export earnings, but it also lowered the stakes of politics in the country. Because winning elections did not grant access to massive revenues from the energy spigots, politicians and their entourages were less obsessed with seizing and maintaining power.

Kyrgyzstan's relative poverty also meant that it did not have the luxury of spending lavishly on a praetorian guard to protect the president, on gleaming capital cities designed to instill pride and awe in the populace, or on social services or subsidized goods that could assuage a discontented nation. In other words, Kyrgyzstan's government didn't have the means to buy off or easily impress or suppress its people. It was in part this recognition of the country's economic and political vulnerability that encouraged President Akaev to open up to the West in the 1990s and to lay the foundations of a liberal order, a foundation that has admittedly revealed serious cracks over the years.

Even before the introduction of extensive formal checks and balances in the 2010 Constitution, Kyrgyzstan's demographic divisions served as an informal constraint on the accumulation of power by the president. In a visit to Florida at the end of 2016, Kyrgyzstan's ambassador to the United States, Kadyr Toktogulov, reminded my students that for all its negative features, the North-South political divide prevented a narrowly based regional elite from consolidating authoritarian control over the country. Once a region felt itself sufficiently disenfranchised, its leaders and citizens rose up against the existing order, as the South did in 2005 when it overthrew Akaev, and as the North did in 2010 when the target was the Bakiev regime. The hope now is that under the new parliamentary system, which distributes political influence across a range of parties and ministries rather than concentrating it in the hands of a president, regional resentments will decrease and disputes over policy and personnel will be resolved in the corridors of state power rather than in the streets.

The first quarter-century of Kyrgyzstan's statehood has left many fundamental issues unsettled about its direction of development. Disputes continue over the country's identity, its geopolitical orientation, its political institutions, and even its borders. But the very uncertainty of Kyrgyzstan's future path is in part testimony to the country's openness to the world and to vigorous domestic debates and protests. Of course, amid this relentless cycle of political and financial crises, Kyrgyzstan must eventually find a way to realize its economic potential, to establish an independent judiciary, to reduce corruption, and to ensure that the understandable desire to nurture Kyrgyz language and traditions does not prevent minority groups from participating fully in the country's political, economic, and cultural life. Failing to resolve these issues will only play into the hands of the growing number of

Islamists in the region who promise to replace the avarice and incessant squabbling of the country's political class with a more just and stable social order. As one local scholar told me in an interview almost a decade ago, if something isn't done we'll have two types of Kyrgyz in fifteen to twenty years, and one will be pro-Islamist.[3]

The turbulence of the post-communist era in Kyrgyzstan stands in marked contrast to life in the Soviet Kirgizia that my friend Bolot Djigitekov and others grew up in so many decades ago. It is almost surely not the country that Bolot would have imagined, or perhaps even wanted; nor is it the future that Kyrgyzstan's leaders or citizens envisioned when I arrived for my first visit in the innocent, romantic days following the demise of communism. Yet for all the disappointments, Kyrgyzstan continues to defy the pessimists in Moscow, Washington, and in Kyrgyzstan itself who have, at various moments, despaired of the country's prospects and, in some cases, even its viability. Despite being sandwiched between China, the Russian world, and the Middle East, Kyrgyzstan has managed, against all odds, to keep alive the hope for open societies and accountable governments in Central Asia. It may not have become the Switzerland of Asia, but it proved that in one of the world's toughest neighborhoods, it could resist the authoritarian temptation and carve out its own path of political and economic development.

Thanks to the chance encounter with Bolot in Moscow almost forty years ago, the arc of my scholarly career followed the birth and development of one of the Soviet Union's most physically beautiful and politically intriguing legacies. The world of Soviet courts and lawyers' offices that had been the focus of my early research expanded to include the corridors of power in a new state, whose leaders introduced me to the inner workings of their minds as well as the institutions in which they functioned. In the course of my encounters in Kyrgyzstan, I found that the natural sentiments undergirding human empathy overcame my formal training, which had encouraged scientific detachment toward the subjects of one's research. In short, I developed a bond with the people and the country I studied, and a concern for their fate. I also came to appreciate that individuals matter as much as institutions—a commonplace for most but a form of heresy for some in the social sciences.

Just as Bolot could not have envisioned the future of his native land, I could not have imagined that my life journey would take me from a Cold War childhood in a small town in Central Florida to a post-communist country a half a world away. Nor, for that matter, could I have imagined pursuing a scholarly life, never mind one that offered such a range of experiences beyond the office and the classroom. Whatever lies ahead for Kyrgyzstan, witnessing the emergence of this small, contrarian land has been for me a life-defining and life-affirming experience.

Notes

1. CONVERSATIONS WITH BOLOT

1. Ironically, the Soviet regime was responsible for creating a modern Kirgiz identity through the granting to the Kirgiz of a fixed territory, a standardized language, an officially recognized nationality, and a national history. For the standard Soviet work on the controversies surrounding the emergence of the Kirgiz as a people, see S. M. Abramzon, *Kirgizy i ikh etnogeneticheskie i istoriko-kul'turnye sviazi* (Leningrad: Izdatel'stvo nauka, 1971).

2. After Stalin's death in 1953, the Soviet government began to allow limited foreign travel to the Kirgiz capital and its environs, but large areas of the republic remained closed to foreigners. Central Intelligence Agency, Intelligence Report: Soviet Restrictions on Travel by Foreigners (December 1966). https://www.cia.gov/library/readingroom/docs/CIA-RDP79S01008A000100080001-4.pdf

2. FROM MOSCOW TO BISHKEK (OR KIRGIZIA, KIRGIZSTAN, KYRGYZSTAN)

1. For more on Aitmatov's life and literature, see Joseph P. Mozur, *Parables from the Past: The Prose Fiction of Chingiz Aitmatov* (Pittsburgh: University of Pittsburgh Press, 1994), and Jeffrey B. Lilley, *Have the Mountains Fallen? Two Journeys of Loss and Redemption in the Cold War* (Bloomington: Indiana University Press, 2018).

2. Pervyi s'ezd narodnykh deputatov SSSR, den' pervyi, zasedanie vtoroe, May 25, 1989. http://www.agitclub.ru/vybory/gor89/sten/sten03.htm

3. *The USSR First Congress of People's Deputies*, vol. II, ed. Rolf Theen (New York: Paragon House, 1991), 332. Aitmatov had gone so far as to argue that "the great service that the Soviet Union had performed for the rest of the world was to demonstrate how not to go about constructing socialism." Archie Brown, *The Gorbachev Factor* (Oxford: Oxford University Press, 1996), 314.

4. "Chingiz Aitmatov: Kakoi iz menia kosmopolit s takim litsom?," *Trud* 107 (June 16, 2008). www.trud.ru/issue/article.php?id=200806161070801

5. Theen, *USSR First Congress*, 333.

6. Theen, 334.

3. THE PRESENT IS HISTORY

1. At the end of Soviet rule, there was a balkanization of the economy, with the Kirgiz largely relegated to jobs in agriculture, education, and government service. With industrial jobs dominated by the Slavs, Kirgiz accounted for only 6.3 percent of those employed in the electric energy sector, 11 percent in machine construction and metalworking, and 15.3 percent in construction. R. Osmonalieva, "Ob'ektiven li voliuntarizm?," *Kommunist Kirgizstana* (October 1990): 79–83.

2. Mikhail Guboglo, "Demography and Language in the Capitals of the Union Republics," *Journal of Soviet Nationalities* 1, no. 4 (Winter 1990–1991): 2–42.

3. N. Zenkov, "Budut li garantii?," *Slovo Kyrgyzstana*, September 22, 1990, 1. In the first six months of 1990—that is, a year-and-a-half before the collapse of the USSR—the outflow of Russians from Kirgizia was already more than two-and-a-half times that of the previous year.

4. A year later, in the summer of 1993, among the seventy-two schools in Bishkek, there were seven using only Kyrgyz-language instruction, nineteen with a mixed Russian and Kyrgyz format, and forty-six offering Russian-only classes. Interview with Makil' Imankulova (Deputy Minister of Education), June 8, 1993, Bishkek. The figures for the entire country were as follows: of 1,796 schools in all, 1,122 used Kyrgyz, 142 Russian, 120 Uzbek, 2 Tajik, and 409 were mixed. Interview with Suiunduk Oljobaev (Head, Department of State Language, Ministry of Education), June 10, 1993, Bishkek.

5. Eugene Huskey, "Kyrgyzstan: The Politics of Frustration," in Ian Bremmer and Ray Taras, eds., *Nations and Politics in the Soviet Successor States* (Cambridge: Cambridge University Press, 1993), 405. Russians also took a disproportionate share of places in higher education, with over 55 percent of Russian applicants accepted compared to less than 30 percent of Kyrgyz. R. Achylova, "Natsiia—sub'ekt, a ne rudiment istorii," *Kommunist Kirgizstana* (June 1990): 35–39. In terms of membership in the Communist Party, however, Kyrgyz were represented in numbers that were roughly equal to their share of the overall republican population, 48.2 percent in 1990 compared to the Russian share of 29.9 percent in that year. "Natsional'nyi sostav kompartii Kirgizii," *Kommunist Kirgizstana* (July 1990): 49.

6. Aizada Kuitieva, "Sestra Chingiza Roza Aitmatova napisala memuarnuiu knigu 'Belye stranitsy istorii'," March 31, 2008, 24.kg. http://www.centrasia.ru/newsA.php?st=1206993840

7. For a brief personal account in English of the Stalinist terror in Kirgizia, see Azamat Altay, "Kirgiziya During the Great Purge," *Central Asian Review* 12, no. 2 (1964): 97–107.

8. "Usubaliyev Gives Report to Kirgiz CP Congress," Foreign Broadcast Information Service, February 4, 1981, R46.

9. Roza Aitmatova, *Belye piatna istorii (moi vospominaniia)* (Bishkek: V.R.S. Company, 2013).

4. HOPE ABOUNDS

1. The exchange took me back to a train journey I had made from Moscow to the Polish border at the end of 1988. I had shared a compartment with a collective farm chairman from Belarus who was returning from a conference where reform-oriented Soviet economists explained market mechanisms used in Western agriculture. The one stumbling block for him was pricing. When I tried to assure him that prices in capitalist economies reflected, in large measure, the interplay of supply and demand in the market, he insisted that that was impossible. No powerful country like the US, he argued, would allow anyone but the government to set prices.

2. Interview with Djypar Djeksheev, June 18, 1992, Bishkek.

3. Interview with Asan Ormushev, June 19, 1992, Bishkek.

4. Osmon Ibraimov, "Neizvestnyi genotsid," *Slovo Kyrgyzstana*, April 20, 1991, 10; "Narod, predavshii zabveniiu proshloe, obrechen . . . ," *Slovo Kyrgyzstana*, July 4, 1991, 1.

5. Taken together with the revolutionary upheavals that followed, the Urkun devastated the local economy, with the number of horses, sheep, and goats declining by half from 1914 to 1924. A. Dzhumanaliev, *Politicheskoe razvitie Kyrgyzstana (20-30-e gody)* (Bishkek: Ilim, 1994), 16. The definitive work in English on the Urkun is Edward Dennis Sokol's *The Revolt of 1916 in Russian Central Asia* (Baltimore: Johns Hopkins University Press, 2016), published originally in 1954 and reissued in 2016.

5. TRAVELING THE CHU VALLEY

1. Eugene Huskey, "Kyrgyzstan Leaves the Ruble Zone," *RFE/RL Research Report* 35, no. 2 (July 1993): 38–43.

2. Among others on this trip who alerted me to the importance of regional differences among the Kyrgyz was Alikbek Jekshenkulov, a member of parliament. Interview with Alikbek Jekshenkulov, June 10, 1993, Bishkek.

3. See Eugene Huskey, "Eurasian Semi-presidentialism: The Development of Kyrgyzstan's Model of Government," in *Semi-presidentialism Outside Europe: A Comparative Study*, ed. Robert Elgie and Sophia Moestrup (Abingdon, UK: Routledge, 2007), 161–81.

4. Besides the publication of several unflattering articles on the Kirgiz party leadership in official Moscow-based newspapers, most notably *Komsomolskaia pravda*, there appeared in the Soviet capital in this period a damning pamphlet, entitled *Unknown Republic* (*Neizvestnaia respublika*), which was produced by a delegation from the reform-oriented Moscow Popular Front upon their return from a fact-finding mission to the Kirgiz Republic in 1990.

5. Absamat Masaliev, *Stranitsy zhizni i bednoe nashe otechestvo* (Bishkek: Az-mak, 1993), 312–13.

6. Roza Otunbaeva told me that Aitmatov had also approached her about being nominated for the presidency, but she refused. She believed that Aitmatov's intervention was important but not decisive for the selection of Akaev. Interview with Roza Otunbaeva, September 25, 1992, Washington, DC. Although Aitmatov represented the small progressive wing of the Kirgiz Communist Party, he had not been supportive of the demonstrations that were bringing more and more people onto the streets of the Kirgiz capital at the end of the Soviet era. In February 1990, the Communist Party leadership in Moscow enlisted Aitmatov to appear on television to discourage the formation in Kirgizia of the kind of "national front" organization that was advocating greater autonomy in many other Soviet republics. He reminded his fellow Kirgiz in that appearance that we are not like the Baltic peoples. "That's Europe, an advanced society with the achievements of democracy behind it. And who's behind us? China, with its almost feudal dictatorship." "Obrashchenie k molodezhi," *Slovo Kyrygzstana*, February 17, 1990, 3.

7. The idea of aristocracy doesn't fit comfortably with the nomadic traditions of the Kyrgyz, though there were leaders of certain families, called bai, that enjoyed an elevated reputation. This is what Levitin had in mind.

6. THE POWER OF WORDS

1. Vystuplenie Prezidenta Kyrgyzskoi Respubliki A. Akaeva na lanche s predstaviteliami delovykh i finansovykh krugov, New York City, May 17, 1993. Original mimeograph in possession of the author.

2. Vystuplenie Prezidenta Kyrgyzskoi Respubliki A. Akaeva na obede ot imeni Foruma svobody, Rosslyn, Virginia, May 18, 1993. Original mimeograph in possession of the author.

3. "Vot tak 'politika'," *Slovo Kyrgyzstana*, June 24, 1994, 1.

4. "Stavki ochen' vysoki," *Slovo Kyrgyzstana*, September 24, 1994, 4.

5. Zamira Sydykova describes her criminal conviction and its aftermath in the opening pages of her book, *Gody ozhidaniia i poter'. Vremia peremen* (Bishkek, 2003).

6. Z. Kurmanov, "Soros prekrasno znaet tsenu liudiam i ikh kachestvam," Posviashchaetsia istoriku Chinare Zhakypovoi, TsentrAziia, August 15, 2005. http://www.centrasia.ru/newsA.php?st=1124135280

7. KYRGYZSTAN GOES TO THE POLLS

1. Ian Pryde, "Kyrgyzstan's Slow Progress to Reform," *The World Today* (June 1995): 16.

2. This is not to say that they are politically benign in the United States. Efforts at minority vote dilution, which include gerrymandering and voter suppression, have illustrated the nakedly partisan uses of electoral rule changes.

3. V. Uleev, "Chem vymoshchena nasha doroga," *Res Publica*, August 22, 1995, 3.

4. Interview with Kamil' Baialinov, May 19, 2000, Bishkek.

5. Interview with Myktybek Abdyldaev, July 29, 2008, Bishkek.

6. D. Evlashkov, "Pochem senatorskoe kreslo?," *Slovo Kyrgyzstana*, February 18, 1995, 5.

7. Kanybek Imanaliev, "Litsom k litsu," *Slovo Kyrgyzstana*, July 8, 1995, p. 5.

8. K. Bokonbaev, "Pust' traibalizm posluzhit delu," *Slovo Kyrgyzstana*, January 14, 1995, 7.

9. For an analysis of the ways in which referendums shifted power from the prime minister to the president in the 1990s, see Gulnara Iskakova's magisterial study of Kyrgyzstan's political institutions, *Vybory i demokratiia v Kyrgyzstane: Konstitutsionnyi dizain prezidentsko-parlamentskikh otnoshenii* (Bishkek: 2003), 420–34.

10. See President Akaev's attempt to present the past and present of Kyrgyzstan through the lens of the Manas legend in Askar Akaev, *Kyrgyz Statehood and the National Epos 'Manas'* (New York: Global Scholarly Publications, 2003).

8. CENTRAL ASIA THROUGH STUDENTS' EYES

1. "50 vedushchikh politikov Kyrgyzstana v kontse 1999 goda," *Res Publica* (Bishkek), January 18–24, 2000, 5.

2. Office for Democratic Institutions and Human Rights (OSCE), Kyrgyz Republic Parliamentary Elections, 20 February and 12 March 2000, Final Report (Warsaw: April 10, 2000).

3. Poppy Brady, "Nightmare Flight," *Evening Mail* (Birmingham, UK), January 23, 1999, 11.

4. By 2017, there had been a dramatic transformation in the background of the workforce, with 98 percent of the personnel drawn from citizens of Kyrgyzstan—2,533 of a total of 2,601 workers at the mine. http://www.kumtor.kg/en/category/announcements/jobs/ The ownership of the company had also changed, with most of the shares purchased by Centerra Gold in 2009 while a minority ownership share was transferred to Kyrgyzaltyn JSC, pursuant to an agreement with the Kyrgyzstani government.

5. Phillip Whish-Wilson, "The Aral Sea Environmental Health Crisis," *Journal of Rural and Remote Environmental Health* 2, no. 1 (2002): 29–34.

6. "Istoriia pamiatnikov na tsentral'noi ploshchad' Ala-Too v Bishkeke," Akipress Kultura, August 6, 2014. http://culture.akipress.org/news:8566

7. Zamira Sydykova, *Est' u revolutsii nachalo, net u revoliutsii kontsa* (Bishkek: 2011), 106–7.

9. FALSIFICATION AND CONCILIATION

1. Interview with Daniiar Usenov, May 24, 2000, Bishkek.
2. Interview with Omurbek Tekebaev, May 24, 2000, Bishkek; interview with Melis Eshimkanov, May 29, 2000, Bishkek.
3. A. Galunichev, "Tri chernykh dnia avgusta v Bishkeke," *Slovo Kyrgyzstana*, August 27, 1991, 3.
4. Two of these refused to take the language examination, insisting that it would be administered unfairly.
5. IFES Press Release, Final Report, Monitoring of Electronic Mass Media in Kyrgyzstan during the Election Campaign (October 2–October 29, 2000). Copy in possession of the author. See also Statement of Preliminary Findings and Conclusions, OSCE/ODIHR Election Observation Mission, Kyrgyz Republic-Presidential Elections, 29 October 2000 (Bishkek: October 30, 2000).
6. "Melis Eshimkanov: u menia khvataet muzhestva pozdravit' Akaeva s pobedoi!," *Delo No* (Bishkek), November 1, 2000.
7. R. F. M. J. Cleven and M. van Bruggen, "The Cyanide Accident in Barskoon (Kyrgyzstan)," National Institute of Public Health and the Environment (Netherlands), February 2000. http://rivm.openrepository.com/rivm/bitstream/10029/9591/1/609026001.pdf

10. BORDERS AND REGIONS BEDEVIL A PRESIDENT

1. For a detailed account of this episode, see Zamira Sydykova, *Gody ozhidaniia i poter'*, 146–7 and passim.
2. Alisher Khamidov, "Dispute over China-Kyrgyz Border Demarcation Pits President vs. Parliament," Eurasianet.org, June 27, 2001.
3. Interview with Roza Otunbaeva, April 11, 2009, Bishkek.
4. Madeleine Reeves, "Travels in the Margins of the State: Everyday Geography in the Ferghana Valley Borderlands," in *Everyday Life in Central Asia: Past and Present*, ed. Jeff Sahadeo and Russell Zanca (Bloomington: Indiana University Press), 281.
5. Greg Child, "Fear of Falling," *Outside* (November 1, 2000). http://www.outsideonline.com/1928676/fear-falling; Viktoriia Panfilova, "V ogne protivostoianiia: nesoglasovannost' deistvii i sopernichestvo gosudarstv regiona povyshaiut opasnost' rasprostraneniia religioznogo ekstremizma," *NG Sodruzhestvo*, February 28, 2001; Martha Brill Olcott, "The War on Terrorism in Central Asia and the Cause of Democratic Reform," *Demokratizatsiya: The Journal of Post-Soviet Democratization* 11, no. 1 (2003): 86–95; Matthew Stein, "The Goals of the Islamic Movement of Uzbekistan and Its Impact on Central Asia and the United States," FMSO-JRIC Analyst, US Army (Camp Leavenworth, Kansas, January 2013).
6. By the beginning of 2010, the Manas Transit Center was transiting 30,000 military personnel a month into Afghanistan and 600 short tons of cargo. Embassy Bishkek, "Scenesetter for SRAP Holbrooke's Visit to Kyrgyzstan," WikiLeaks Cable: 10BISHKEK113_a, dated February 16, 2010. https://wikileaks.org/plusd/cables/10BISHKEK113_a.html

11. THE TULIP REVOLUTION

1. By far the best account of the mobilization efforts that led to the Tulip Revolution is Scott Radnitz's *Weapons of the Wealthy: Predatory Regimes and Elite-Led Protests in Central Asia* (Ithaca, NY: Cornell University Press, 2010), 131–66.

2. "Kyrgyzstan's Tulip Revolution: Interview with Roza Otunbaeva," *Demokratizatsiya: The Journal of Post-Soviet Democratization* 13, no. 4 (Fall 2005): 485.

3. International Crisis Group (ICG), "Kyrgyzstan: After the Revolution," Asia Report no. 97 (May 4, 2005), 11.

4. Temir Sariev, *Shakh kyrgyzskoi demokratii* (Bishkek: Salam, 2008), 113.

5. Il'ia Poroshenko, "Ot bitvy 'maidanov' k bitve 'kabinetov'," *Rossiiskie vesti*, November 15, 2006, 7.

6. ICG, "Kyrgyzstan: After the Revolution," 6, footnote 31.

7. Askar Akaev, *Diplomacy of the Silk Road (A Foreign Policy Doctrine)* (New York: Global Scholarly Publications, 2003); Askar Akaev, *Trudnaia doroga k demokratii* (Moscow: Mezhdunarodnye otnosheniia, 2002), 307–410; Eugene Huskey, "Foreign Policy in a Vulnerable State: Kyrgyzstan as a Military Entrepot between the Great Powers," *China and Central Asia Forum Quarterly* 4 (2008): 5–18.

8. Statement of H.E. Mr. K. Bakiev, The President of the Kyrgyz Republic, at the General Debate of the 60th Session of the General Assembly, September 17, 2005. http://www.un.org/webcast/ga/60/statements/kyr050917eng.pdf

9. "Kyrgyzstan's Tulip Revolution," 486.

12. THE REVOLUTION BETRAYED

1. International Crisis Group, "Kyrgyzstan: A Faltering State," Asia Report no. 109 (December 16, 2005).

2. Interview with Azimbek Beknazarov, April 15, 2009, Bishkek.

3. In such an environment, personal jealousies and grudges can play an outsized role. On the long-simmering personal feud between Tekebaev and Bakiev, see Sydykova, *Est' u revoliutsii nachalo*, 118–19.

4. Interview with Joomart Saparbaev, April 20, 2009, Bishkek.

5. Roza Otunbaeva admitted that finding a role in government was vital after struggling in the opposition. According to the human rights activist, Tolekan Ismailova, at one point Roza commented that "I'm tired of marching in the streets; I've run through so many shoes that I'm fed up with marching, and, of course, I needed a place, and so I'm thankful to be in Parliament." A similar motivation explained Zamira Sydykova's decision to become an ambassador under Bakiev. In response to a reproach from Ismailova about working with Bakiev, Zamira replied: "What are you, crazy? I have no money, I'm poor." Interview with Tolekan Ismailova, July 25, 2008, Bishkek.

6. Interview with Sergei Masaulov, April 14, 2009, Bishkek. As one prominent oppositionist admitted, for a Kyrgyz, status is more important than money. Interview with Kubatbek Baibolov, October 13, 2008, DeLand, Florida.

7. Viktoriia Panfilova, "V tsentre Bishkeka snova budet zharko," *Nezavisimaia gazeta*, May 23, 2006, 13.

8. Andrei Baryshev, "Revoliutsiia, den' sed'moi," *Gazeta*, November 9, 2006, 3.

9. Mekhman Gafarly, "Tiul'pany dvazhdy ne tsvetut," *Novye izvestiia*, November 9, 2006, 4.

10. Baryshev, "Revoliutsiia, den' sed'moi."

11. Feliks Kulov, *Na perevale* (Moscow: Vremia, 2008), 224.

12. Sariev, *Shakh kyrgyzskoi demokratii*, 136. It is hard to overstate the disappointment among opposition activists when Kulov refused to challenge Bakiev in late 2006. Interview with Raia Kadyrova, April 13, 2009, Bishkek.

13. "Feliks Kulov otkryl svoi front protiv Prezidenta Kirgizii," Gazeta.kg, February 21, 2007. http://www.toptj.com/news/2007/2/23/feliks_kulov_otkryl_svoy_front_protiv_prezidenta_kirgizii

14. "Radikal'naia oppozitsiia v formirovanii novogo pravitel'stva uchastiia prinimat' ne budet," *Regnum*, March 29, 2007.

15. "Militsia spetssredstvami razognala miting oppozitsii u Doma pravitel'stva Kirgizii," NewsRu.com, April 19, 2007. http://www.newsru.com/world/19apr2007/bishkek.html

16. On the importance of clan, local, and regional identity in elections in the early post-independence period, see Abylabek Asankanov, *Kyrgyzy: rost natsional'nogo samosoznaniia* (Bishkek: Muras, 1997), 7–29.

17. Viktoriia Panfilova, "Oppozitsiia Kirgizii ne poidet ni na kakie kompromissy," *Nezavisimaia gazeta*, March 30, 2007, 6.

18. Viktoriia Magda, "Militsiia pereshla na storonu oppozitsii," *Nezavisimaia gazeta*, April 12, 2007, 9.

19. Arkadii Dubnov, "Svetlyi put' dlia Kirgizii," *Vremia novostei*, December 17, 2007, 5.

20. Between election day and the announcement of the final results, Bakiev's chief of staff, Sadyrkulov, reportedly sought to negotiate with Tekebaev to award some seats to Ata-Meken, but Tekebaev apparently refused to engage in this horse trading, which would have required Ata-Meken to have kept several political heavyweights from the top of his party list out of the parliament. Interview with Peter Sondergaard (Resident Country Director, International Republican Institute), April 9, 2009, Bishkek.

13. FEAR STALKS THE LAND

1. U. Midinova and E. Turaliev, "O 'piknikakh,' dlinnykh ocherediakh . . . i drugikh malopriiatnykh veshchakh," *Literaturnyi Kirgizstan* 1 (1990): 123–6. The criticisms of Russians by Midinova prompted a lively set of letters in subsequent issues of this journal.

2. The episode is described in detail in Philip Shishkin, *Restless Valley: Revolution, Murder, and Intrigue in the Heart of Central Asia* (New Haven, CT: Yale University Press, 2013), 128–38.

3. Interview with Omurbek Tekebaev, August 5, 2008, Cholpon-Ata, Kyrgyzstan.

4. See the official parliamentary report on the incident at Postanovlenie Zhogorku Kenesha ot 21 sentiabria 2006 goda No. 1262-III, Ob utverzhdenii Zakliucheniia deputatskoi komissii po fakty zaderzhaniia 5 sentiabria 2006 goda v aeroportu g. Varshava deputata Zhogorku Kenesha Kyrgyzskoi Respubliki Tekebaeva, O.Ch., Paragraf (Informatsionnaia sistema).

5. Interview with Kubatbek Baibolov, December 2, 2016, DeLand, Florida. For a collection of his articles and speeches produced in the period from 2000 to 2004, see Kubatbek Baibolov, *Nash narod dostoin luchshei zhizni* (Bishkek, 2004).

14. TALK OF KINSHIP, GENDER, AND ISLAM

1. Interviews with Tursunbek Akun, July 30, 2008, and April 11, 2009, Bishkek.

2. For a hagiography of President Bakiev and his brothers, see Omurzak Tolobekov, *Zhizn', posviashchennaia revolutsii ili brat'ia Bakievy* (Bishkek: Uchkun, 2007). The work devotes considerable attention to President Bakiev's brother Jusup, who died in 2006.

3. This perspective on family rule was shared by all of the respondents with whom I spoke, and some of them had worked in government under Bakiev. The former minister of defense, for example, noted that it was common for government ministers to turn to the son rather than the father to resolve their problems. In these informal institutional arrangements, the son was not acting so much as an agent of the President but as the leader of his own mini-fiefdom within the presidential firmament. Interview with Ismail Isakov, October 2, 2009, Bishkek.

4. Interview with Tursunbek Akun, July 30, 2008, Bishkek.

5. Interview with Miroslav Niazov, August 2, 2008, Bishkek.

6. Interview with Baktybek Beshimov, July 28, 2008, Bishkek.

7. Interview with Erkin Bulekbaev, July 30, 2008, Bishkek.

8. Russell Kleinbach, Mehrigiul Ablezova, and Medina Aitieva, "Kidnapping for Marriage (ala kachuu) in a Kyrgyz Village," *Central Asian Survey* 24, no. 2 (June 2005): 191–202. For a revealing, and disturbing, video on the practice, see "Kyrgyzstan: The Kidnapped Bride," *Frontline/World*, PBS (March 25, 2004). http://www.pbs.org/frontlineworld/stories/ kyrgyzstan/thestory.html

9. Interview with Bolot Alymkulov, April 21, 2009, Bishkek. The best work on clans in Central Asia may be found in Kathleen Collins, *Clan Politics and Regime Transitions in Central Asia* (Cambridge: Cambridge University Press, 2006), and Edward Schatz, *Modern Clan Politics: The Power of "Blood" in Kazakhstan and Beyond* (Seattle: University of Washington Press, 2004).

10. Interview with Myktybek Abdyldaev, July 29, 2008, Bishkek.

11. For a detailed account of the Aitmatov funeral, see the report of the American Embassy's Chargé d'Affaires published by Wikileaks. Embassy Bishkek, "Kyrgyzstan Honors Author Chingiz Aitmatov with State Funeral," WikiLeaks Cable: 08BISHKEK614_a, dated June 17, 2008. https://wikileaks.org/plusd/cables/08BISHKEK614_a.html

12. The other religious proselytizers in Kyrgyzstan were Protestant groups, most of whom were supported in some way by Western religious organizations. Such activity provoked anger among many, not just in the Muslim community but in the Russian Orthodox Church, who viewed the foreign-supported Christian groups as unwelcome competition. Compared to neighboring countries, Kyrgyzstan's central government put few barriers in the way of religious activity, though frequently local officials would intervene to discourage proselytizing by some Muslim and Christian groups. See Igor Rotar, "Kyrgyzstan: Religious Freedom Survey— January 2004," Forum 18 News Service (Oslo), January 7, 2004. http://www.forum18.org/ Archive.php?article_id=222

13. Interview with Ulugbek Babakulov, July 30, 2008, Bishkek.

14. One of the best-informed and most astute Western observers of Kyrgyzstan in this period, Paul Queen-Judge, had a similar view of the contrast between a hopelessly divided political opposition and the well-organized and purposeful cells of Hizb ut-Tahrir members. Ol'ga Vlasova and Ekaterina Kudashkina, "Komu nuzhna Kirgizii," *Ekspert* (April 14, 2008): 92–96.

15. Nathan Hamm, "Tursunbai Bakir uulu, Defender of the Faith," Registan, August 18, 2006.

15. TAKING THE LONELY ROAD HOME

1. Kyrgyzstan's Minister of Defense during the Russo-Georgian War, Ismail Isakov, stated that Russia's military intervention marked a turning point in its relations with the post-communist world. Interview with Ismail Isakov, October 2, 2009, Bishkek. For more on the Georgian conflict as a factor in the worsening relations between Russia and the United States over the Manas Air Base, see Embassy Bishkek, "Kyrgyzstan under 'Enormous Pressure' from Russia to Close Manas Air Base," WikiLeaks Cable: 08BISHKEK1002_a, dated October 2, 2008. https://wikileaks.org/plusd/cables/08BISHKEK1002_a.html

16. THE NETHERWORLD OF THE OPPOSITION

1. The news would not have come as a surprise to foreign policy experts in the White House. The American ambassador in Bishkek had been apprised in January by the Russian ambassador and Bakiev's chief of staff that a large Russian aid package was in the offing. Embassy Bishkek, "Russian Ambassador Confirms Proposed $2.5 Billion Economic Package for Kyrgyzstan," WikiLeaks Cable: 09BISHKEK85_a, dated January 29, 2009. https:// wikileaks.org/plusd/cables/09BISHKEK85_a.html

2. Embassy Bishkek, "Kyrgyzstan: Provisional Agreement Reached to Continue Operations at Manas," WikiLeaks Cable: 09BISHKEK299_a, dated April 4, 2009. https://wikileaks.org/plusd/cables/09BISHKEK299_a.html

3. Prices for heroin and other drugs were far lower in Kyrgyzstan than in most other post-communist countries, given Kyrgyzstan's proximity to major sources of heroin in Afghanistan and the Kyrgyzstani government's light touch on the drug trade, which was explained by widespread corruption in the courts and law enforcement agencies.

4. Shishkin, *Restless Valley*, 94–96, offers a gripping account of Sadyrkulov's last hours. *Restless Valley* also gives harrowing detail about the murder a few months later in Almaty of Kyrgyzstani journalist, Gennadii Pavlyuk, which was part of a campaign of intimidation against journalists carried out by the Bakiev regime (156–59). In early June 2010, the head of the MVD confirmed that the case was still being investigated, and that there was evidence that Pavlyuk was killed because he was providing sensitive information to Omurbek Tekebaev, the leader of the Ata-Meken Party. Interview with Bolot Sher, June 5, 2010, Bishkek. On the persecution of journalists in this period, see also Embassy Bishkek, "Kyrgyzstan: Growing Concern about Attacks on Journalists," WikiLeaks Cable: 09BISHKEK1331_a, dated December 24, 2009. https://wikileaks.org/plusd/cables/09BISHKEK1331_a.html

5. Interview with Azimbek Beknazarov, April 15, 2009, Bishkek.

6. Beknazarov interview, 2009.

7. Almazbek Atambaev, Tri interv'iu zhurnalistu Leile Saralaevoi (Bishkek: March 31, 2009).

8. Interview with Almazbek Atambaev, April 16, 2009, Bishkek.

9. As Kelly McMann has shown, however, corruption in Central Asia is endemic in part because of Islamic organizations' "inabilities to meet material needs." Kelly M. McMann, *Corruption as a Last Resort: Adapting to the Market in Central Asia* (Ithaca, NY: Cornell University Press, 2014), 123.

10. Embassy Bishkek, "CODEL Reid's Meetings in Kyrgyzstan," WikiLeaks Cable: 08Bishkek836_a, dated August 15, 2008. https://wikileaks.org/plusd/cables/08BISHKEK836_a.html

11. Several days later, an energetic entrepreneur leveled more criticism against the American government, noting that it somehow found the time to submit an official note protesting the removal of the fence around the Hyatt Hotel but could not be bothered to lodge complaints about the antidemocratic moves of Bakiev's government. Interview with Bolot Alymkulov, April 21, 2009.

12. As someone who knew only a smattering of Kyrgyz, I was fortunate to have acquaintances in the crowd who were willing to interpret for me.

13. Kyrgyz with whom I have spoken over the years often claimed that Atambaev could not speak Kyrgyz, but like most other Russified Kyrgyz who entered politics, Atambaev gradually improved his abilities in his native tongue. By 2010, it was virtually impossible for ethnic Kyrgyz to succeed in politics or government without having some fluency in the Kyrgyz language.

14. As the prominent opposition politician Asiya Sasykbaeva noted, what united the opposition in this period were the actions of the authorities. Interview with Asiya Sasykbaeva, April 10, 2009, Bishkek.

15. For a taste of the methods used by Bakiev to ensure his reelection, see Embassy Bishkek, "Kyrgyzstan: Abuse of Administrative Resources in Presidential Campaign, Part II," WikiLeaks Cable: 09BISHKEK894_a, dated August 7, 2009. https://wikileaks.org/plusd/cables/09BISHKEK894_a.html

16. OSCE/ODIHR, Kyrgyz Republic Presidential Election, 23 July 2009, Election Observation Mission, Final Report (Warsaw: October 22, 2009), 12. http://www.osce.org/odihr/elections/kyrgyzstan/39923?download=true

17. Five months later, four members of the Social Democratic Party were sentenced to four years in prison for participating in the protests, and fifteen more persons received several years of probation each. Embassy Bishkek, "Kyrgyzstan: Balykchy Defendants Guilty—Another Blow to the Opposition," WikiLeaks Cable: 10Bishkek5_a, dated January 4, 2010. https://wikileaks.org/plusd/cables/10BISHKEK5_a.html

17. BAKIEV FALLS, WASHINGTON REACTS

1. Interview with Roza Otunbaeva, August 2, 2008, Bishkek.
2. Interview with Ismail Isakov, October 2, 2009, Bishkek.
3. Interview with Dinara Oshurakhunova, April 14, 2009, Bishkek.
4. Kyrgyzstan National Opinion Poll, October 2008, International Republican Institute (Bishkek, 2008), 12.
5. As Zamira Sydykova writes, these plans were not designed merely to influence the regime but to overthrow it. Sydykova, *Est' u revolutsii nachalo*, 84.
6. The Interim Government set out the ground rules for the transition period in Decree No. 1 of the Interim Government, signed on April 7, 2010. http://cbd.minjust.gov.kg/act/view/ru-ru/ 202765?cl=ru-ru
7. Eric McGlinchey, "Running in Circles in Kyrgyzstan," *New York Times*, April 9, 2010, A23. http://www.nytimes.com/2010/04/10/opinion/10mcglinchey.html?_r=1
8. In fact, Secretary of State Hillary Clinton had spoken to Roza Otunbaeva on April 10 and dispatched Assistant Secretary of State Robert Blake to the region for consultations. https:// www.state.gov/r/pa/prs/ps/2010/04/139968.htm
9. Deidre Tynan, "US Lost Sight of Enduring Democratic Values in Bishkek—Experts," Eurasianet.org, April 22, 2010. http://www.eurasianet.org/node/60917
10. http://play.webvideocore.net/popplayer.php?it=dgsk2tcezvkk&is_link=1&w=720&h= 405&pause=1&title=1509025+-+Venice+Commission+25+Years-&skin=3&repeat=& brandNW=1&start_volume=100&bg_gradient1=&bg_gradient2=&fullscreen=&fs_mode=0& skinAlpha=80&colorBase=%23202020&colorIcon=%23FFFFFF&colorHighlight= %23fcad37&direct=true&no_ctrl=&auto_hide=1&viewers_limit=0&cc_position=bottom&cc_ positionOffset=70&cc_multiplier=0.03&cc_textColor=%23ffffff&cc_textOutlineColor= %23000000&cc_bkgColor=%23000000&cc_bkgAlpha=0.7

18. REVOLUTIONARY LEGALITY VERSUS TRANSITIONAL JUSTICE

1. Ob osvobozhdenii ot ugolovnoi otvetstvennosti, Dekret VP no. 36, 30 aprelia 2010, Vremennoe Pravitel'stva Kyrgyzskoi Respubliki.
2. For a detailed account of the violence written by the local KGB, see "KGB i oshkaia tragediia [k massovym besporiadkam v oshkoi oblasti (Dokument Upravleniia KGB po oshkoi oblasti ot 24.06.1990 g.)]," *Literaturnyi Kirgizstan* (November 1990): 93–100. See also Valery Tishkov, "'Don't Kill Me, I'm a Kyrgyz!': An Anthropological Analysis of Violence in the Osh Ethnic Conflict," *Journal of Peace Research* 32, no. 2 (1995): 133–49.
3. Widely held assumptions, in Kyrgyzstan and the West, about the superior economic position of the Uzbeks in southern Kyrgyzstan are challenged in a careful study of household income and wealth among Kyrgyz and Uzbeks by Damir Esenaliev and Susan Steiner, "Are Kyrgyz Better off Than Uzbeks? Measuring and Decomposing Horizontal Inequality," Deutsches Institut für Wirtschaftsforschung, Discussion Paper 1252 (Berlin, 2012). https://www.diw. de/documents/publikationen/73/diw_01.c.411250.de/dp1252.pdf
4. Embassy Bishkek, "Kyrgyzstan: Update on Hyatt Hotel's Dispute with City of Bishkek," WikiLeaks Cable: 08BISHKEK969_a, dated September 3, 2009. https://wikileaks.org/ plusd/cables/09BISHKEK969_a.html
5. Interview with Dmitrii Kabak, May 31, 2010, Bishkek. On the Nookat controversy, see the report, Monitoring of Compliance with Human Rights, Related to the Events in Nookat on October 1, 2008 (copy in possession of the author). Mr. Kabak was a member of the ombudsmen's commission that submitted this report.

6. Spisok privlechennykh General'noi prokuraturoi Kyrgyzskoi Respubliki k ugolovnoi otvetstvennosti gosudarstvennykh i inykh lits po sobytiiam 6-7 aprelia 2010 goda (copy in possession of the author).

7. Interview with Bolot Sher, June 5, 2010, Bishkek.

8. Tursunbai Bakir uulu, "Nedalekie rektory vystupaiut protiv svobody veroispovedeniia," Gezitter.kg, October 25, 2012. http://m.gezitter.org/interviews/15322_tbakir_uulu_nedalekie_rektoryi_vyistupayut_protiv_svobodyi_veroispovedaniya/

9. Interview with Cholpon Jakupova, May 31, 2010, Bishkek. While I was in Edil' Baisalov's office in early June, 2010, Masaliev's wife called him on his personal cell phone to beg him to release her husband from house arrest.

10. For a fuller version of this report, updated to include the tragic events that transpired in mid-June, see Marcie Mersky, Bogdan Ivanišević, and Eugene Huskey, "Assessing a Transitional Justice Approach for Kyrgyzstan, Kyrgyzstan Mission Report May 30–June 6, 2010," International Center for Transitional Justice (New York: August 2010). https://ictj.org/sites/default/files/ICTJ-Kyrgyzstan-TJ-2010-English.pdf

11. Interview with Nazgul Turdubekova, May 31, 2010, Bishkek.

19. JUNE 2010

1. Morgan Y. Liu, in *Under Solomon's Throne: Uzbek Visions of Renewal in Osh* (Pittsburgh: University of Pittsburgh Press, 2012), reveals the patterns of everyday life in Uzbek *mahallas* in Osh.

2. Aibek Mirsidikov and Kadyrjon Batyrov had in recent years been adversaries, though both were Uzbek. See Iurii Vasil'ev, "Kirgiziia: za chto ubit Chernyi Aibek?" Radio Svoboda, June 7, 2010. http://www.svoboda.org/content/article/2064618.html

3. In a careful study from the early 2000s of attitudes of Kyrgyz, Russians, and Uzbeks toward each other, Regina Faranda and David Nolle found that while the Uzbeks were most open to close relations with other ethnic groups in the country, the Kyrgyz were the least willing to accept Uzbeks as relatives by marriage or even as close friends. Kyrgyz attitudes to Russians indicated much less social distance between those two groups. Faranda and Nolle, "Ethnic Social Distance in Kyrgyzstan: Evidence from a Nationwide Opinion Survey," *Nationalities Papers* 31, no. 2 (June 2003): 177–210.

4. For detailed accounts in English of the inter-ethnic violence in Osh, see Kyrgyzstan Inquiry Commission, "Report of the Independent International Commission of Inquiry into the Events in Southern Kyrgyzstan in June 2010" (2011). https://reliefweb.int/sites/reliefweb.int/files/resources/Full_Report_490.pdf, and Norwegian Helsinki Committee, Memorial Human Rights Center, and Freedom House, "A Chronicle of Violence: The Events in the South of Kyrgyzstan in June 2010 [Osh Region]" (2012). The reports were based on extensive interviewing of eyewitnesses to the events. http://www.nhc.no/filestore/Publikasjoner/Rapporter/2012/Rapport_2_12_ENG_nett.pdf . See also Bruce Pannier, "Kyrgyzstan: Anatomy of a Conflict," Radio Free Europe/Radio Liberty, July 2, 2010, which contains videos and photos of the events. https://www.rferl.org/a/Kyrgyzstan_Anatomy_Of_A_Conflict/2089464.html

5. Interview with Felix Kulov, July 21, 2010, Bishkek.

6. "V Kirgizii ob'iavlena chastichnaia mobilizatsiia," Russkaia sluzhba BBC, June 13, 2010. http://www.bbc.com/russian/international/2010/06/100612_kyrgyz_russia_peace keepers_request.shtml

7. One source insists that the Russian government demanded that, as a condition for intervention, Kyrgyzstani officials abandon the June 27 referendum as well as their plans to introduce a parliamentary system of government. Kerim Kerimbaliev and Vasilii Markov, "Iiunskii koshmar: mezhetnicheskie stolknoveniia v Kirgizii," *Novoe vremia*, June 21, 2010 (https://newtimes.ru/articles/detail/23431/), referenced in Zamira Sydykova, *Est' u revoliutsii nachalo*, 86–87.

8. Interview with Akhmatbek Kel'dibekov, July 23, 2010, Bishkek.

9. "Where Is the Justice? Interethnic Violence in Southern Kyrgyzstan and Its Aftermath," Human Rights Watch, August 16, 2000, footnote 47. HRW specialists on the ground interviewed several employees and students from the dormitory in question and they noted that several windows were broken in the initial violence but the rioters did not gain access to the students. https://www.hrw.org/report/2010/08/16/where-justice/interethnic-violence-southern-kyrgyzstan-and-its-aftermath

10. Andrew E. Kramer, "Kyrgyz Tensions Rooted in Class, not Ethnicity, Experts Say," *New York Times*, June 14, 2010. http://www.nytimes.com/2010/06/15/world/asia/15ethnic.html?_r=0

11. Kyrgyzstan Inquiry Commission, "Report of the Independent International Commission of Inquiry," p. 40.

12. Alisher Khamidov, "Naselenie na iuge Kyrgyzstana nedovol'no deistviiami silovikov," VOA, June 21, 2010. http://www.golos-ameriki.ru/a/kyrgyz-police_2010_06_21-96811499/185907.html

13. See OSCE/ODIHR, The Kyrgyz Republic, Constitutional Referendum, 27 June 2010 (OSCE: Warsaw, July 27, 2010). http://www.osce.org/odihr/elections/70938?download=true

20. "WE EITHER HAVE FAIR ELECTIONS, OR WE HAVE VIOLENCE"

1. Interview with Kamchibek Tashiev, July 23, 2010, Bishkek.

2. During the interview, Tashiev didn't fully grasp how the new electoral rules worked. He assumed that the share of the seats would be won region by region, whereas the seats would in fact be apportioned based on how parties did over the whole country. Tashiev interview, 2010.

3. Interview with Akhmatbek Kel'dibekov, July 23, 2010, Bishkek.

21. FIRST STEPS ON THE PARLIAMENTARY ROAD

1. Even with the same-day registration option, only 55 percent of eligible voters cast a ballot, which meant that parties had to receive approximately 9 percent of the actual votes cast in order to cross the five-percent threshold.

2. Eugene Huskey and David Hill, "Regionalism, Personalism, Ethnicity, and Violence: Parties and Voter Preference in the 2010 Parliamentary Election in Kyrgyzstan," *Post-Soviet Affairs* 29, no. 3 (June 2013): 237–67.

3. Four years later, however, women occupied less than 21 percent of the seats. Because women tended to be placed in every fourth position on a party list, when they resigned from parliament—a common occurrence after 2010—the next person on the party list—a man—usually filled the vacant slot. "Dolia zhenshchin sredi deputatov s 2010 g. sokratilas' na 10%," *Argumenty nedeli Kyrgyzstan*, May 12, 2014. http://argumenti.kg/novosti/politika/6905-dolya-zhenschin-sredi-deputatov-zhogorku-kenesha-s-2010-goda-sokratilas-na-10.html

4. "Deputaty K. Tashieva i T. Sulaimanova publichno pomirilis'," AKIPress, April 11, 2011. http://www.for.kg/news-149466-ru.html; "Obzor raboty Zhogorku Kenesh za 2011 god," KNews, December 31, 2011. http://knews.kg/2011/12/31/obzor-rabotyi-jogorku-kenesha-za-2011-god/

5. "V Oshe sozhgli knigi 'Chas shakala'," Janyryk Apta, May 19, 2010, p. 2, translated in Gezitter.org, May 23, 2010. http://www.gezitter.org/society/2816_v_oshe_sojgli_knigu_chas_shakala/

22. WITHOUT ABUSE, POWER LOSES ITS CHARM

1. Iuliia Mazykina, Debaty kg. "A pogovorit'-to, ne o chem," 24.kg, October 18, 2011. https://24.kg/archive/ru/election2011/111815-debatykg-a-pogovorit-to-i-ne-o-chemhellip.html/

2. David Hill and Eugene Huskey, "Electoral Stakes, Labor Migration, and Voter Turnout: The 2011 Presidential Election in Kyrgyzstan," *Demokratizatsiya: The Journal of Post-Soviet Democratization* 23, no. 1 (2015): 3–30.

3. On this point, see Radnitz, *Weapons of the Wealthy*, 123.

4. "Kyrgyzstan: politicheskoe bankrotstvo spikera parlamenta mozhet izmenit' rasklad sil v klanovoi bor'be," Ferghana.ru, May 29, 2008. http://www.fergananews.com/article.php?id=5724

23. GOODBYE TO MANAS

1. Embassy Bishkek, "Kyrgyzstan: Next Steps on Manas Air Base Issues," WikiLeaks Cable: 07BISHKEK1201_a, dated September 28, 2007. https://wikileaks.org/plusd/cables/07BISHKEK1201_a.html

2. Interview with Temirbek Shabdanaliev (Head of the Public Advisory Councils attached to the Ministry of Economics and the Manas Air Base), June 19, 2013, Bishkek.

3. Kyrgyzstan National Opinion Poll, February 4–February 27, 2012, International Republican Institute, Bishkek, 2012.

4. NS IPTEK, Otsenka sistemy gosudarstvennykh zakupok v OAO 'National'naia elektricheskaia set' Kyrgyzstana' i v OAO 'Elektricheskii stantsii za 2010 god' (Bishkek: November 2011). My thanks to Maia Gogoladze for providing this source.

5. Interview with Baktybek Ashirov (Head of Committee for Fighting Economic Crimes), June 13, 2014, Bishkek.

6. Interview with Aziza Abdirasulova, June 13, 2013, Bishkek.

7. Powerful political forces had thrown a wrench in the works, however, by convincing Atambaev to shift responsibility for the oversight of the public advisory boards from the presidential staff to the prime minister's apparatus. However, before that transfer occurred, the supporters of renewing the mandate for the boards succeeded in getting the president to sign a decree extending the life of the initiative. The second generation of public advisory boards began their work in 2014, with some turnover of personnel on the boards.

24. IN OSH THE PAST IS NEVER DEAD

1. David Trilling, "Kyrgyzstan: Indian Medical Students Caught in Diploma Mill?," Eurasianet.org, December 6, 2011. http://www.eurasianet.org/node/64644

2. Elly Harrowell, "From Monuments to Mahallas: Contrasting Memories in the Urban Landscape of Osh, Kyrgyzstan," *Social and Cultural Geography* 16, no. 2 (2014): 203–25. In 2014, Kurmanjan Datka was the subject of one of the country's most ambitious film projects. Regarding Kurmanjan Datka's place among the handful of women whose memories have been woven into the national narrative, see Helge Blakkisrud and Nuraida Abdykapar kyzy, "Female Heroes in a Man's World: The Construction of Female Heroes in Kyrgyzstan's Symbolic Nation-Building," *Demokratizatsiya: The Journal of Post-Soviet Democratization* 25, no. 2 (January 2017): 113–35.

3. Daniyar Muradilov, "Istoriia i kul'ture v religioznoi sfere v Kyrgyzstane," Islam v SNG, November 20, 2014. http://www.islamsng.com/kgz/pastfuture/8383

25. PREPARING FOR A PRESIDENTIAL AFTERLIFE

1. http://www.internetlivestats.com/internet-users/kyrgyzstan/
2. "Prezident Kyrgyzstana Roza Otunbaeva: posle 20 let, 'Nam dvadtsat' let neuiutno v novoi skorpule," KirTag, September 2011. http://kyrtag.kg/interview/prezident_kyrgyzstana_roza_otunbaeva_nam_dvadtsat_let_neuyutno_v_novoy_skorlupe
3. In 2010, Thomas Lahusen, Gulzat Egemberdieva, and Andre Loersch made *The Interim Country*, a twenty-seven-minute documentary film about Kyrgyzstan that included revealing interviews with ordinary Kyrgyzstanis and striking footage from the inter-ethnic violence in Osh in 2010. The film, which I narrated, attracted well over 150,000 views in its first years on YouTube. It is now available through Chemodan Films. http://www.chemodanfilms.com/the-interim-country/
4. Anna Kapushchenko, "Atambaev raskritikoval Otunbaevu i eks-ministrov za nedovol'stvo popravkami k Konstitutsiiu," Kloop Media, August 31, 2016. http://kloop.kg/blog/2016/08/31/atambaev-raskritikoval-otunbaevu-i-eks-ministrov-iz-za-popravok-v-konstitutsiyu-glavnoe/
5. Eugene Huskey, "Plebiscitarianism and Constitution-Making: The December 11, 2016 Referendum in Kyrgyzstan," Presidential Power blog, December 15, 2016. http://presidential-power.com/?p=5770
6. Eugene Huskey, "Kyrgyzstan—A Setback for Democracy: The 2017 Presidential Election," Presidential Power blog, October 17, 2017. http://presidential-power.com/?p=7070

26. A STAN LIKE NO OTHER

1. One of the objections to this line of analysis is that, in Central Asia, the titular peoples of Kazakhstan and Turkmenistan are also traditionally nomadic, and yet those countries, and particularly Turkmenistan, have been more authoritarian than Kyrgyzstan. Many Kyrgyz would retort that their mountainous surroundings have created a distinct form of nomadic culture.
2. See Radnitz, *Weapons of the Wealthy*.
3. Interview with Kanybek Imanaliev (Pro-Rector for International Relations, Kyrgyz-Russian Slavic University), July 25, 2008, Bishkek. In fact, as David W. Montgomery points out in his *Practicing Islam: Knowledge, Experience, and Social Navigation in Kyrgyzstan* (Pittsburgh: University of Pittsburgh Press, 2016), there are many ways in which Islam is understood and practiced in Kyrgyzstan, and a simple bifurcation of Muslims into radical and moderate camps does not do justice to the diversity of religious expression in Kyrgyzstan.

Selected Bibliography

BOOKS AND OFFICIAL REPORTS

Abramzon, S. M. *Kirgizy i ikh etnogeneticheskie i istoriko-kul'turnye sviazi*. Leningrad: Izda-tel'stvo nauka, 1971.

Aitmatova, Roza. *Belye piatna istorii (moi vospominaniia)*. Bishkek: V.R.S. Company, 2013.

Akaev, Askar. *The Diplomacy of the Silk Road*. New York: Global Scholarly Publications, 2003.

———. *Kyrgyz Statehood and the National Epos 'Manas'*. New York: Global Scholarly Publi-cations, 2003.

———. *Trudnaia doroga k demokratii*. Moskva: Mezhdunarodnye otnosheniia, 2002.

Anderson, John. *Kyrgyzstan: Central Asia's Island of Democracy?* Amsterdam: Harwood, 1999.

Asankanov, Abylabek. *Kyrgyzy: rost natsional'nogo samosoznaniia*. Bishkek: Muras, 1997.

Collins, Kathleen. *Clan Politics and Regime Transitions in Central Asia*. Cambridge: Cam-bridge University Press, 2006.

Cooley, Alexander. *Great Games, Local Rules: The New Great Power Contest in Central Asia*. New York: Oxford University Press, 2012.

Cooley, Alexander, and John Heathershaw. *Dictators Without Borders: Power and Money in Central Asia*. New Haven, CT: Yale University Press, 2017.

Cummings, Sally. *Symbolism and Power in Central Asia: Politics of the Spectacular*. Abing-don, UK: Routledge, 2010.

Dzhumanaliev, Akylbek. *Politicheskoe razvitie Kyrgyzstana (20-30-e gody)*. Bishkek: Ilim, 1994.

Gullette, David. *The Genealogical Construction of the Kyrgyz Republic: Kinship, State, and "Tribalism."* Folkestone, UK: Global Oriental, 2010.

Iskakova, Gulnara. *Vybory i demokratiia v Kyrgyzstane: Konstitutsionnyi dizain prezidentsko-parlamentskikh otnoshenii*. Bishkek, 2003.

Kulov, Feliks. *Na perevale*. Moscow: Vremia, 2008.

Kyrgyzstan Inquiry Commission. "Report of the Independent International Commission of Inquiry into the Events in Southern Kyrgyzstan in June 2010." 2011. https://reliefweb.int/sites/reliefweb.int/files/resources/Full_Report_490.pdf

Landau, Jacob M., and Barbara Keller-Heinkele. *Politics of Language in the Ex-Soviet Muslim States*. Ann Arbor, MI: University of Michigan Press, 2001.

Laruelle, Marlene, and Johann Engvall, eds. *Kyrgyzstan Beyond "Democracy Island" and "Failing State": Social and Political Changes in a Post-Soviet Society*. Lanham, MD: Lexington Books, 2015.

Laruelle, Marlene, and Sebastien Peyrouse. *The Chinese Question in Central Asia: Domestic Order, Social Change, and the Chinese Factor*. London: Hurst and Company, 2012.

Lilley, Jeffrey B. *Have the Mountains Fallen? Two Journeys of Loss and Redemption in the Cold War*. Bloomington: Indiana University Press, 2018.

Liu, Morgan Y. *Under Solomon's Throne: Uzbek Visions of Renewal in Osh*. Pittsburgh: University of Pittsburgh Press, 2012.

Luong, Pauline Jones. *Institutional Change and Political Continuity in Post-Soviet Central Asia: Power, Perceptions, and Pacts*. New Haven, CT: Yale University Press, 2002.

McGlinchey, Eric. *Chaos, Violence, Dynasty: Politics and Islam in Central Asia*. Pittsburgh: University of Pittsburgh Press, 2011.

McMann, Kelly M. *Corruption as a Last Resort: Adapting to the Market in Central Asia*. Ithaca, NY: Cornell University Press, 2014.

———. *Economic Autonomy and Democracy: Hybrid Regimes in Russia and Kyrgyzstan*. New York: Cambridge University Press, 2006.

Marat, Erica. *The State-Crime Nexus in Central Asia: State Weakness, Organized Crime, and Corruption in Kyrgyzstan and Tajikistan*. Washington, DC, and Uppsala, Sweden: Silk Road Paper, October 2006.

Masaliev, Absamat. *Stranitsy zhizni i bednoe nashe otechestvo*. Bishkek: Az-mak, 1993.

Mersky, Marcie, Bogdan Ivanišević, and Eugene Huskey. "Assessing a Transitional Justice Approach for Kyrgyzstan, Kyrgyzstan Mission Report May 30–June 6, 2010." International Center for Transitional Justice. New York: August 2010. https://ictj.org/sites/default/files/ICTJ-Kyrgyzstan-TJ-2010-English.pdf

Montgomery, David W. *Practicing Islam: Knowledge, Experience, and Social Navigation in Kyrgyzstan*. Pittsburgh: University of Pittsburgh Press, 2016.

Mozur, Joseph P. *Parables from the Past: The Prose Fiction of Chingiz Aitmatov*. Pittsburgh: University of Pittsburgh Press, 1994.

Norwegian Helsinki Committee, Memorial Human Rights Center, and Freedom House. "A Chronicle of Violence: The Events in the South of Kyrgyzstan in June 2010 [Osh Region]." 2012. http://www.nhc.no/filestore/Publikasjoner/Rapporter/2012/Rapport_2_12_ENG_nett.pdf

Olcott, Martha Brill. *Central Asia's Second Chance*. Washington, DC: Carnegie Endowment for International Peace, 2010.

Radnitz, Scott. *Weapons of the Wealthy: Predatory Regimes and Elite-Led Protest in Central Asia*. Ithaca, NY: Cornell University Press, 2010.

Sariev, Temir. *Shakh kyrgyzskoi demokratii*. Bishkek: Salam, 2008.

Schatz, Edward. *Modern Clan Politics: The Power of "Blood" in Kazakhstan and Beyond*. Seattle: University of Washington Press, 2004.

Shishkin, Philip. *Restless Valley: Revolution, Murder, and Intrigue in the Heart of Central Asia*. New Haven, CT: Yale University Press, 2013.

Sokol, Edward Dennis. *The Revolt of 1916 in Russian Central Asia*. Baltimore: Johns Hopkins University Press, 2016.

Sydykova, Zamira. *Est' u revolutsii nachalo, net u revoliutsii kontsa*. Bishkek, 2011.

———. *Gody ozhidaniia i poter'. Vremia peremen*. Bishkek, 2003.

ARTICLES AND BOOK CHAPTERS

Altay, Azamat. "Kirgiziya During the Great Purge." *Central Asian Review* 17, no. 2 (1964): 97–107.

Blakkisrud, Helge, and Nuraida Abdykapar kyzy. "Female Heroes in a Man's World: The Construction of Female Heroes in Kyrgyzstan's Symbolic Nation-Building." *Demokratizatsiya: The Journal of Post-Soviet Democratization* 25, no. 2 (January 2017): 113–35.

Brubaker, Rogers. "Nationalizing States Revisited: Projects and Processes of Nationalization in Post-Soviet States." *Ethnic and Racial Studies* 34, no. 11 (2011): 1785–1814.

Commercio, Michele E. "The Politics and Economics of 'Retraditionalization' in Kyrgyzstan and Tajikistan." *Post-Soviet Affairs* 31, no. 6 (2015): 529–56.

Esenaliev, Damir, and Susan Steiner. "Are Kyrgyz Better off Than Uzbeks? Measuring and Decomposing Horizontal Inequality." Deutsches Institut für Wirtschaftsforschung, Discussion Paper 1252 (Berlin, 2012). https://www.diw.de/documents/publikationen/73/diw_01.c.411250.de/dp1252.pdf

Faranda, Regina, and David Nolle. "Ethnic Social Distance in Kyrgyzstan: Evidence from a Nationwide Opinion Survey." *Nationalities Papers* 31, no. 2 (2003): 177–210.

Fierman, William. "Identity, Symbolism, and the Politics of Language in Central Asia." *Europe-Asia Studies* 61, no. 7 (September 2009): 1207–28.

Fumagalli, Matteo. "Framing Ethnic Minority Mobilisation in Central Asia: The Cases of Uzbeks in Kyrgyzstan and Tajikistan." *Europe-Asia Studies* 59, no. 4 (June 2007): 567–90.

Gullette, David. "Theories on Central Asian Factionalism: The Debate in Political Science and Its Wider Implications." *Central Asian Survey* 26, no. 3 (2007): 373–87.

Gullette, David, and John Heathershaw. "The Affective Politics of Sovereignty: Reflecting on the 2010 Conflict in Kyrgyzstan." *Nationalities Papers* 43, no. 1 (2015): 122–39.

Handrahan, Lori M. "Gender and Ethnicity in the 'Transitional Democracy' of Kyrgyzstan." *Central Asian Survey* 20, no. 4 (2001): 467–96.

Harrowell, Elly. "From Monuments to Mahallas: Contrasting Memories in the Urban Landscape of Osh, Kyrgyzstan." *Social and Cultural Geography* 16, no. 2 (2014): 203–25.

Heathershaw, John. "Of National Fathers and Russian Elder Brothers: Conspiracy Theories and Political Ideas in Post-Soviet Central Asia." *Russian Review* 71, no. 4 (2012): 610–29.

Hierman, Brent, and Navruz Nekbakhtshoev. "Whose Land Is It? Land Reform, Minorities, and the Titular 'Nation' in Kazakhstan, Kyrgyzstan, and Tajikistan." *Nationalities Papers* 42, no. 2 (2014): 336–54.

Hill, David, and Eugene Huskey. "Electoral Stakes, Labor Migration, and Voter Turnout: The 2011 Presidential Election in Kyrgyzstan." *Demokratizatsiya: The Journal of Post-Soviet Democratization* 23, no. 1 (2015): 3–30.

Huskey, Eugene. "An Economy of Authoritarianism? Askar Akaev and Presidential Leadership in Kyrgyzstan." In *Power and Change in Central Asia*, edited by Sally Cummings. London: Routledge, 2002, 74–96.

———. "Competing Visions of Nation in Kyrgyzstan." In *Nations and States in the Post-Soviet Space*, edited by Peter Rutland and Ray Taras. Cambridge: Cambridge University Press, forthcoming.

———. "Eurasian Semi-presidentialism: The Development of Kyrgyzstan's Model of Government." In *Semi-presidentialism Outside Europe: A Comparative Study*, edited by Robert Elgie and Sophia Moestrup. Abingdon, UK: Routledge, 2007, 161–81.

———. "The Fate of Political Liberalization in Kyrgyzstan." In *Conflict, Cleavage, and Change in Central Asia and the Caucasus*, edited by Karen Dawisha and Bruce Parrott. Cambridge: Cambridge University Press, 1997, 242–76.

———. "Foreign Policy in a Vulnerable State: Kyrgyzstan as a Military Entrepot between the Great Powers." *China and Central Asia Forum Quarterly* 6, no. 4 (2008): 5–18.

———. "Kyrgyzstan: The Politics of Demographic and Economic Frustration." In *New States, New Politics: Building the Post-Soviet Nations*, 2d edition, edited by Ian Bremmer and Ray Taras. Cambridge: Cambridge University Press, 1997, 654–76.

———. "The Politics of Language in Kyrgyzstan." *Nationalities Papers* 23, no. 3 (1995): 549–72.

Huskey, Eugene, and David Hill. "Regionalism, Personalism, Ethnicity, and Violence: Parties and Voter Preference in the 2010 Parliamentary Election in Kyrgyzstan." *Post-Soviet Affairs* 29, no. 3 (2013): 237–67.

Huskey, Eugene, and Gulnara Iskakova. "The Barriers to Intra-Opposition Cooperation in the Post-Communist World: Evidence from Kyrgyzstan." *Post-Soviet Affairs* 26, no. 3 (July–September 2010): 228–62.

Ilkhamov, Alisher. "Neopatrimonialism, Interest Groups and Patronage Networks: The Impasses of the Governance System in Uzbekistan." *Central Asian Survey* 26, no. 1 (2007): 65–84.

International Crisis Group. "Political Transition in Kyrgyzstan: Problems and Prospects." Asia Report no. 81 (11 August 2004): 7–10.

Karagiannis, Emmanuel. "Political Islam and Social Movement Theory: The Case of Hizb ut-Tahrir in Kyrgyzstan." *Journal of Religion, State, and Society* 33, no. 2 (2005): 137–50.

"KGB i oshkaia tragediia [k massovym besporiadkam v oshoi oblasti (Dokument Upravleniia KGB po oshkoi oblasti ot 24.06.1990 g.)]." *Literaturnyi Kirgizstan* (November 1990): 93–100.

Kleinbach, Russell, Mehrigiul Ablezova, and Medina Aitieva. "Kidnapping for Marriage (ala kachuu) in a Kyrgyz Village." *Central Asian Survey* 24, no. 2 (2005): 191–202.

Kuehnast, Kathleen. "From Pioneers to Entrepreneurs: Young Women, Consumerism, and the 'World Picture' in Kyrgyzstan." *Central Asian Survey* 17, no. 4 (1998): 639–54.

Kynev, Alexander. "Kyrgyzstan do i posle 'tiul'panovoi revoliutsii'." Mezhdunarodnyi institut gumanitarno-politicheskikh issledovanii. http://igpi.ru/info/people/kynev/1128082583.html

"Kyrgyzstan's Tulip Revolution: An Interview with Roza Otunbaeva." *Demokratizatsiya: The Journal of Post-Soviet Democratization* 13, no. 4 (2005): 483–90.

Laruelle, Marlene. "The Paradigm of Nationalism in Kyrgyzstan: Evolving Narrative, the Sovereignty Issue, and Political Agenda." *Communist and Post-Communist Studies* 45, nos. 1–2 (2012): 39–49.

Marat, Erica. "Imagined Past, Uncertain Future: The Creation of National Ideologies in Kyrgyzstan and Tajikistan." *Problems of Post-Communism* 55, no. 1 (2008): 12–24.

———. "'We Disputed Every Word': How Kyrgyzstan's Moderates Tame Ethnic Nationalism." *Nations and Nationalism* 22, no. 2 (2016): 305–24.

Megoran, Nick. "On Researching 'Ethnic Conflict': Epistemology, Politics, and a Central Asian Boundary Dispute." *Europe-Asia Studies* 59, no. 2 (2007): 261–74.

Murzakulova, Asel, and John Schoeberlein. "The Invention of Legitimacy: Struggles in Kyrgyzstan to Craft an Effective Nation-State Ideology." *Europe-Asia Studies* 61, no. 7 (2009): 1229–48.

Ó Beacháin, Donnacha. "Roses and Tulips: Dynamics of Regime Change in Georgia and Kyrgyzstan." *Journal of Communist Studies and Transition Politics* 25, nos. 2–3 (2009): 199–226.

Radnitz, Scott. "Paranoia with a Purpose: Conspiracy Theory and Political Coalitions in Kyrgyzstan." *Post-Soviet Affairs* 32, no. 5 (2016): 474–89.

———. "What Really Happened in Kyrgyzstan?" *Journal of Democracy* 17, no. 2 (2006): 132–45.

Reeves, Madeleine. "Travels in the Margins of the State: Everyday Geography in the Ferghana Valley Borderlands." In *Everyday Life in Central Asia: Past and Present*, edited by Jeff Sahadeo and Russell Zanca. Bloomington: Indiana University Press, 281–300.

Ryabkov, Maxim. "The North–South Cleavage and Political Support in Kyrgyzstan." *Central Asian Survey* 27, nos. 3–4 (2008): 301–16.

Schatz, Edward. "The Soft Authoritarian Tool Kit: Agenda-Setting Power in Kazakhstan and Kyrgyzstan." *Comparative Politics* 41, no. 2 (2009): 203–22.

Suny, Ronald Grigor. "Constructing Primordialism: Old Histories for New Nations." *Journal of Modern History* 73, no. 4 (2001): 862–96.

Temirkoulov, Azamat. "Tribalism, Social Conflict, and State-Building in the Kyrgyz Republic." *Berliner Osteuropa Info* 21 (2004): 94–100.

Tishkov, Valery. "'Don't Kill Me, I'm a Kyrgyz!': An Anthropological Analysis of Violence in the Osh Ethnic Conflict." *Journal of Peace Research* 32, no. 2 (1995): 133–49.

Wachtel, Andrew Baruch. "Kyrgyzstan between Democratization and Ethnic Intolerance." *Nationalities Papers* 41, no. 6 (2013): 971–86.

Wimmer, Andreas. "Nation Building: A Long-Term Perspective and Global Analysis." *European Sociological Review* 31, no. 1 (2015): 30–47.

FEATURE FILMS

Atanyn Kereezi (*A Father's Will*). Directed by Bakyt Mukul and Dastan Zhapar uulu (2016).
Belye gory (White Mountains). Directed by Melis Ubukeev (1964).
Beshkempir (*The Adopted Son*). Directed by Aktan Abdykalykov (1998).
Boz Salkyn (*Pure Coolness*). Directed by Ernest Abdyzhaparov (2007).
Djamilia. Directed by Irina Poplavskaia (1969).
Kurmanjan Datka (*Queen of the Mountains*). Directed by Sadyk Sher-Niiaz (2014).
Ochkarik (*Four-eyes*). Directed by Al'gimantas Vidugiris (1972).
Salam, N'iu Iork (*Hello, New York*). Directed by Ruslan Akun (2013).
Sunduk Predkov (*The Wedding Chest*). Directed by Nurbek Egen (2006).
Sutak (*Heavenly Nomadic*). Directed by Mirlan Abdykalykov (2015).
Svet-ake (*The Light Thief*). Directed by Aktan Abdykalykov (2010).
Volch'ia iama (*Wolf Trap*). Directed by Bolot Shamshiev (1983).

DOCUMENTARY FILMS

Flowers of Freedom. Directed by Mirjam Leuze. Brave Hearts International (2014). https:// vimeo.com/117153311
Grazhdanin zemnogo shara (Citizen of the Globe). Directed by Ol'ga Chekalina. Kinokompa-niia Tigr (2009).
The Interim Country. Directed by Thomas Lahusen, Gulzat Egemberdieva, and André Loersch. Chemodan Films (2010). http://www.chemodanfilms.com/the-interim-country/
Kyrgyzstan: The Kidnapped Bride. Directed by Petr Lom. *Frontline/World*, PBS (March 25, 2004). http://www.pbs.org/frontlineworld/stories/kyrgyzstan/thestory.html
Kyrgyzstan: The Other Silk Road. Directed by Kazu Ahmed. Swiss National Centre of Compe-tence in Research, NCCR North-South (2008). https://www.youtube.com/watch?v= tuBFWbOn1yM
The Kyrgyzstan Project. Directed by Jim Aikman and Matt Segal (2012). https://www.youtube. com/watch?v=OW5O1TR06V0
Moscow's Little Kyrgyzstan. Directed by Chingiz Narynov. Journeyman Pictures (2017). https:/ /www.youtube.com/watch?v=IVaqcE1NlU8

Index

Abdirasulova, Aziza, 197
Abdrisaev, Baktybek, 148
Abdumamunova Street, 107
Abdyldaev, Duishon, 160–161
Abdyldaev, Myktybek, 117–119
Academy of Sciences of Kyrgyzstan, 11, 15, 37
Academy of Tourism. *See* travel and tourism
Achebe, Chinua, 190
Adilet (Justice) Party, 84
Aeroflot (Soviet Airlines), 11
Afghanistan, xi, 81, 82, 90, 91, 109, 130, 133, 193, 194
Afghan War, 82
"against all" option. *See* elections
Air Kyrgyzstan, 203
Aitmatov, Chingiz Torekulovich, 15, 17, 18, 119, 224n11; critique of Soviet socialism, 7, 217n3; early life of, 6; literary achievements of, 7, 16; political and diplomatic activity of, 7–8, 10, 38, 219n6; views on ethnic minorities in the USSR, 8; visit to Florida, 8–10
Aitmatov, Torekul: discovery and reinterment of remains of, 17–18, 18; as a leader of Soviet Kirgizia, 17; mystery surrounding fate of, 17; secret trial and execution of, 8, 17
Aitmatova, Maria, 10
Aitmatova, Roza, 16–17, 17, 18

Aitmatov Club, 15
Akaev, Askar, 22, 54; early career of, 37, 213; effort to create cult of, 54; foreign policy doctrine of, 91; political use of Manas epic, 56, 220n10; as president, 32, 36, 37, 38–39, 41, 51, 52, 54, 60, 70–73, 79–80, 83, 84, 85, 87, 90, 109, 151, 214, 219n6; removal and exile of, 88, 89; visit to US, 43–44. *See also* elections; "family rule"; referendums
Akaeva, Bermet, 83–84, 85
Akaeva, Mairam, 66, 83
Ak-Buura River, 205, 206
akim (head of local or regional administration), 32–33, 38, 52, 55, 81, 89, 98, 184
akimiat (local or regional government headquarters), 33, 85, 89, 142–143
Ak Jol (Bright Path) Party, 102–103
Akmataliev, Melis, 15–16
Akmataliev, Ryspek, 90
Akmatbaev, Tynychbek, 90
aksakal (gray beard), 34, 177, 185
Aksy district, 79, 82, 83, 85, 95
Akun, Tursunbek, 113–115, 117, 118, 120
Ala-Archa National Park, 40, 105, 108, 175
Alai district, 205
ala kachuu (bride kidnapping), 116
Ala-Too Mountains, 13, 22, 55, 135, 204
Ala-Too Square (Bishkek), 63, 64

238 *Index*

Alga, Kyrgyzstan! (Forward, Kyrgyzstan!)
  Party, 84
Al'ianchikov, Alexander, 45
Al Jazeera, 167
Alma-Ata riots (1986), 8
Almaty, Kazakhstan, 14, 46, 109, 124, 127,
  130
Al-Qaeda, 81, 82
Altai region, 55
American ambassador, 133, 146, 192
American Embassy (Bishkek), 21, 133,
  144, 146, 199–200, 224n1
American Treasury. *See* Treasury
  Department (US)
American University of Central Asia
  (AUCA), 63, 66–67, 69, 129–130, 148,
  191–192
Amu Darya River, 60
APCs (armored personnel carriers), 165
April Revolution (2010), 143–144, 158,
  172, 214; consequences of, 153–154,
  164; victims' defense movement
  following, 172–173
Aragon, Louis, 6
Aral Sea, 62
Arashan, Kyrgyzstan, 134, 138
Ariston water heater, 63, 207
Armenia, 194
Armenians. *See* ethnic minorities
Ar-Namys (Fatherland) Party, 71, 180,
  182, 183, 185
Article 12 of the United Nations
  Convention Against Torture (UNCAT).
  See torture
Arzu (Bishkek restaurant), 120
Asaba (Flag) Party, 26–27
Ashar (social movement), 15
Ashirov, Baktybek, 196
Asr (the afternoon prayer), 165
Ata-Jurt (Fatherland) Party, 83, 177, 182,
  183, 184, 185
Atambaev, Almazbek, 52, 131–134, 133,
  138, 139, 142, 176, 178, 187, 189, 190,
  225n13; early career of, 132; as
  president, 191, 193, 194, 198, 210–212,
  229n7; as prime minister under Bakiev,
  99, 132; as prime minister under
  Otunbaeva, 183–184, 186, 188; as
  reluctant ex-president, 211–212. *See*

also elections; referendums
Ata-Meken (Motherland) Party, 96, 102,
  103, 108, 109, 135, 176, 182, 183, 212,
  223n20, 225n4
Audis, 46
automobiles in Kyrgyzstan. *See specific
  names of automobiles*
Azerbaijan, 5, 119

Babakulov, Ulugbek, 119–120
Babanov, Omurbek, 184, 185, 212
Bactrian camel, 74
Baekova, Cholpon, 102
bai (prominent Kyrgyz in pre-
  revolutionary era), 38
Baialinov, Kamil', 53
Baibolov, Kubatbek, 83, 109–111, 111,
  173, 175–177, 189
Baikonur, Kazakhstan, 8–10
Baisalov, Edil', 120, 157–158, 176, 227n9
Bakiev, Janysh, 108, 109, 114
Bakiev, Jusup, 223n2
Bakiev, Kurmanbek, 83, 85, 88, 136, 177,
  222n3; accession to power, 89–90; as
  instigator of counter-coup of May 2010,
  155; as president, 91, 95, 96, 96–102,
  105–106, 106, 108, 114, 117, 129, 132,
  134, 139, 151, 222n12; removal and
  exile of, 143, 172; visit to US, 91–93.
  See also elections; "family rule";
  referendums
Bakiev, Maxim, 114, 141
Bakir uulu, Tursunbai, 120
Balykchy, Kyrgyzstan, 139
Barskoon, Kyrgyzstan, 76–77
Baryktabasov, Urmat, 89
Batken region, 80, 81, 179
Batyrov, Kadyrjon, 156, 178
Beknazarov, Azimbek, 79–80, 85, 95, 98,
  131, 154, 177
Belarus, 194
Bernshtein, Boris, 40
beshbarmak, 31. *See also* food and drink
Beta Stores, 88
Big Man (in politics), 85, 89, 90, 96, 100,
  117, 134
Bin Laden, Osama, 133
Birmingham, UK, 61

About the Author

Eugene Huskey is the William R. Kenan, Jr. Chair in Political Science and Russian, East European, and Eurasian Studies at Stetson University. Trained in Soviet politics and legal affairs at the London School of Economics and Political Science, he has written extensively on post-communist Russia and Kyrgyzstan, covering subjects ranging from the presidency and political leadership to elections, legal reform, and the politics of language. A student of Kyrgyzstan since the end of the 1980s, he has witnessed and chronicled each stage in the history of this new country. In addition to his academic work, Huskey has published popular articles on Kyrgyzstani politics and foreign policy and given testimony and briefings on developments in Kyrgyzstan to the US Congress and executive agencies.

www.ingramcontent.com/pod-product-compliance
Lightning Source LLC
Chambersburg PA
CBHW030646270326
41929CB00007B/224